E

TEREST

TO SERVE
THE PUBLIC INTEREST

EDUCATIONAL
BROADCASTING
in the
UNITED STATES

ROBERT J. BLAKELY

Foreword by
McGEORGE BUNDY

SYRACUSE UNIVERSITY PRESS   •   1979

Copyright © 1979 by Syracuse University Press
Syracuse, New York 13210

Published with assistance from the Ford Foundation

Library of Congress Cataloging in Publication Data

Blakely, Robert J
   To serve the public interest.

   Includes bibliographical references and index.
   1. Educational broadcasting—United States—History.
I. Title.
LB1044.8.B55   384.54   78-25751
ISBN 0-8156-2198-1
ISBN 0-8156-0153-0 pbk.

Manufactured in the United States of America

To Alta Eckhoff Blakely

Robert J. Blakely was a vice-president of the Fund for Adult Education, a subsidiary of the Ford Foundation, 1951–61, and is a member of the National Association of Educational Broadcasters and the Adult Education Association of the U.S.A. He is also the author of *The People's Instrument: A Philosophy of Programming for Public Television* and *Adult Education in a Free Society*. Blakely is Adjunct Professor of Adult Education, School of Education, Syracuse University.

CONTENTS

TABLES

FOREWORD

THE STORY of noncommercial broadcasting in the United States is not well known. Quite a lot that is not so has been printed, and much that has happened along the way is known to very few. In this book Robert Blakely has provided the first reliable general survey from the beginning to 1978.

Not everyone will share all his judgments—I myself still prefer the term "Public Broadcasting" to his choice of "Educational Broadcasting." But Mr. Blakely's knowledge and experience give him every right to judge, and he has allowed those with other views to speak for themselves in his accounts of such startling moments as the effort of commercial broadcasters to prevent allocation of frequencies to noncommercial stations and the effort of the Nixon White House to eliminate national public affairs programming.

Mr. Blakely's central theme, as I read him, is that noncommercial broadcasting owes its very life, and most of its present strength, to the individual citizens who have cared enough to fight for it. Certainly foundations have helped, but they have helped because such citizens persuaded them. There is a direct line of succession among these caring citizens that runs from the seven leaders of the 1940s with whom Mr. Blakely begins down through Ralph Rogers of Dallas. What gives me confidence for the future, more than the notable achievements of particular stations or programs, more even than the understanding and support that have increased so markedly in Washington, is that the citizens who truly care can now be numbered in the millions.

This kind of broadcasting, which is really both public and educational, will certainly have no free ride to the future its friends now covet for it. But it will be surprising if future obstacles are any more testing than those overcome by the pioneers. This book offers both encouragement and instruction to everyone who cares about the next chapter.

New York, N.Y.   McGeorge Bundy
December 1978

PREFACE

M Y ASSOCIATION with educational broadcasting began in 1922. During my childhood and youth, radio station WOI, Iowa State College, was a source of entertainment and information for our entire family in Onawa, Iowa. Later, in high school and then in college, I engaged in discussions and debates carried over WSUI, the State University of Iowa. Between 1933 and 1937 I occasionally participated in America's earliest and most extensive educational experiment in television, conducted by the State University of Iowa's WGXKIU. At that time I also came to know several faculty radio leaders in the Big Ten universities who were among the pioneers of educational radio.

As an officer of the Ford Foundation's Fund for Adult Education (1951–61), I took part in the founding of educational television (ETV). Representing the Fund, I conducted preliminary negotiations with universities and nonprofit community corporations in the central third of the United States that were activating ETV stations on the channels reserved for that purpose by the Federal Communications Commission (FCC). I also attended sessions where directors of the Fund and leaders of the National Association of Educational Broadcasters (NAEB) decided about grants-in-aid to the stations that were preparing to broadcast and where leaders discussed establishing a national program exchange center to serve those stations. The tenor of this movement at that time, as one participant put it, was like trying "to learn to ride a bicycle while inventing it." The leaders of educational radio and the pioneers of educational television during the fifties were my colleagues, and the anecdotes I relate are intended to give the reader a slight sense of having been there, too.

During 1969 and 1970 while researching a book on the philosophy of public television, I visited many stations and talked with local managers and directors as well as officers of national educational broadcasting organizations. These first-hand observations and conversations made me a partisan for educational broadcasting—always for its potential, if not always for its performance.

Commercial broadcasting stations and networks have two purposes. One, according to law and the stations' licenses, is to serve the
public interest. The other, according to the need of private business, is to
make a profit. The goal of most commercial broadcasting is not to entertain or inform but to attract the largest possible audience and to *sell*—not
just the programs themselves (which are the bait) but also the commercials (which are the hook). The educational component of our total national broadcasting service, however, has but a single purpose—to serve
the public interest. This service can treat audiences as receptive, interested persons, not potential customers, and can acknowledge their needs.

Although the histories of educational radio and educational television may *seem* separate because educational radio preceded educational
television by thirty years, both radio and television have emerged from
the physical science called electromagnetism. Americans working for sixty
years have succeeded in transforming American broadcasting from an almost exclusively commercial system into a combination public (noncommercial) and private (commercial) system. Other countries, including
Canada, Great Britain, West Germany, Italy, and Japan, also have combination broadcasting systems made up of both public and private components. But only in the United States was public broadcasting established
primarily through the voluntary, cooperative initiatives and sustained efforts of private citizens.

The purpose of this book is to tell the story of that achievement.
This history of educational (public) broadcasting is necessarily a kind of
history of broadcasting in the United States. It describes landmark events
such as Marconi's invention of wireless telegraphy in 1894, the Radio Act
of 1927, the Communications Act of 1934, and the Federal Communication Commission's suspension of licensing television stations in 1948.
But it includes many things that a general history of broadcasting might
not, such as the details of educational radio as well as educational television, and the details of broadcasting for instruction as well as broadcasting for general audiences.

This history begins in the middle of things. The first chapter deals
with a dramatic change that occurred in the prospects for educational
broadcasting between 1948 and 1951. On September 29, 1948, when the
Federal Communications Commission suspended the processing of
licenses for TV stations, it had reserved no channels for educational stations. Until late 1950 educators showed little interest in making a con-
certed effort to win reservations of TV channels for educational stations
after licensing was resumed. Yet between October 16, 1950, and January
30, 1951, American educators, organized in the Joint Committee on

Educational Television (JCET), prepared and presented such persuasive arguments in FCC hearings that on March 21, 1951, the Commission proposed to reserve 209 noncommercial educational channels.

Chapters two and three recount the preceding developments of both the commercial and educational broadcasting systems in the United States between 1922 and 1948.

Chapter four resumes the story after the FCC's 1951 proposal to reserve channels for educational stations. It relates the educators' activities, supported and guided by the Fund for Adult Education, newly established by the Ford Foundation, in getting 212 television channels permanently reserved for educational stations; in activating the first sixteen ETV stations; and in founding and operating the Educational Television and Radio Center (ETRC), a national program exchange and distribution service for ETV stations. It also tells of the increased vitality of educational radio stations and the establishment of their network of taped programs distributed by mail.

Chapter five recounts the financial and legislative support educational broadcasting received from 1956 to 1963 and the activities this support made possible. Chapter six then details the period from 1964 through 1966, including the nationwide expansion of the educational broadcasting system, the federal aid it received, and the appointment of the Carnegie Commission on Educational Television.

Chapter seven analyzes the swift flow of events in 1967—from the release of the Carnegie Commission's recommendations in January to President Johnson's signing of the Public Broadcasting Act in November.

The final chapter recounts the history of public broadcasting from 1968 to mid-1978 and describes the prospects of public broadcasting in the United States as of mid-1978.

This history, I hope, will help the reader clearly see the need for a component of the American system of telecommunications that has a single purpose: to serve the public interest, as mandated in the Communications Act of 1934. The reader, I hope, will also gain an understanding of the hard struggle against heavy odds that brought public broadcasting into being. And the reader will, I hope, have a stronger commitment to help public broadcasting fulfill its potential in the precarious future that it faces.

Chicago   Robert J. Blakely
Fall 1978

ACKNOWLEDGMENTS

THE PEOPLE who have helped me are too numerous to mention, but two groups merit special appreciation.

First, the U.S. Office of Education, the Ball State University Foundation, Muncie, Indiana, and the Marks Foundation, Washington, D.C., provided grants to the National Association of Educational Broadcasters (NAEB) that made it possible for me to begin this book. The grants were sufficient to motivate me to write a long history of educational broadcasting in the United States instead of the medium-length history of public television which I undertook to write. James Fellows of the NAEB, Thomas D. Clemens of the U.S. Office of Education, Edmund F. Ball of the Ball State University Foundation, and Leonard Marks were understanding and forbearing as the work progressed.

Second, I gratefully acknowledge the invaluable aid of the individuals who, in various drafts, read all or parts of this book: James Fellows, Robert B. Hudson, Willard D. Rowland, Jr., David M. Davis, Walter B. Emery, C. Scott Fletcher, G. H. Griffiths, William G. Harley, Richard B. Hull, Arthur Hungerford, Fritz Jauch, Chalmers M. Marquis, Harold B. McCarty, Burton Paulu, Saul Rockman, Harry J. Skornia, Terry Turner, I. Keith Tyler, and John F. White. Alta Eckhoff Blakely read the entire manuscript in its final draft. Each of these people saved me from errors, corrected my perceptions, and tested my judgments. To them, all credit and thanks, and no responsibility for errors and shortcomings, which is mine alone.

TO SERVE
THE PUBLIC INTEREST

SEIZING THE LAST CHANCE

Until late 1950 the chance seemed small that the American people would ever have a choice between a national commercial broadcasting service and a national noncommercial broadcasting service.

By that time television had eclipsed radio in the attention of both the public and broadcasters. Educators had learned from experience with AM radio that they needed channels reserved specifically for noncommercial stations because they could not compete for licenses with commercial broadcasters in the open market. When, on March 18, 1947, the Federal Communications Commission (FCC) resumed licensing television stations, which had been interrupted by World War II, it reserved no channels for noncommercial educational stations because educators had expressed little interest in them. In contrast, the commercial broadcasters' drive to get television licenses and put stations on the air was like a gold rush. During 1948 alone the number of TV stations on the air increased from seventeen to forty-one. By the fall of that year the FCC concluded that it must change its rules governing television: first, because its plan for allocating TV channels was resulting in interference in the reception of signals; second, because the twelve TV channels, all VHF (very high frequency), would clearly be far from enough to satisfy the demand for licenses; and third, because the question of what rules should govern color television needed more study. Therefore, on September 29, 1948, the Commission stopped licensing applications for television stations. This action was called the "freeze." The 108 stations already licensed could continue operation or construction, but all other applications were "frozen."

The prospects for educational broadcasting in radio were better than in television, but still they were not good. No AM radio channels had ever been reserved for educational stations, and the AM band was filled with stations. Of the 202 AM licenses that had been granted to educational institutions since 1922, only thirty-six were still on the air at the end of 1936, and the number continued to decline to fewer than thirty. The Federal Communications Commission did, on June 27, 1945, finally reserve FM channels for noncommercial educational radio stations—the first 20 of 100 FM channels. But the growth of educational FM stations had been retarded, mainly because the growth of commercial FM stations and the buildup of markets for sets that could receive FM signals had been slow.

The national obsession with television, the lack of TV channels reserved for educational stations, the declining number of educational AM radio stations, the slow growth of educational FM radio stations—these were not the only reasons why the future of educational broadcasting looked bleak throughout the 1940s. Another reason was that educators in the United States had shown little evidence that they would try to persuade the FCC to reserve any of the highly valued VHF channels for educational stations. The FCC had scheduled hearings just before the freeze. After reporting that Chairman Wayne Coy had issued two separate invitations to educators to appear at those hearings to request reservations, *Billboard,* August 21, 1948, concluded:

> Last chance for educational institutions to get into television broadcasting is seen now resting with the Federal Communications Commission's September hearings on upstairs [UHF, ultra high frequency] video. All but crowded out of the television field, educational institutions are expected then to push vigorously for reservations of channels in the upper [UHF] band. With present channels approaching the saturation point, it appears certain that saturation of spectrum space in the low [VHF] band will find universities holding no more than six stations.[1]

No educators accepted the invitations to appear at those hearings. The freeze, which was expected to last only several months, went on and on without any organized initiative from educators to argue for reservations when the freeze was ended. Before ending the freeze, the FCC scheduled final hearings, beginning in December 1950, and the educators immediately went into action.

On October 16, 1950, seven national educational organizations formed the Ad Hoc Joint Committee on Educational Television (JCET) to try to persuade the FCC to reserve TV channels for educational stations. They were the American Council on Education, the Association for Education by Radio, the Association of Land-Grant Colleges and Universities, the National Council of Chief State School Officers, the National Association of Educational Broadcasters (NAEB), the National Association of State Universities, and the National Education Association. During the FCC hearings, the educators presented their case so effectively and the commercial broadcasters presented their opposition so poorly that the FCC, on March 21, 1951, proposed the reservation of 209 noncommercial channels—both VHF and UHF—within a table of allocations that covered most of the nation. In 1952 the Commission provisionally reserved an even larger number of reserved TV channels and in 1953 made those reservations permanent. Thus the formation of the Joint Committee on Educational Television marked a turning point in the development of educational broadcasting in the United States.

Four factors explain the sudden vitality of organized education that resulted in the formation and persuasive performance of the JCET. First, a cadre of able leaders emerged in educational broadcasting. Second, the National Association of Educational Broadcasters began to develop into an effective organization. Third, at two seminars held at the Allerton House, the University of Illinois, in the summers of 1949 and 1950, educators and educational broadcasters visualized a new role for educational broadcasting and for the kinds of programming it could do. Finally, a new member of the FCC, Frieda B. Hennock, came forth as a powerful champion of reserving television channels for educational stations.

SEVEN LEADERS

One of the educators' strength in the struggle to win television channels reserved for educational stations was that people in many organizations, institutions, and agencies were able to work together for the common good. It was crucial, however, that strong, skillful leadership to extend educational broadcasting into the field of television come from within the National Association of Educational Broadcasters. It was made up of the persons and institutions that were already experienced in and had the facilities for radio broadcasting. Sketches of seven of the persons who provided leadership to the NAEB illustrate that between the fall of 1948 and the fall of 1950 educators and educational broadcasters developed a sense of common commitment that enabled them to seize the opportunity to win the reservation of television channels for educational stations. The contributions of Richard Hull, Harold McCarty, and Seymour Siegel must be told in the context of the NAEB.

On November 12, 1925, a group of educational broadcasters attending the fourth national Radio Conference in Washington formed the Association of College and University Broadcasting Stations (ACUBS). Its purpose was "the dissemination of knowledge to the end that both the technical and educational features of broadcasting may be extended to all." Membership was open to all educational broadcasting institutions, whether they sold air time or not. The ACUBS in 1925 had only forty-one members—less than one-half of the educational institutions then holding broadcast licenses. The twenty-five members at the first ACUBS convention on July 1 and 2, 1930—held in conjunction with the first Institute for Education by Radio (IER)—sent a telegram to the State Governors' Annual Conference urging the governors to press for the "reservation of channels for broadcasting stations owned and operated by the states and by colleges and universities" and for "such hours and amounts of power as may be necessary." The ACUBS had by then identified three main goals: the reservation of channels; a national headquarters, ideally in Washington, D.C.; and a means for program exchange, ideally network connections. None of these goals had been attained by 1934, when the ACUBS changed its name to the National Association of Educational Broadcasters. The reservation of radio channels became a reality when the FCC set aside FM channels (five in 1940, and twenty in 1945) for noncommercial educational broadcasting stations. When the NAEB opened its active membership to institutions holding FM construction permits and closed it to stations selling time (with dues ranging from $10–20 a year, according to transmitting power), membership began to climb— from twenty-three in 1944, to thirty-eight active members (owning and operating stations), thirty-two associate members (broadcasting over commercial stations or planning radio activities), and six individual associate members in 1948. Measured by the past, this growth was progress, but it was sadly inadequate for the new tasks that faced the NAEB. With reserved radio channels, the association was called upon to promote the activation of FM stations. With the FCC's proposal not to reserve television channels, the NAEB was called upon to help organize the vastly more difficult effort to reverse the decision. The obstacles were not merely that commercial interests were certain to offer opposition, but that some of the NAEB members, who were oriented to radio, were certain to offer opposition also. Many members were so preoccupied with the problems of day-to-day programming and year-to-year survival that the proposal to invade the field of television seemed overwhelming. It was essential, therefore, that the leaders who made the proposal be fully accepted by the NAEB, which had become a kind of closed "club." Three of the leaders fitting this prescription were Richard B. Hull, Harold B. McCarty, and Seymour N. Siegel.

Richard B. Hull was elected president of the NAEB in the crucial years 1947–49. He was director of radio station WOI, Iowa State College, Ames, Iowa, which had successfully competed since April 28, 1922, with commercial stations for large audiences, not only in farm and home services programming, but also with public affairs and cultural programming, particularly classical music. Hull's predecessor, W. J. Griffith, had developed a twenty-year plan for WOI which included FM radio (added soon after World War II) and television. Following a memorandum written by Hull, university President Charles E. Friley applied for a television license in 1947. Because of hesitation by commercial applicants, the FCC granted a commercial license (the only one in central Iowa) to Iowa State College. WOI TV went on the air February 21, 1950 —the sole television channel owned and operated by an educational institution during the freeze. Moreover, for a while it enjoyed the best of both worlds in that it was able to select programs from all three networks, able to sell time, and able to use the earnings to develop noncommercial programming and to purchase facilities. Because it provided for experimentation and internships, WOI TV became a bridge across which educational broadcasters passed from radio to television. From such a background, Richard Hull brought impeccable credentials to the leadership of NAEB. Only he had experience in AM radio, FM radio, and television.

Harold B. McCarty also brought extensive expertise to the task of leading the radio-oriented NAEB into the field of television. The tradition of public service at the University of Wisconsin is rooted in the partnership between Charles R. Van Hise, president of the university from 1903 to 1918, and Robert M. La Follette, governor of Wisconsin from 1901 to 1906 and U.S. senator from then until 1925. During these decades the "Wisconsin Idea" developed—an idea that a state university should not only meet the educational and cultural needs of all the people of the state but also actively help them solve their day-to-day problems. Broadcasting was a part of this policy. Broadcasting began with the licensing of experimental station 9XM in 1916, operated by Professor Earle M. Terry and his coterie of students, including Malcolm Hanson, later chief radio engineer on Byrd's first expedition to Antarctica, 1929. Station 9XM served the U.S. Navy in training during World War I and began regularly scheduled voice and music broadcasts to the public in 1919. In 1922 the call letters WHA were assigned to the station, and Professor William H. Lighty was appointed program director. Lighty stressed the mission of taking the university to the people. From Lighty McCarty adopted the "Wisconsin Idea," beginning in 1929 when he was a student-announcer. In 1931 he became program director of WHA, and Harold Engel became assistant director. WHA inaugurated the "Wisconsin School of the Air" in November of that year and the "Wisconsin College of the Air" two years later. Political broadcasting was started in 1932, when WHA began to provide free time to all qualified candidates for state offices in primary and general elections, and soon the station was broadcasting events from the state government.

In 1945 an act of the state legislature incorporated a plan for an educational broadcasting network of AM and FM stations and established the State Radio Council. In March 1947, WHA FM was inaugurated— the first of the planned statewide network. McCarty was NAEB president for 1935 and 1936, and as such he was a member of the Federal Radio Education Committee (which the FCC sponsored and U.S. Commissioner of Education John W. Studebaker chaired) and a participant in the First National Conference on Educational Broadcasting in 1936. Following the 1948 convention of the NAEB, President Hull appointed McCarty chairman of a television study committee to explore the advisability of asking the FCC to set aside TV frequencies for educational stations. Thus, like Hull, McCarty stood on a solid base of university radio broadcasting as he worked to maneuver the association into television.

Hull and McCarty came from the type of Midwest land-grant college stations that dominated educational broadcasting. The story of Seymour N. Siegel must be told within the context of New York City's municipal radio station, WNYC. Rodman Wanamaker, of the Wanamaker stores, and Grover Whalen, a former Wanamaker executive, succeeded in 1924 in establishing WNYC with an appropriation from the New York City government. This move had been obstructed for two years by the American Telephone and Telegraph Company, which wanted the city to buy time on its commercial station, WEAF. WNYC's programming from the beginning has been strong in community service—news, information, in-service training for city employees (including policemen), and classical music.

The station was a delight to Mayor Fiorello La Guardia, whose reading of the comics over the air during a 1937 newspaper strike is remembered by many. La Guardia swore in Siegel's predecessor, Morris S. Novik, as program director of WNYC (with conditions guaranteeing the station's political independence) on February 9, 1939. Novik immediately made WNYC a member of the NAEB and became a director of the association that same year. He brought experiences in urban ethnic, economic, political, and intellectual life to the NAEB that were strikingly different from the relatively insulated experiences of the state university station directors. A story told by both Novik and Hull makes this point. Novik's first meeting as a director of NAEB was at Iowa State College on September 1, 1939, a day of "fine corn weather." The directors, sweating in a basement classroom, observed the uniformed legs of a man striding past their open window. Then an Iowa state patrolman came to the door. "Is M. S. Novik here? The mayor of New York City wants him to come back right away. Hitler has invaded Poland."

Novik's assistant program director was Seymour Siegel, who became program director of the station and a member of the NAEB board in 1947. The son of a Republican congressman from New York City, he had left WNYC to be a commander in Navy communications during World War II and returned to WNYC deeply aware of the possibilities of electromagnetic tape recording, which had been developed during the war. Moreover, through his access to the intellectual and cultural resources of New York City and to the substantial staff and equipment of WNYC, he helped the NAEB achieve its long-time goal of program exchange. Siegel succeeded Hull as president of the association in 1950 and 1951.

I. Keith Tyler, although not a member of the NAEB, was a leader highly valued for his achievements in three roles. First, he had been an officer of the Institute for Education by Radio since 1936. Held each spring beginning in 1930 at Ohio State University, this institute provided a forum to clarify the objectives and further the techniques of education by radio. The presentations and annual proceedings, *Education on the Air,* are the best record of statements, discussions, arguments, reports on fact-finding and research, and, in short, the intellectual history of educational broadcasting from 1930 until the mid-1950s, when more specialized national meetings began to eclipse its importance. As the person primarily responsible for planning and conducting the institute programs, Tyler was the most knowledgeable person in the nation concerning the issues, the interests, and their spokesmen.

Second, Tyler was a member of the OSU Bureau of Educational Research and an outstanding researcher. He was director of the Evaluation of School Broadcasts project, a research and service activity that between 1937 and 1943 analyzed the educational values of radio in classrooms and studied the social and psychological effects of radio upon children and young people.[2] Finally, as a special assistant to OSU's long-time president, Howard L. Bevis, Tyler frequently wrote influential position papers voiced by Bevis, not only for his university but also in his role as spokesman for the National Association of State Universities and the Association of Land-Grant Colleges and Universities.

There were three "mavericks" in this group of NAEB leaders— Probst, Schramm, and Hudson. George Probst was never an officer or director of NAEB, but his institutional credentials, although unconventional, were unique. The University of Chicago was the first major private university to enter broadcasting. "The University of Chicago Round Table" was broadcast weekly over commercial radio from February 1, 1931, until June 12, 1955. On October 15, 1933, it became a Sunday afternoon feature of NBC, and it was a most successful combination of serious informal adult education and radio broadcasting. At its peak, it was broadcast over eighty-eight commercial stations and twenty educational stations in the United States, over the stations of the Canadian Broadcasting Corporation, and (by recording) throughout the United Kingdom via the British Broadcasting Corporation. Beginning in 1937, its audience in the United States was estimated to be between two and three million, and the printed program transcripts, started in May 1938, were sent to the twenty thousand people who requested them weekly. For twelve years, beginning in 1938, an annual grant of $50,000 from the Sloan Foundation paid for speakers and a full-time director, and it subsidized the publication of transcripts. George Probst, a historian in his own right, became director of "The University of Chicago Round Table" in 1945, and under him it reached its highest excellence. His personal relations with Robert M. Hutchins, who resigned as president of the University of Chicago in 1951 to become an associate director of the Ford Foundation, helped secure large-scale financial support to educational broadcasting.

Wilbur Schramm is known to students of education and communication for his theory and research relating the technologies of communication to their effects upon human behavior. In the late 1940s he became director of the Institute of Communications Research at the University of Illinois. A person of both imagination and charm, Schramm initiated two projects that had far-reaching consequences for educational broadcasting. His approach to the Rockefeller Foundation resulted in the two Allerton House Seminars of 1949 and 1950, and his approach to the W. K. Kellogg Foundation led to the 1951 grants to the NAEB for a headquarters and radio program exchange at Urbana, Illinois. Moreover, he helped persuade Robert Hudson to move from commercial to educational broadcasting.

Robert B. Hudson was listed in the 1949 Allerton House Seminar as a consultant, Director of Education and Opinion Broadcast for the Columbia Broadcasting System (CBS)—a position he had held since 1945. At the 1950 Allerton House Seminar he was listed as general chairman and director of university broadcasting at the University of Illinois, which had operated station WILL AM since 1922 and was the first university to operate an FM station. Before joining CBS, Hudson had been director of the Denver Adult Education Council, had organized and directed the Rocky Mountain Radio Council, and had been a radio consultant to the Office of War Information during World War II. Like Probst, he had not served as officer or director of the NAEB. Nevertheless, he quickly won acceptance and exerted quiet but strong influence. He insisted that educational broadcasting be both effective broadcasting and honest education, and he drew upon experience in adult education, in local and regional noncommercial broadcasting, and in national commercial broadcasting to make it so.

NAEB'S HEADQUARTERS AND PROGRAM EXCHANGE

The seven men whose backgrounds have been sketched above gave leadership to the NAEB not only toward entering the new field of television but also toward reaching two other goals—a national headquarters and a means of program exchange. The NAEB had been a weak organization, but the 1948 convention, held in Urbana, Illinois, October 10–12, marked a new era for educational broadcasting. President Richard Hull and his board of directors initiated an aggressive set of plans. A committee of Hull, Probst, and McCarty planned to establish a central service for sharing programs, one or more regional FM educational networks, and a central administrative office. These plans were discussed at the 1949 convention, October 15–17, at Ann Arbor, Michigan. Elected president a third time, Hull requested funds from several foundations. Seymour Siegel began a program exchange by making five sets of recordings of the 1949 *Herald Tribune* Forum available to twenty-two member stations of NAEB. By the next year this "bicycle network" (so-called because the tapes were mailed to the stations one after another) had expanded to include programs from numerous member stations, the Canadian Broadcasting Corporation, and the British Broadcasting Corporation, in addition to others from WNYC, totaling four hours of programs daily. At the 1950 convention Siegel was elected president, and Wilbur Schramm formally proposed a plan for the NAEB network to locate an office at the University of Illinois. Through Schramm's efforts the W. K. Kellogg Foundation made a grant of $245,350 on May 23, 1951, to establish a permanent NAEB headquarters and a tape network and to hold training seminars and conduct research. The headquarters and the tape network were to be at the University of Illinois, and the operations were to be self-supporting at the end of five years. In August 1951, James S. Miles, Director of WBAA, Purdue, became director of the Kellogg Radio Project.

Thus the NAEB was developing into an effective national association that furthered the progress of educational radio as well as the events that led to the founding of educational television. At the beginning of 1951 the association had a total membership of 105 institutions, 67 of which operated stations.

THE ALLERTON HOUSE SEMINARS

Two seminars held at the University of Illinois stated the purposes of educational broadcasting in such a way as to help educational broadcasters, educators, scholars, and government officials define common goals, and they explored new ways of advancing education through broadcasting. The seminars were the outcome of conversations between Wilbur Schramm, director of the Institute of Communications Research, University of Illinois, and John Marshall, assistant director of the Rockefeller Foundation.[3] Because of the response to the first seminar on philosophy and purpose in 1949, a second seminar on programming was held in 1950. The Rockefeller Foundation underwrote the expenses for both seminars, and the University of Illinois provided its secluded Allerton House Conference Center, near Urbana.

The 1949 Seminar (June 29–July 12)

The first seminar assembled the most vigorous directors of educational radio stations and university program-production centers, together with some advisers and public members, to take stock of educational broadcasting. There were twenty-two directors or managers of stations or centers, almost an equal number of advisers and public members, and also invited guests from Denmark, Great Britain, Japan, Korea, and the Philippines.

Most of the directors and managers had met many times, but never before had they come together to think solely and systematically about mission and strategy. They discussed the purposes, goals, future, and needs of educational broadcasting in this country. According to participant Robert B. Hudson:

It seemed that suddenly a great truth had been revealed which had long haunted every man present but which had seldom escaped from deep in his subconscious—the truth that educational radio not only had a job to do, but it was capable of doing it. The sheer relief in getting at this matter was electrifying: the wall of repression, buttressed by years of rationalizations and expediencies, came tumbling down and educational radio, for the first time in its turbulent history, was on the move.[4]

In their report, "Educational Broadcasting: Its Aims and Responsibilities," the twenty-two directors and managers, defining broadcasting to include AM and FM radio, television, and facsimile (transmission of images by slow-scan TV), expressed the philosophy and strategy they had fashioned: educational broadcasting in a democracy is an essential part of and a supplement necessary to both education and public communications; the improvement and expansion of educational broadcasting are imperative. This idea linked educational broadcasting stations and educational institutions, broadcasting and other methods of education, systematic instruction and informal education at all levels, and educational broadcasting and commercial broadcasting.

The 1950 Seminar (June 2–19)

The seminar assembled educational program and production directors from both noncommercial and commercial broadcasting as well as specialists in academic disciplines, education, and communication to analyze and study educational radio program production in subject areas that had been neglected or inadequately treated. Robert Hudson was general chairman, and the participants were young men and women responsible for building programs at educational stations. The participants drafted summaries and daily reports, which grew into a catalog of ideas and analyses for new program series, later used by many educational stations. One specific proposal by anthropologist Robert Redfield resulted in the series "The Ways of Mankind" and another by historian Allan Nevins in the series "The Jeffersonian Heritage."

The first Allerton House seminar created a sense of common mission and direction, the second a sense of capabilities for programming. "In many respects the supreme kudos to the Allerton House group is this: it sparked the development of a unique and innovative system of public communication. The corollary is that the new system attracted to its service able people from many fields to apply their knowledge and skills: people from education, commercial radio and television, films, theater, performing arts, social sciences, government, not to mention specialists in nearly every substantive field."[5]

Such development takes time, but it began immediately. For the persons who took part in the 1949 Allerton House Seminar the situation could not have been more dramatic. On the concluding day news was received that the FCC had proposed a new television allocations table which made no reservations for educational stations in either VHF or UHF, but that Commissioner Frieda B. Hennock had proposed a 25 percent reservation in both. On that day—the end of the first Allerton House Seminar and the beginning of the end of the freeze on licensing TV stations—the "development of a unique and innovative system of public communications" began, and Frieda Hennock was the chief catalyst for movement into television.

COMMISSIONER HENNOCK

The only dissenting opinion in the Commission's proposed allocations plan was voiced by Commissioner Frieda Hennock. In a history-making plea for the reservation of television channels to meet the present and future needs of education, Commissioner Hennock provided the legal and moral platform on which the educational establishment was subsequently to act; she also became the "mother protector" image of the educational television movement, perhaps its most widely known advocate and an effective champion of almost fanatical zeal.[6]

Frieda Barkin Hennock was the first woman member of the Federal Communications Commission. Brought to the 1948 Institute for Education by Radio by Clifford Durr (whom she succeeded as commissioner), she knew little about broadcasting at first but learned rapidly. She seized upon the issue of reserved television channels as a means toward the goal of increasing competition and public responsibility in broadcasting. She had a practical command of politics, an intuitive grasp of policies, and a definite concept of a national educational television system. Hennock ignited the movement toward educational television and inspired educators to enlist.

FORMATION OF THE JCET

The meeting representatives of seven national educational agencies that organized the Ad Hoc Joint Committee on Educational Television took place on October 16, 1950. It was called by Richard Hull, president of the NAEB, and Franklin Dunham, chief of radio-television, U.S. Office of Education. The group agreed that there should be a common effort by an "organization of organizations" to present a unified case for reserving television channels for educational stations. The members compromised on two basic differences: the request should be for "preferential treatment in VHF" and space in the UHF band, and the station designation should be "nonprofit and/or noncommercial." I. Keith Tyler was elected chairman and Belmont Farley, head of the press-radio division of the National Education Association, secretary-treasurer. A "strategy committee" was formed, consisting of Robert Hudson, from the University of Illinois; Edgar Fuller, executive secretary of the National Council of Chief State School Officers; George Probst, director of "The University of Chicago Round Table"; and Stuart Haydon, from the University of Chicago. The "organization of organizations" represented the American Council on Education, the Association for Education by Radio, the Association of Land-Grant Colleges and Universities, the National Council of Chief State School Officers, the National Association of Educational Broadcasters, the National Association of State Universities, and the National Education Association.

At the suggestion of Frieda Hennock, Tyler and Farley asked General Telford Taylor to be legal counsel. Taylor, who had been chief counsel for the FCC and had recently returned from service as U.S. Prosecutor in the Nuremberg trials, accepted and enlisted the aid of former FCC colleague Seymour Krieger, although the JCET was able to pay only token fees to Taylor, Krieger, and their law firms.

THE PREPARATION OF THE JCET CASE

For more than two years FCC members had been dealing with technical problems under constantly mounting pressures from the industry, the public, politicians, government agencies, and Congress to resume licensing TV stations. Now, just when they had completed all the major technical inquiries, the commissioners were asked to delay decision even longer while they considered philosophical questions such as the compatibility of private and public interests and the roles of commercial and noncommercial broadcasting. Under these circumstances, glib expressions of educators' "interest" in educational television would not be enough to secure reservations. The JCET would have to present weighty evidence that there was a good probability of developing a useful educational television service.

The task of the JCET officers Tyler and Farley, strategists Hull,

Probst, Haydon, and Fuller, and counselors Taylor and Krieger was to design on short notice a coherent argument for the reservation of channels and to recruit and marshal witnesses to support it. Because the scheduling of the sessions and the availability of witnesses (both subject to change) had to be synchronized, presenting the JCET case was like assembling a jigsaw puzzle. Every evening before a session, the counselors and staff questioned the next day's witnesses to determine how best to offer or elicit their particular contributions. The JCET held plenary meetings on December 7, 1950, the eve of the last session before the holiday recess, and on December 30. In both the smaller and larger huddles, results were assessed and plans laid.

The period of the hearings was divided into four stages: first, the JCET presentations on November 27–30 and December 5–8, which were not subjected to cross-examination by representatives of commercial broadcasting (although counsel was present); second, the recess between December 9 and January 21; third, the JCET presentations on January 22–24, which were subjected to cross-examination by counsel for opponents; and, fourth, the presentations by the opponents on January 24–30, which were subjected to cross-examination by JCET counsel.

THE HEARINGS

The record[7] reveals that the FCC commissioners were extraordinarily concerned with the JCET's situation and had granted an initial postponement to give the JCET time to prepare its case. They had hoped to finish the hearings early in December, yet they not only continued them to the end of January but also postponed resumption for a week to enable the JCET to complete its monitoring study of the programs being broadcast by the seven commercial stations in New York City. Each of the seven commissioners attended from one to all of the fourteen sessions —a large attendance in light of the Commission's wide responsibilities, particularly those of the chairman.

The proponents and opponents of reserved channels were as unevenly matched as they had been in the 1934 FCC hearings on the proposal to reserve AM radio channels for educational stations—except that the imbalance was reversed. The JCET presented seventy-one witnesses, sixty-four exhibits, and took up almost eleven days; the opposition offered five witnesses, six exhibits, and used almost four days. All witnesses favoring reservations were organized by the JCET, although thirty-one of them officially represented other institutions, organizations, agencies, or themselves. They covered a wide range of interests: all levels of education, both public and private; the U.S. Office of Education, state regents, and local school boards; U.S. senators, state governors, and municipal officials; national and local lay organizations; organized labor and organized medicine; urban and rural areas in various parts of the country; and general education for citizens and special education for handicapped persons. The five opposing witnesses, who did not appear under unified sponsorship, represented the National Association of Broadcasters, CBS, and NBC-RCA.

The commercial broadcasters seemed overconfident at first and were unprepared. Moreover, they were a divided group: those with TV stations wanted reservations in order to reduce competition; those that did not have stations or (like CBS) that wanted more stations or other stations with more desirable frequencies opposed reservations.

The November–December Sessions

Testimony favoring reserved channels filled all eight sessions between November 27 and December 8, during which the JCET presented its complete case (although supplementary evidence was presented after the recess). The case was presented in five parts: (1) which reservations were being requested; (2) the principles and precedents that justified reservations; (3) the reasons for reservations; (4) the prospects of how and when the reserved channels would be used; and (5) the potential of educational television.

1. The Request. The JCET asked for at least one VHF educational channel in every standard metropolitan area and every major educational center, and also for at least 20 percent of all UHF channels. These channels should be reserved for noncommercial educational stations, except that channels should be reserved for nonprofit educational stations in cities where only one channel was allocated.

This request was a refinement of the rough compromises that the ad hoc group had reached on October 16. VHF reservations were needed because only VHF sets were then available. The development of UHF was uncertain, and experience in VHF would prepare educators to use UHF channels when they were available. A "standard metropolitan area" was one with a population of fifty thousand or more. A "major educational center" was a community outside a metropolitan area having a university or college with a minimum enrollment of five thousand or with the largest enrollment in the state. (The JCET took no position on reservations in the "closed" cities such as New York and Los Angeles, where all VHF channels were occupied, because it could not agree upon a position.) These requests were submitted to the FCC as guidelines. The formula added up to requests for 168 VHF reservations in metropolitan areas and another 46 in educational centers—numbers which demonstrated widespread need and also provided a reasonably precise estimate.

The JCET followed the advice of Taylor and Hennock that the general request be for noncommercial classification rather than nonprofit (in which some air time could be sold) for three reasons. First, previous attempts to get nonprofit AM reservations had failed, whereas previous attempts to get noncommercial FM reservations had succeeded. Second, a general bid for nonprofit reservations would have been opposed by many educators and by all commercial interest. Third, a bid for noncommercial reservations would unite educators and divide commercial interests. At the same time, the exception—the request for a nonprofit reservation in a city where only one channel was allocated—would provide the people in that area with both educational and commercial service.

2. The Justification. Television channels should be reserved because the electromagnetic spectrum is a natural resource belonging to the people (so said the Communications Act of 1934); because the FCC's responsibility was to administer the act in the public interest; because the FCC's 1935 decision not to reserve AM channels had not been in the public interest; and because the 1945 decision to reserve FM channels had been in the public interest.

The JCET considered any reservation of a natural resource in American history a precedent applicable to the reservation of television channels. For example, Belmont Farley, representing the National Education Association (NEA), reviewed the reservation of land in the public interest. He found that since the 1659 Massachusetts grants for grammar schools more than 154,000 square miles of land had been reserved for education. Other national reservations in the public interest included 154 forests, 28 parks, and 185 monuments. Ohio State University President Howard L. Bevis, representing the Association of Land-Grant Colleges and Universities and the National Association of State Universities, concluded that the principles of the Morrill Act (which established land-grant colleges) applied: "In the public domain of broadcasting we are asking that these same principles be applied—(1) the reservation of a portion of the television spectrum for the use of educational institutions when they are able to develop the necessary facilities, and (2) the encouragement of education by providing usable television channels to educational institutions" (24:16366).

Commissioner Rosel Hyde thought the analogy was inaccurate.

While some natural resources could be depleted, "the radio frequencies continue on for use regardless of what immediate use might be made of them. . . . Hence the opportunity for the educator is always open, you might say" (24:16148). The rejoinder was that commercial appropriation of a channel could close opportunity to educators as effectively as the physical depletion of a resource, as evidenced by the FCC's 1935 decision against reserving AM channels. When Harold McCarty, of the University of Wisconsin's WHA, referred to the FCC statement to Congress on January 22, 1935, justifying the decision against reserving AM channels, Commissioner Hennock insisted that he read most of it aloud. Then she exclaimed, "How can I get 100,000 copies made immediately to remind us not to do it again?" (25:16125). When McCarty said the FCC had avoided its responsibilities by creating the Federal Radio Education Committee (FREC), on which he had served, Commissioner Hyde asked whether participation on FREC "had not lagged on all camps." McCarty answered: "I should say that interest has lagged particularly on the part of the Commission. . . . The Commission's participation in the deliberations of the Federal Radio Education Committee has been purely nominal and frequently we have had meetings without representation from the Commission" (24:16131).

The reservations of FM channels for educational stations in 1940 and 1945 were both a precedent for reserving television channels and an indication of the prospects that education would use reserved channels. Farley said that by 1950 more than seventy-five educational organizations were giving radio service which had been made possible through the reservation of twenty FM channels.

3. The Need. This factor entailed both exclusive right and time to exercise it. Educators needed the exclusive use of television channels because commercial stations could not or would not provide adequate access and because educators wanted control of program scheduling, sequence, and development. Educators need time because, by the nature of their wide responsibilities and the slow processes of their accountability, they cannot move as fast as commercial agents.

Witnesses documented the breaking or nonfulfillment of many promises that the networks and commercial stations had made in 1934 to give time to educational institutions, and they predicted that new promises by the networks and stations to do so could not be depended upon in television. For example, Robert Lewis Shayon, producer of many commercial network programs, said that educational and cultural programming would never realize significant potential through commercial stations or networks because commercial broadcasters were forced to maximize profits. The president of the Radio and Television Council of Greater Cleveland reported that local stations imposed their own standards for programming and usually ignored community expressions of interests and needs.

Throughout the hearings Commissioner Hyde insisted that the 1935 decision against reserving AM channels had never prevented educators from applying for an AM broadcasting license. In direct response, Harold McCarty told of an application by the University of Wisconsin in 1933 for a clear-channel, shared-time license. Led on by questions from Commissioner Hennock, he gave details: NBC had sent a vice-president, legal counsel, and a Midwest representative to see the governor of Wisconsin, telling him that they would spend a million dollars to oppose the license, and so intimidating the governor that "he advised withdrawal of the application, and it was never pressed" (24:16077).

Several spokesmen wanted educators to be able to schedule programs during hours and in sequences that fitted educational purposes, both in schools and in homes, without interruptions, shifts, censorship, or influence. Louis B. Hoyer, superintendent of the Philadelphia public schools, predicted that available time on commercial television would decrease, as it had in radio, but more rapidly: "If educational television is to survive and expand, there must be safeguards against this eventuality. Some provisions must be made, too, for the teacher training of college students who wish to learn the techniques of educational television. This cannot be done satisfactorily in busy commercial stations" (24:15832).

The need for time to take advantage of reservations was stressed by several witnesses, beginning with U.S. Commissioner of Education Earl James McGrath. Educators are responsible to all segments of the community, he said; the decision-making process is necessarily complicated and slow; without reserved channels all the best channels would be occupied by the time educators would be ready. "Educators and those who are responsible for financing education must plan and operate in terms of decades and generations rather than in terms of months or weeks" (24:15790).

4. The Prospects for Use. The record of educational radio and the preparation for the use of educational television were both presented as encouraging. Without reserved channels financing would be impossible; with them financing would be possible.

Anticipating that at some point S. E. Frost, Jr.'s book *Education's Own Stations*[8] would be used as a weapon against the request for the reservation of TV channels, McCarty analyzed the book's cases in detail, concluding: "The record, so far as my study leads me to conclude, is rather a very heartening one instead of a damaging and disgraceful one" (24:16082). Morris Novik, representing the American Federation of Labor and speaking also from his experience with New York City Municipal Broadcasting System, warned the Commission: "Please don't judge the educational radio stations of 1950 with the stations of 1924–34. They have grown up. They have seen the light. The stations are no longer adjuncts of engineering departments; they are now integral parts of the entire campus" (25:16790). Howard Bevis gave two reasons why educational FM radio had grown slowly: the scarcity of FM receiving sets and the shorter radius of FM stations' coverage. Then a number of spokesmen presented records of impressive educational radio service.

Still, radio was not television. What were educators doing in television? At that time the only television station owned and operated by an educational institution was WOI TV, Iowa State College. It was also the only television station in central Iowa. On a nonprofit basis it was broadcasting both educational programming and the best offerings of all the commercial networks. WOI director Richard Hull cited examples of both educational and commercial programming that were providing the area with both educational and commercial television service. After the freeze, when more commercial stations began in central Iowa, Hull said, WOI TV would become a full-time educational station. In the meantime, it was using its earnings to add studios and equipment for local educational program production. Here was a justification for the exception that the JCET provided for in its request—nonprofit educational stations in communities where only one channel was allocated so that both educational and commercial programming would be offered.

While Commissioner Hennock was without doubt glad Iowa State College had a television station, she was opposed to the nonprofit status and scornful also of a concern for mass audiences. When Hull said some of the better programs from the networks helped establish large audiences for educational programs, she asked, "Why should you care about a substantial audience?" Hull replied, "That is the purpose of mass communications." Unless they reach a large audience, "you had better use some other technique" for reaching the smaller audiences (25:16948). (This argument over the size of audiences for educational stations continues to boil to the present day.)

Howard Bevis reported from a survey he had made of land-grant colleges and state universities that of forty-nine institutions responding, forty-six planned either immediate or future development of an educational TV station and none opposed reserved channels. President John A. Hannah reported that Michigan State College had already approved $110,000 for television equipment and operating expenses.

With the nonprofit status ruled out, except in unusual and probably temporary circumstances, the question of how educational television stations would be financed was crucial. The considerable testimony, queries, and replies led to the conclusion that without reserved channels, there was little hope for financing.

Merlin H. Aylesworth testified that without reservations financing would not be available, but with them support was possible from people who "could endow a television station as well as a law library or a building" (24:16190). In producing Aylesworth as a witness, the JCET was using the divide-and-conquer tactic that the commercial industry had devastatingly used in the 1934 hearings by parading many educators who opposed AM reservations. Aylesworth had been the first president of NBC, and as such had testified before the FCC in 1934 that AM reservations were unnecessary because 20 percent of the programs over his network had educational purpose and another 30 percent had educational value. When educators "are ready we will place our facilities at their disposal without charge," he said. "Our guilt lies in having been too big-hearted in our desire to help educators." By 1950, however, Aylesworth had changed his mind.

5. The Potential of Educational Television. The testimony presented a wide range of programming and services that educational television could perform. Included were programs for children both in and out of school in the fields of music, languages, and philosophy. Experiments and field trips for college and university students were projected, as were news analyses and extension courses and services for adults in rural, urban, and suburban areas.

The Holiday Recess

From the first session of the hearings, commercial broadcasters had become aware that the 1950 proponents of reserved TV channels were much more persuasive than the 1934 proponents of reserved AM channels had been. *Broadcasting* for January 15, 1951, editorialized: "Almost too late organized radio and TV will seek to balance the record on the demands of organized educators who would have Uncle Sam reserve at least 20 percent of available TV spectrum space for pure, unadorned education. Until quite recently there were no comers from the commercial side of TV. Most of them felt they couldn't oppose education any more than they could favor sin." A few commercial interests had filed to be heard after the recess.

The full JCET held a strategy meeting on December 30 to find ways of filling holes in their argument. The members decided that their case had two major weaknesses. First, it had not presented a table showing that it was physically possible for the FCC to allocate specific channels in specific locations to meet the general JCET request for reservations according to a formula based upon need and population and/or student body size. Second, the case had not presented specific evidence to substantiate the frequent assertion that commercial TV programming was unsatisfactory from informational, educational, and cultural points of view.

To fill the first hole the JCET ideally ought to prepare an allocations table for the entire country that would take into account both the needs for reserved channels and the coverage areas of stations. There was not time to draw up such a map for the entire country. Moreover, to calculate the coverage areas of television stations was a highly technical engineering task, made more difficult by the facts that the FCC was considering the use of both the VHF and UHF bands, that 108 VHF stations had already been licensed, and that many features of UHF broadcasting were still unknown. Therefore, the JCET decided to limit its efforts to the highly populated eastern section of the United States (which posed the most allocations problems) and to UHF channels (none of which had yet been licensed).

Francis J. Brown of the American Council on Education and I. Keith Tyler drew up a map (Exhibit 644) showing the need for reserved channels based on city and suburban populations and student enrollments in educational institutions. An electronics engineer whom the JCET commissioned drew up two coverage contour maps (Exhibits 645, 646) to indicate possible UHF noncommercial assignments of channels that would fit the educational needs revealed in the population and enrollment map. The most the JCET could hope to do was to indicate that the matching of need and allocation was physically possible and to suggest an approach that the FCC could follow in making its own allocations table.

The second major task for the JCET during the recess was to gather evidence that commercial television service was inadequate. The NAEB was already planning a monitoring study of network stations' programs. When Taylor heard of these plans at the December 30 meeting of the JCET he and Hull urged that the study be completed in time to present the results at the January sessions. Action was begun the next day. Dallas W. Smythe, chairman of studies for the NAEB and a research professor at

the University of Illinois, directed the study with Donald Horton, a research associate in sociology at the University of Chicago, who had previously been head of television audience research at CBS.

The purpose of the research was to find out the kinds of television
programs being broadcast, the total and the distribution of the time
given to each (hour-by-hour for a week), the number and length of commercials, and the proportion between advertiser sponsored and network
or station supported programs. New York City was chosen as the site of
the study because it was a closed city (with all seven allocated television
channels occupied) and the nation's richest resource for educational and
cultural programming. Seymour Siegel arranged for eight television receiving sets in a hotel suite. Twenty-one volunteers were hired to monitor
the programming. Briefed on the purpose and procedures, equipped with
stop watches, and using special forms, the monitors recorded information on each program which they classified according to seventeen prede-
termined categories (which did not include an "educational" classification
because Smythe judged it too vague—a judgment that later arguments
confirmed). The period monitored was from sign-on to sign-off by each
of the seven stations between January 4 and January 10, 1951. The monitoring studies received wide publicity in the press, which built up interest
in the hearings, so the FCC postponed resumption of the hearings from
January 15 to January 22 to give the JCET time to collate and analyze
the results.

The January Sessions

The JCET presentation lasted for almost three days, beginning January 22 and ending mid-afternoon of January 24. The industry's presentation then began and continued for three full days, ending January 30.
Witnesses for each side were cross-examined by counsel for the other, as
well as by commissioners and their counsel.

1. The JCET Engineering Study. The main points that emerged
from the cross-examination concerned the JCET request for reservations
in both VHF and UHF. Thad Brown, counsel for the Television Broadcasters Association, asked why all educational reservations should not be
UHF. Tyler replied that the future of UHF was very uncertain and that
educators were unwilling to settle for UHF alone. Brown then asked why
educators should want any reservations in the admittedly inferior UHF
band. Farley answered: "You think there may be a possibility there and
if there is, we want to say now that we would like to be protected there"
(26:17609).

2. The JCET Monitoring Study. In spite of its hasty execution and several small errors in tabulation (exposed in cross-examination), the results of the monitoring study obviously impressed the FCC. The study showed that the performance of seven commercial TV stations in the country's largest city was unsatisfactory in terms of informational, educational, and cultural programming and therefore, that noncommercial educational television stations were needed to provide such programming to the public.

The documented description of commercial television programming that the FCC received from the JCET study in 1951 was in the sharpest contrast to the description of radio programming that the Commission had heard from the commercial radio broadcasters in 1934. The decline in quality and the rise of commercialism in radio programming (documented by the FCC in 1946) had carried over into television programming. The commissioners knew, from the number of applications for TV licenses they had received, that the television industry would not be able to give the access to educators that the radio industry in 1934 (with large blocks of time then unsold) had promised to give to educators.

The study revealed that less than one percent of the programming was specifically designed for children. One-fifth of the programs broadcast during hours when children were most likely to watch television was westerns. There was almost no broadcasting of sculpture, painting, graphic arts, decorative arts or architecture, and only one-half hour of programming was sponsored by an educational institution. Newscasts took up 5 percent of the total time monitored, but there was little analysis of events and very little treatment of local problems. There was no in-school programming, no special education programs for the handicapped, no extension courses, and no adult or vocational education courses. Regular commercials took up more than fifty-five hours (10 percent), each averaging seventy-three seconds in length, and there were another twenty-eight hours (depending on how one counted the mix of commercial identification with program content) of "continuous commercials" not included in the 10 percent of regular commercials.

In cross-examination commercial counsel attacked the categorizing system, particularly its lack of a classification for education; the overlooking of program segments (skits and songs within variety entertainment programs); and the concept of the "continuous commercial." Counsel also implied that the reason for insufficient cultural programs and the lack of instructional programs was that educational institutions were uncooperative.

3. The Industry's Presentation. The five witnesses opposing reser-

vations were Kenneth H. Baker, NAB; Charles Church, NAB, Justin Miller, NAB, Frank Stanton, CBS; and Raymond C. Guy, NBC and RCA.

The first witness was Kenneth Baker, director of research for NAB. His intent was to prove, with the aid of exhibits (662–65), that educators had a "poor" broadcasting record in both AM radio and FM radio and that in metropolitan areas where there were educational radio stations commercial radio stations were doing more educational broadcasting than educational stations. Baker criticized the monitoring study's program classification, particularly its omission of a category for educational programming. In a long series of questions Commissioner Hennock elicited Baker's opinion that each kind of program considered was "educative." By the end of the afternoon, lacking evidence to counter the JCET study, Baker changed his judgment: "I am positive it is one of the best studies of its kind, well, the first of its kind ever done in television. It is the only one, absolutely, and the best of its kind" (26:17680). The study was, indeed, the first of a new kind of educational research into program monitoring—a shift from research for the sake of research to research for practical application. The NAEB was soon to make other such monitoring studies, supported by the Fund for Adult Education.

Baker made his formal presentation the next morning. He contended that "with one or two noteworthy exceptions, the educators' experience with radio, both AM and FM, has been a dismal failure . . . not only in in-school, formalized instruction but also in the utilization of the supplemental educational values in standard commercial radio" and that "educators as a group have not evidenced the willingness or the competence in using radio that would justify the reservation to them of any part of the broadcast spectrum" (27:17706–50). He based his conclusion of educational broadcasters' "dismal failure" in AM radio upon Frost's *Education's Own Stations,* which he did not know had been analyzed by McCarty in an earlier session. JCET counsel Telford Taylor led the witness into damaging admissions or reversals. For example, the "one or two noteworthy exceptions" to "dismal failure" grew, specific station by specific station, into many exceptions. The growth in numbers of commercial FM stations which Baker reported failed to mention that most of them were AM-FM operations broadcasting the same programs. The "superior" educational service of commercial stations was based upon Baker's rationale that anything could be educational. Commissioner Hennock elicited the fact that Baker's figures on the "relatively few" educational FM stations had omitted about eighty 10-watt stations. By the noon recess Baker was thoroughly discredited, and the succeeding witnesses for commercial broadcasting carefully avoided accusing educational broadcasters of incompetence.

Frank Stanton, president of CBS, argued that the FCC's major concern should be to promote a strong commercial television system, which would thereby provide the necessary foundation for later development of an educational service. He gave three reasons why noncommercial reservations would not be in the public interest: "(1) the overriding importance of a general television service; (2) the need for a sound and competitive service; (3) the very real danger that the reservations may result in non-use which would waste spectrum space" (27:18070). In cross-examination, Taylor elicited from Stanton qualifications or concessions on each point.

Justin Miller, president of NAB, prefaced his remarks with the criticism that few commercial broadcasters could testify because they had not been given time to prepare. Under questioning by several commissioners and Taylor, Miller amended his remarks to mean that his attention had not been called to the notice of appearance filed by the Office of Education on August 26, 1949, or to the supplementary notice filed by the JCET on November 20, 1950—another indication that the industry had not taken the educators' capabilities seriously. Miller argued against reservation of channels: devices other than television offered greater flexibility for the specialized areas of education; to meet increased enrollments educational institutions needed more teachers and buildings rather than the "luxury" of television; educators were not ready for VHF; and by the time they were ready to use television, the UHF band would probably be considerably improved.

Charles Church, Jr., director of education and research, KMBC, Kansas City, speaking for the NAB, reverted to the 1934 arguments against reservations—they would be a waste, and educators should either cooperate with commercial facilities or compete for licenses with commercial applicants on equal terms. The preservation of natural resources, he said, did not prohibit utilization.

THE COINCIDENCE OF MARCH 22, 1951

On March 21, 1951, the FCC issued the "Third Notice" proposing the reservations of 209 noncommercial educational channels within a national allocations table.

News of the "Third Notice" was made public on March 22. That was the first day of a two-day conference that Arthur Adams, president of·the American Council on Education, called for the representatives of the seven organizations that had made up the Ad Hoc Joint Committee on Educational Television. (In February Richard Hull had written to Adams that, although the Ad Hoc JCET had "ceased to exist on January 30, at the hour when the FCC closed the hearings on the educational phase of the current proceedings," a continuing organization was needed.) To consider the need Adams had called the meeting. It opened in elation over the FCC's proposal. When it closed on March 23, the JCET had been reorganized as a permanent agency. The history of broadcasting in the United States had taken a sharp turn.

THE U.S. LAISSEZ FAIRE
BROADCASTING SYSTEM

THE FEDERAL COMMUNICATION COMMISSION'S 1951 proposal to reserve television channels for educational stations was the first formal step toward withdrawing from commercial use a significant part of the electromagnetic spectrum in the United States that commercial broadcasters valued. Although the Commission in 1940 and 1945 had previously reserved bands in the higher radio frequencies for noncommercial educational broadcast stations, commercial interests did not much value these channels because they were not ready for rapid development. These commercial interests highly valued the VHF channels that the FCC in 1951 proposed to reserve.

The commercial nature of the American radio broadcasting system was well described by Armstrong Perry, of the National Committee on Education by Radio, after attending the 1931 World Conference on Radio in Vienna and inspecting broadcasting services in twenty-nine countries. He was quoted in the *Congressional Record* of February 18, 1932, as saying: "The information gathered indicated that the United States stands almost alone among the nations of the world in its policy of placing radio channels in the hands of commercial concerns to be used as they see fit. . . . Advertisers are permitted to buy time in some countries, but they do not dominate the air."

How did such a system develop in the United States? This "flashback" chapter will try to answer that question.

27

THE NEED TO REGULATE BROADCASTING

Governments must regulate broadcasting for two reasons. The first is that, by national laws and international agreements, they must regulate the traffic of the signals so that the many uses of the spectrum do not interfere with one another. The second reason is that broadcasting has great power to affect the behavior of individuals and groups.

Once a government has recognized the need to regulate broadcasting, it must answer three questions: (1) To what uses will broadcasting be put? (2) Who will control the content of the broadcasts and how? (3) Who will support the costs of broadcasting and how? Each government has answered these questions in its own special way, and therefore the broadcasting system of each nation is unique. However, national broadcasting systems can be categorized into at least four clearly identifiable types, which are often combined in various ways. These types may be tagged "state control," "public corporation," "state-private partnership," and "laissez faire."

In the first type, the state uses, controls, and supports broadcasting; the system of the USSR is an example. In the second type, the state establishes a public corporation and, within the limits of a charter, provides for the corporation to have monopolistic use, control, and support of broadcasting autonomous of the government; the British broadcasting system from 1927 to 1954 was an example. In the third category the state enters into a partnership with a private corporation and, in exchange for a share of the profits, grants the private corporation exclusive use and control of broadcasting; Radio Luxembourg is an example. Fourth, in the laissez faire type the government, with a minimum of regulation, permits individual licensees to use, control, and support broadcasting; the U.S. broadcasting system was of this type until the period 1952–67, when a national public educational component was gradually added to the national private commercial component.

Because contrast with and comparison to other types of broadcasting systems may help Americans better understand the unique characteristics of their own system, I will now briefly sketch the developments until the end of World War II of broadcasting in several other countries.[1]

STATE CONTROL

The Soviet Union

When the Bolsheviks seized and used the Moscow radio station early in the 1917 civil war, they set the basic pattern for broadcasting in Russia even before the Communist system was established. The Communist party and state have direct and exclusive use, control, and support of broadcasting. Most programming is propagandistic, including many large informational, educational, and cultural segments.

After experimentation the first Soviet broadcasting station operating on a regular schedule went on the air in 1922. Its first program was an all-Russian musical concert. The recorded speeches of Lenin were being broadcast by December 1922, and by 1924 the fare also included theatrical performances, news, political speeches, and lectures. By 1926 the government linked Moscow and several other cities through short wave. During the next decade it constructed an extensive radio network throughout the country and stressed group listening in factories, "houses of culture," stores, and dormitories. It was slow to enter television; in 1960 there were only five million TV sets in the Soviet Union. By 1975 the number was fifty-five million. In 1978 almost two-thirds of the nation's households had TV sets. "Saturation" is planned in time for the 1980 Olympics in Moscow.[2]

Not all state-controlled broadcasting systems have been as uncomplicated and stable as that of the USSR, as evidenced by the systems of Fascist Italy, Imperial Japan, and Nazi Germany.

Fascist Italy

When Mussolini took power in October 1922, he began the organized use of propaganda by the press, cinema, and radio to shape both domestic and foreign opinion. A royal decree of February 8, 1923, declared that the Ministry of Posts and Telegraphs, in consultation with the army and the navy, had jurisdication over broadcasting.

The state had an official censor in every station, and all news programs not provided by Mussolini's press agency had to be approved by a local party representative. The state granted a broadcasting license to a limited company, *Unione Radiofonica Italiana* (URI), giving it exclusive authority to broadcast in Italy for six years. The company installed a central transmission facility in Rome and regional stations in Naples, Palermo, and Milan and had authority to establish additional stations in other cities.

The state arranged for financial support through the terms of URI's capitalization, income, and fees. A tax was imposed on the sale of radio parts to citizens, 10 percent of which went to the state and 90 percent to the company. Sellers of receiving sets paid the company license fees in proportion to their business. The company paid the Ministry of Communications an annual fee for each station in operation and also other fees it collected from those individuals and companies who used radio receivers.

Mussolini made several important changes in the control of radio before World War II, including the replacement of URI by a new broadcasting company, *Ente Italiano Audizioni Radiofoniche* (EIAR) in 1926, and the addition of *Ente Radiorurale* (ER) in 1933. ER was a rural radio agency designed to encourage the purchase of radio sets by rural people and thereby improve their farming methods. But such changes did not alter the state's control over all communications media by "private" corporations. This trend was formalized in 1936 with the establishment of a Ministry of Press and Propaganda, which controlled all mass media, including broadcasting.

Imperial Japan

Another version of state controlled broadcasting evolved in Japan. Broadcasting began in that country in 1925 over stations in Tokyo, Osaka, and Nagoya owned and operated by various private companies, principally local newspapers. In 1926 these three stations were merged into a single corporation, the predecessor of the present Japan Broadcasting Corporation (NHK). The system that developed until Japan was defeated in World War II was not a private enterprise, although it was commercially owned and operated and supported by fees on receiving sets. It was not a state-syndicalist corporation in the fascist model, although it had a state monopoly. Broadcasting in Japan developed at a time when a veneer of modernization overlay a bedrock of feudalism, when degrees of freedom were granted as privileges from the state, with sovereignty residing in the emperor exercised through a complex of governmental agencies—legislative, executive, and military. As wars were begun and escalated the result was that, along with all other forms of communication—indeed, all other aspects of individual and social life—broadcasting was an instrument of a totalitarian military state system, no less complete than were the broadcasting systems of the Soviet Union, Fascist Italy, and Nazi Germany.

Nazi Germany

The Weimar Republic developed an elaborate "nonpolitical" broadcasting system which combined state supervision and private control, and centralized and regionalized programming. The Ministry of Posts built the radio transmitters, but privately licensed companies provided the programming. The system was financed by an annual license tax on receivers, with the revenue shared equally by the federal government and the private broadcasting companies.

The first broadcasting license was granted in 1923 to a Berlin company, and the next year eight other companies were licensed to provide programs from studios in Leipzig, Munich, Frankfurt, Hamburg, Stuttgart, Breslau, Konigsberg, and Cologne. In 1926 a national broadcasting company was founded in which the Ministry of Posts held 51 percent of the stock, with the rest held by private interests. That same year the national company established a station in Berlin and assumed economic control of all the broadcasting stations in the republic. Regional governments appointed "cultural committees" to advise the stations and studios on programming. A "supervisory committee" of three members (one representing the federal government, the other two the region) was appointed in each region to guard against partisan material. News was provided by DRADAG, a company in which the federal government held a majority of the stock.

Preparation to convert this nonpartisan system into a centralized political instrument for the federal state began with the Papen government in 1932. When Adolph Hitler became chancellor and Joseph Goebbels his minister of propaganda early in 1933, the German broadcasting system and all other systems of communication came entirely under the control of the state.

PUBLIC CORPORATION CONTROL

The concern of British leaders over the use, control, and support of broadcasting was a symptom of an important social evolution following World War I. An aristocratic society governed by people whose interests were global and imperial seized on domestic broadcasting as an important instrument to retain continuity and guide development during a period of profound internal change. The "common people" had for decades been making claims to political, economic, and social rights that after 1918 could not be denied. Broadcasting, both as a service that the people wanted and as a force that would profoundly affect their lives, could not be ignored. The British leaders closely watched the American experience with broadcasting between 1920 and 1926, and feared the consequences of a laissez faire system in Great Britain. They therefore directed broadcasting toward the intellectual and cultural progress of the people in the democratic atmosphere that was emerging in Great Britain.

Although the British Broadcasting Corporation (BBC) as a public body with a royal charter was not established until 1927, the essential principles and features of the British broadcasting system began with the formation of the private British Broadcasting Company in December 1922. Soon after World War I commercial interests (led by the Marconi Company) were authorized to begin broadcasting news, weather reports, and music. For a short time it appeared that commercial broadcasting would develop in Great Britain similar to the way it was booming in the United States. But the postmaster general, who had authority to grant radio licenses, believed that it would be better for the various companies to form a single company rather than to compete. Therefore, the British Broadcasting Company was established, and on January 18, 1923, it was authorized to construct and operate eight broadcasting stations. All the commercial interests that were, or could be permitted to become, members of the company were manufacturers of radio equipment, and their sole interest in broadcasting was to present programs that would induce the people to buy sets. Every owner of a receiving set was assessed an annual license fee of ten shillings, half of which went to the company and half to the government.

The British Broadcasting Company was considered experimental and was granted a license for two years only. Nevertheless, the principles on which the company was authorized were to characterize the British broadcasting system for more than thirty years. The principles were: the radio spectrum is in the public domain and the government should exercise control over both transmission and reception; the postmaster general should license all transmitters and receiving sets; and the system should be financed by annual license fees on receiving sets rather than by the sale of time for advertising.

In response to protests against monopoly and unfair competition with newspapers, the postmaster general appointed a committee to study the situation and make recommendations. The committee reaffirmed the basic principles of the experimental arrangement, and the license of the British Broadcasting Company was renewed for another two years, until December 31, 1926.

Broadcasting developed so rapidly and concern over entrusting such power to a private monopoly grew so keen that the postmaster general appointed a second committee. The major recommendation of this committee was that a public corporation replace the private company to serve as "trustee for the national interest in broadcasting."

Adopting this recommendation, the government petitioned that the charter for a public corporation be granted by the Crown, explaining that the public would regard a Crown corporation as a public institution with the "greatest possible latitude" rather than as a creature of Parliament. And on January 1, 1927, the British Broadcasting Company became the British Broadcasting Corporation and was chartered for ten years. Despite the transition, there was no discernible change in BBC policy or programming. In fact, the first major change in the British broadcasting system was the formation in 1954 of another public corporation, the Independent Television Authority (ITA), also under the jurisdiction of the postmaster general, to introduce commercial television into Great Britain.

STATE-PRIVATE PARTNERSHIP COMMERCIAL CONTROL

Radio broadcasting in Luxembourg is an example of exclusive commercial use, control, and support. In that country the government exercises jurisdiction but enters into contractual agreement with a monopolistic commercial company, the Luxembourg Broadcasting Company, to share in the profits. The company determines the programming. The pattern was set in 1929, and (except for difficulties during and immediately after World War II) the monopolistic state-commercial partnership has continued and been profitable for both partners. Since 1966 the government's share of the profits from commercial broadcasting has been one of its largest sources of revenue.

Luxembourg's broadcasting system must be regarded as a supplementary type rather than an exclusively alternative type. Luxembourg, with fewer than one thousand square miles and almost 350,000 people, could not on its own provide much broadcasting service to its people alone. However, it borders on Belgium, Germany, and France, and its people are bilingual and widely multilingual. They have had access to the radio broadcasting from neighboring countries, and, in turn, their commercial broadcasting has been a supplementary source of radio broadcasting to the citizens of neighboring countries. For over forty years Radio Luxembourg has been a source of commercial radio programming to Great Britain, France, Belgium, the Netherlands, Germany, and the Scandinavian countries as well as its own people. It has been a major influence in the introduction of commercial broadcasting into the systems of Great Britain and several Western European countries that at first did not have it.

The fact that the broadcasting areas of many European countries overlap sufficiently to give their peoples familiarity with several types of programming provides an important contrast with the broadcasting situation in the United States. For all its many stations and great resources, the American broadcasting system kept the American people generally parochial in their awareness of potential choices. The more pervasive and dominant commercial broadcasting became, the more deeply it was incorporated into the mind-set of the American people.

LAISSEZ FAIRE

Unlike the preceding systems of national broadcasting, the American system developed with little government interference. By 1950 it had developed into a preponderantly commercial system supported by advertising with a minimum of governmental regulation.[3] The formative developments took place in the prebroadcasting period (until 1920, when previously the primary use of radio was point-to-point communication) and before the passage of the first law to regulate broadcasting—the Radio Act of 1927. That law ratified a system already formed by the workings of free competition. The succeeding Communications Act of 1934 was a re-enactment of the portions of the Radio Act of 1927 and an addition of authority to include the regulation of telephone and telegraph as well. The broadcasting system and the regulatory agencies (the Federal Radio Commission from 1927 to 1934 and the Federal Communications Commission from 1934 to date) continued into the age of television unchanged in any important way.

RADIO IN THE UNITED STATES BEFORE 1920

The United States had no law regulating broadcasting as such until 1927. The Radio Act of 1912, the governing law until 1927, was designed to control point-to-point communications. The practical use of radio in 1912 was to communicate between ships, between ships and shore stations, and between stations on land.

A main reason for the 1912 act was to eliminate unnecessary interference by amateur radio operators with governmental, military, and commercial point-to-point communications. The United States was late in enacting such regulation. Great Britain had adopted radio laws in 1904; the Berlin Convention of 1906 had recommended the prevention of interference with distress signals. Events in 1912 brought action in Congress. A U.S. Navy admiral was unable to communicate with a Navy yard "because of amateur clamor," and rescue work in the Titanic disaster had been hampered by signals irrelevant to the rescue.

The 1912 act reserved a segment of the spectrum for government use —between wavelengths of 1600 and 600 meters, or, translated into frequencies, between 187 and 500 kilocycles (kc.). This is the band in which radio signals carry the farthest. Although unforeseeable at that time, this reservation in the band for governmental use forced broadcasting to develop in the upper frequencies. It blocked the development of radio broadcasting stations that could reach thousands of miles. For transmitting beyond the 187–500 kc. band, a person was required to have a license specifying frequency and hours on the air, and at least supervision by a federally licensed operator. Licenses were available upon application from the Secretary of Commerce and Labor (Secretary of Commerce after 1913) to any citizen of the United States or Puerto Rico or to any company incorporated under the laws of a state, Puerto Rico, or territory of the United States. The act did not give the Secretary authority to deny a license to an applicant who met the requirements prescribed by the law. In the year of its passage the Attorney General handed down the opinion that the act gave the Secretary "no general regulatory power." In brief, the Radio Act of 1912 provided a registration procedure for point-to-point radio communications.

Although the act made no explicit recognition that "amateurs" were giving a service recognized as important to the public, they were the ones who would develop broadcasting. In the early days of radio every amateur, one of them wrote, "felt that the world was his to explore." By the end of 1912 there were 1,224 amateur licensees, as compared to 405 ship-station and 123 land-station licensees. Among the amateur licensees were many colleges and universities, some of which already had years of experience in radio behind them. The amateurs were assigned the area above 500 kc., which was to become the range for AM broadcasting. However, the act provided for special licenses to experiment, "using any amount of power or wavelengths, at such hours and under such conditions as will insure the least interference." Other than this provision, no thought was given to the higher frequencies. Yet the later development of the electromagnetic spectrum for broadcasting and other uses spurred the exploitation of the higher frequencies.

World War I

Amateur licensees had increased to 8,562 on the eve of World War

I, and by then they had done or were doing most of what was to become radio broadcasting. They had made no impact upon the general public, however, nor were they to do so until after World War I—and then there would be a new type of "amateur" and a new type of station.

Upon the Declaration of War on April 7, 1917, President Wilson (using authority in the 1912 act) seized all amateur radio apparatus and all commercial radio facilities, delegating control of them to the Navy. The Navy sealed, dismantled, or used the amateur and commercial transmitters for training purposes. Both the Army and the Navy used radio with great effectiveness during World War I, primarily for point-to-point transmission (with the notable exceptions of Wilson's broadcasts of his Fourteen Points to the people of Europe and his appeal to the people of Germany to overthrow their kaiser).

Although patent struggles between private companies were suspended during World War I, radio technology advanced rapidly, both by forced growth at home (particularly improvements of tubes and transmitters) and by inventions captured from the Germans. Hundreds of thousands of young American men in the armed forces became interested and tens of thousands were trained in radio during their service. Many companies, large and small, produced wide varieties and huge quantities of radio apparatus and parts for sale to the government.

After the war the Navy delayed lifting the ban on amateur transmitters until mid-1919 and delayed returning commercial facilities until early 1920. The reason was that some leaders in the Navy, the cabinet, and Congress wanted to perpetuate the Navy's monopoly control over radio for point-to-point communications, or to have the government give a monopoly charter to a single commercial corporation. In preparation for this latter possibility, the Radio Corporation of America (RCA) was formed on October 17, 1919—a creation of Owen D. Young. An alliance of several corporations, at various times it included General Electric, American Telephone and Telegraph Company, Western Electric, and what had been American Marconi. The terms of the alliance provided, among other things, for cross-licensing of patents.

Neither the proposal to perpetuate control of radio by the Navy nor the proposal to grant monopoly control to a corporation received serious congressional consideration in 1918 and 1919, and neither needs to be considered seriously today as an arrangement that would have endured for long if adopted. Both were concerned with establishing a worldwide point-to-point communications system that would give the United States supremacy in world wireless communication. Both were based upon use of the lower and medium frequencies, which required powerful, expensive transmitters, and either arrangement would soon have been made obsolete by the development of the short-wave segment of the spectrum (between 3,500 and 26,100 kc.), using much more simple and economical equipment and much less power.

The decision-makers of 1918 and 1919 could not foresee such developments, of course. Nevertheless, they decided to let the use, control, and support of radio in the United States return to the prewar status—maximum individual freedom under a minimum of government regulation. Their rationale was that American society puts high value on freedom of speech, and radio was regarded as a medium for speech; society also values individual initiative of all kinds, particularly business enterprise, and radio was seen as a proper field for individual initiative and business enterprise; and finally, society recognizes the advantages of competition, and radio was regarded as a fit field for competition.

FORMATION OF THE U.S. SYSTEM OF BROADCASTING

On October 16, 1920, Westinghouse Electric and Manufacturing Corporation applied to the Department of Commerce for a special license to begin broadcasting service in Pittsburgh. The department authorized use of 833.3 kc.—a channel away from the amateurs and comparatively free from interference. The special service began with the broadcast of the returns of the Harding-Cox elections. The instant success of that station, KDKA, and the national publicity it received demonstrated that the American people were hungry for broadcasts of news, information, and entertainment. Soon many individuals and corporations began to apply for licenses to broadcast regular programs to the public over powerful transmitters. In January 1921, the Department of Commerce formally adopted "broadcasting" as a special class of stations and began to issue licenses for such stations. From January through November it issued five; in December it issued twenty-three.

All broadcasting stations were given the same frequency on dial—833.3 kc., the spot allocated for "news, entertainment, and information." Because the 1912 Act had not been designed to deal with this congestion of the air waves, a new law was required to regulate traffic. Seven years passed before a breakdown of the old law forced Congress to enact a new one. However, the decisions that were made and actions that were taken in the interim determined the structures, processes, and contents of American broadcasting. The new law, when it finally came, was a ratification of the results of unrestrained competition.

Financing: The Determining Factor

Anyone who applied and met the requirements of American citizen-ship or incorporation was legally entitled to get a broadcasting license. A breakdown of the ownership of the 576 broadcasting stations licensed as of February 1, 1923, reveals that communication manufacturers and set dealers held 39 percent; educational institutions, 12 percent; publishers, 12 percent; department stores, 5 percent; religious institutions, 2 percent; and "others" (e.g., city governments, automobile dealers, theaters, and banks), 30 percent. There was, however, no overall plan for the use and financing of American broadcasting.

Radio Broadcast raised the question of financial support in its first issue, May 1922. Judging that equipment manufacturers would not bear the mounting costs after the radio-buying boom subsided, the magazine said "some different scheme of financing" would have to emerge, and it mentioned the possibilities of the "endowment of a station by a public-spirited citizen," "municipal financing," and "a common fund . . . controlled by an elected board." But the magazine did not suggest either the sale of time for advertising or financing by state governments.[4] Yet the sale of time for advertising had already been publicly proposed by the American Telephone and Telegraph Company (although its term was "tolls," for the company's long-distance lines linking a network of "radiotelephone" stations), and from the start financing by the states was the source of the most stable educational radio stations.

The Readiness for Commercial Broadcasting

By 1920 all the ingredients were present for the development of a national commercial system of broadcasting based on the sale of time for advertising. Technology was ready, and American business was ready to exploit the potential of broadcasting and to make it into a national sys-tem. The preconditions of mass production, distribution, and communi-cation (including advertising) were ready, as were the preconditions of mass consumption.

American commercial broadcasting arrived at the final solution of financial support through three different routes that eventually con-verged in the sale of time for advertising. These routes and their eventual convergence, which no one saw clearly ahead of the event, can be traced in three case studies.

Westinghouse Electric and Manufacturing Corporation, whose ex-ploration discovered that the American people were ready for radio broadcasting, was driven in its search by the need to find new markets for its electronic products. Its large government market for radio equipment had ended with the war. It could not seek markets in marine and transoceanic communication because General Electric, its chief competitor, already had access to many necessary patents in that area through alliance with RCA. Westinghouse, however, had bought the rights to the Armstrong "heterodyne" circuit, which was to become the basis for improved receiving sets, and it had a government contract to produce lightweight radio transmitters and receivers, which it was doing in Pittsburgh.

Inventor Frank Conrad, a Westinghouse employee, was an amateur radio broadcaster in Pittsburgh, where a department store was advertising his broadcasts in order to sell "amateur wireless sets." Harry P. Davis, a Westinghouse vice-president stationed in Pittsburgh, was astute enough to see in that newspaper ad the possibility of developing a huge American market for receiving sets and parts. Westinghouse applied for and received a special license to broadcast the 1920 presidential election returns. Public interest in the broadcast and demand for sets and parts were spectacular. Westinghouse continued and improved programming on the new station, KDKA, and carefully publicized the demonstration that the American people were ready to receive broadcasting, given good, inexpensive sets and interesting programs. The corporation increased the transmitting power of KDKA and set up other powerful stations in Newark, N.J., and Springfield, Mass.

The American Telephone and Telegraph Company entered broadcasting by a different route, and it did so cautiously to avoid the danger of being eclipsed by a new corporation with a new technology. Yet it wanted both to exploit the business of long-distance telephone service that network broadcasting would require and (to protect its patents) to form radio as much as possible in the image of "radio telephony" rather than "broadcasting." Therefore, on February 11, 1922, AT&T made public a plan for a network of thirty-eight AT&T "radiotelephone stations" linked by its own long-distance lines, all stations operating on a "toll" basis paid by the sender of messages. It would launch a station (later WEAF) in New York City first. The company announced that it would provide no programming of its own but would provide the channels through which anyone with whom it made a contract could send programs. AT&T was trying to stake out exclusive claim to provide the public with radio telephone service—"radio telephone"—on a commercial basis. The plan was called an experiment but, AT&T added, "If this experiment succeeds, a commercial basis for broadcasting will have been established."[5]

John Romulus Brinkley, after a career of transplanting goat glands to men, practicing with a diploma-mill medical degree, entered broadcasting in 1923 to hawk his hospital and nostrum medicines over half the country and beyond. His station, KFKB, Milford, Kansas, started with a 1000-watt station and a preferred position on the dial. The Department of Commerce permitted him to increase his power several times. "We are prospering because our keynote is service," he used to explain. Among his services was the broadcast of the Kansas State College "School of the Air," which by 1924 had for-credit enrollments in thirty-nine states and Canada.

The Founding of Networks

When the Radio Corporation of America saw in the Pittsburgh demonstration the potential of the domestic market for broadcasting, it devised two plans for a national service, one in terms of the sender of programs, the other in terms of the people receiving the programs. The plan in terms of the sender, the AT&T plan, has already been discussed. The plan in terms of the receiver of programs came from David Sarnoff, who was taken over by RCA when it absorbed the Marconi Wireless Company in 1921. In 1916 Sarnoff had outlined to Marconi a plan for developing a "Radio Music Box" that would make radio a "household utility." Marconi ignored the plan, but Sarnoff resubmitted it, elaborated with estimates of future sales, to his new RCA employer, Owen D. Young. In April 1921, Sarnoff became general manager of RCA. Thus RCA, a large and loose alliance, had internal tensions. Would national networking, when it arrived, come through the telephone route or through the broadcasting route? The outcome was shaped by the intra and intercorporate struggles within the RCA alliance and also by actions by the federal government.

On March 23, 1923, Congress requested the Federal Trade Commission to investigate the radio industry to ascertain whether there was possible violation of antitrust laws. In January 1924, the FTC reported that the facts warranted a complaint. It charged the allies—AT&T, RCA, General Electric, Westinghouse, United Fruit, and subsidiaries— with combination and conspiracy to restrain competition and create a monopoly. The FTC began hearings, which put pressure on the accused corporations to settle their differences.

The resolution of the struggle within RCA was the formation of the National Broadcasting Company. The agreements concerning patent and business arrangements that had been made by the members of the RCA alliance in 1919 and 1920 had been written to deal, not with broadcasting, but with wire and wireless telegraphy and telephony. The development of radio broadcasting, however, provoked disagreements. AT&T was interpreting the previous agreements as though they applied only to telephone; RCA, GE, and Westinghouse were interpreting them as though they applied only to broadcasting. The members of the RCA alliance, foreseeing possible disagreements, had set up an arbitration procedure, which they invoked in 1924, each side presenting its case to referee Roland W. Boyden.

After weeks of arguments and testimony, Boyden decided in favor of the radio group (RCA, GE, and Westinghouse). Immediately AT&T, which had sold its stock in RCA, threatened to give evidence against the radio group in the FTC's charge of monopoly. A settlement was made in which AT&T withdrew from broadcasting, RCA bought AT&T's station WEAF, and RCA adopted "toll" network broadcasting, with a contract to use AT&T's long-distance telephone lines exclusively.

On September 9, 1926, RCA incorporated a new company—the National Broadcasting Company. A few days later RCA took full-page newspaper advertisements throughout the country: "ANNOUNCING THE NATIONAL BROADCASTING COMPANY, INC. National radio broadcasting with better programs permanently assured by this important action of the Radio Corporation of America in the interests of the listening public."

RCA avoided reference to the sale of time for advertising. The word is not mentioned in the national announcement even though the newly purchased WEAF was grossing $750,000 a year by 1926 through advertising. The entire announcement is stated in terms of the sale of receiving sets:

> The Radio Corporation of America is the largest distributor of radio receiving sets in the world. . . . The market for receiving sets in the future will be determined largely by the quantity and quality of the program broadcast. . . .
> The purpose of [NBC] will be to provide the best programs available for broadcast in the United States. The National Broadcasting Company will not only broadcast these through station WEAF, but it will make them available to other broadcasting stations in the country so far as it may be practicable to do so, and they may desire to take them.[6]

By January 1927, NBC had two networks on the air—the "Red," fed by WEAF, New York, and the "Blue," fed by WJZ, Newark, N.J. Available stations on each grew rapidly. In 1927 the Columbia Broadcasting System became a competing network. Having no parent company with receiving sets to sell, CBS could not avoid using the word "advertising," but this was an unimportant detail. The fact was that even though AT&T had withdrawn from broadcasting its "tolls," now properly called advertising, had become the economic basis of American commercial broadcasting. Moreover, networking made American commercial broadcasting into a national system. On the one hand, network affiliation became almost indispensable for station profit; on the other hand, network profit depended to a large extent on having local affiliates.

Thus the founding of networks was a major event that determined the structure, processes, and contents of the U.S. broadcasting system, and it occurred before the country had a law specifically designed to regulate broadcasting. In addition to commercial forces, the policies and actions of the federal government shaped broadcasting both locally and nationally between 1921 and 1927.

HOOVER'S CONFERENCES AND ACTIONS

The Department of Commerce had already established broadcasting as a special class of stations when Herbert Hoover became its secretary in March 1921. However, his authority "to regulate radio communications," in the opinion of the Attorney General, gave him "no general regulatory authority." But increasing demands for broadcasting station licenses moved Hoover to hold a Washington Radio Conference on February 27, 1922, "to inquire into the critical situation that has now arisen through the astonishing development of the wireless telephone; to advise the Department of Commerce as to the application of its present powers of regulation; and further to formulate such recommendations to Congress as to the legislation necessary."[7] The twenty-two conferees (radio executives, representatives of government, inventors and engineers, and an amateur representative) recommended that the Secretary of Commerce be given "adequate legal authority" for control. Numerous bills were drafted in response to the conference—one to give all licensing authority without court review to the Secretary of Commerce, one to establish an independent regulatory commission, another to nationalize radio broadcasting, and still another to operate government stations. In all, twenty bills relating to broadcasting were introduced in the 67th Congress of 1921–23.

When Hoover saw that no legislation was going to be passed before the foreseeable "chaos of the air" became a reality, he called three more Washington radio conferences, in 1923, 1924, and 1925. Each succeeding conference was larger than the previous one (the twenty-two conferees in 1922 had grown to four hundred in 1925, including a few representatives of educational stations), each made more explicit recommendations, and each led to action by the Secretary of Commerce.

After the 1922 conference the department opened the 750-kc. frequency to broadcasting stations, in addition to the 833.3 frequency. The 750-kc. stations, which were later called Class B stations, had to operate on power between 500 and 1000 watts and were not permitted to use phonograph records, in order to make them produce original programs. Stations not able to meet these requirements had to remain at the congested 833.3 spot.

After the 1923 conference the department divided stations into three classes. The first class was those stations broadcasting at high power, 500 to 1000 watts or more, serving large areas within which they had no interference. These stations were on various channels between 550 and 1000 kc., and time on the air was shared as necessary. The use of phonograph records was prohibited. The second class of stations had power of 500 watts or less and served smaller areas within which they had no interference. These stations broadcast on various frequencies between 1000 and 1350 kc. and also shared time as necessary. The third group was the remaining stations—low powered, all at the same 833.3 spot on the dial, sharing time as required, and, in many cases, limited to daytime hours.

After the 1924 conference, at the urging of such industrial leaders as David Sarnoff to permit a limited group of strategically located "superpower stations" to serve the entire country, Hoover authorized WJZ and WGY to experiment with 50,000 watts. WJZ, Newark, N.J., was a Westinghouse station; WGY, Schenectady, was a General Electric station (both companies were already under investigation by the Federal Trade Commission for illegal restraint of competition).

After the 1925 conference Hoover finally did what many radio executives had long been urging him to do: he began telling applicants that "all wavelengths are in use" and no more licenses could be issued. This decision introduced trafficking in licenses (the sale and purchase of already licensed stations), which the department encouraged. A spokesman told a Senate committee: "We take the position that the license ran to the apparatus, and if there is no good reason to the contrary, we will recognize that sale and license the new owners of the apparatus." Because licenses were no longer available through the Department of Commerce, pressure to sell was put upon the financially weak commercial stations and the educational stations.

A Pattern Emerges

During the four Washington radio conferences there were developments and refinements in the radio industry's position on advertising, monopolies, and the social role of broadcasting.

One major development concerned the attitude toward the sale of time for advertising as an economic basis for broadcasting. The members of the first Washington Radio Conference (1922) were almost unanimously opposed to advertising. The members of the fourth Washington Radio Conference (1925) generally accepted advertising in principle, although they did not agree upon the standards by which it should be judged or who should judge it.

Another development during the four years concerned monopoly. By 1922 the RCA alliance included General Electric, Westinghouse, AT&T, and others; the members of the alliance had pooled their patent rights and entered into more than twenty licensing, traffic, and sales agreements. The stations of the alliance received most of the preferred Class B allocations that the Department of Commerce made in 1922, and also received most of the preferred first and second group allocations made in 1923. Moreover, as has been mentioned, in 1924 Westinghouse's WJZ, Newark, and General Electric's WGY, Schenectady, received permission to operate with 50,000 watts.

A third development concerned the views of the social role of broadcasting. At each of the four conferences spokesmen hailed broadcasting as an influence that could incalculably improve the intellectual and cultural quality of American life. Secretary Hoover said at the first radio conference: "It is inconceivable that we should allow so great a possibility for service to be drowned in advertising chatter."[8] Nevertheless, the conferees gradually accepted advertising as the economic basis of broadcasting, and they also recommended and approved actions that strengthened the strong commercial stations and weakened the educational stations.

A contradiction appeared at the fourth conference when many members urged the Secretary to cut back on, even to abolish, the numerous low-powered stations clustered at the 833.3 point on the dial, which embraced almost all the educational stations. Yet that same conference passed a resolution calling for the Department of Commerce to give full recognition to the need for educational broadcasting stations and recommending that "adequate, definite, and specific provision should be made for those services within the broadcast band of frequencies." This contradiction revealed the tension of values and goals that would later be partially resolved by the development of a combination commercial-noncommercial system of broadcasting.

The pattern that can be discerned in these developments was the evolution of an overwhelmingly commercial national system of broadcasting supported by advertising and the near disappearance of educational stations. This evolution was furthered by action following each of the four Washington radio conferences. The strong commercial stations could afford to meet the conditions and costs of preferred station classification. The financially weak commercial stations and most of the educational stations could not. When, after the 1925 conference, the department closed licensing through applications and permitted acquiring licenses through the purchase of "apparatus," trafficking in licenses began, and it increased the next year when national commercial networks were founded. An educational institution selling its station was often reassured by the purchaser's promise that he would give the educational institution "free time" to broadcast over the station.

REGULATION BREAKS DOWN

If the Secretary of Commerce had not acted firmly the American airwaves would have become chaotic before 1926. But some persons that were given unfavorable treatment questioned the legality of his actions. When Hoover said he would welcome a test case, Eugene F. McDonald, of Zenith Radio Corporation, intentionally provided one. Zenith had a radio station, WJAZ, Chicago, assigned only two hours a day on a frequency shared with GE station KOA, Denver. Zenith deliberately began broadcasting on a less congested channel—one, moreover, that the United States had ceded to Canada. The Department of Commerce brought suit against Zenith in 1925. The next year a federal court ruled that a station owner could not be punished for disregarding a frequency allocated by the Secretary because the Radio Act of 1912 established no standard by which the discretion of the Secretary was to be controlled. The U.S. Attorney General quickly advised the Secretary that he had no authority to limit the frequency, power, or time used by any station. In effect, the United States had no valid law regulating broadcasting.

Broadcasters responded accordingly. In the less than a year between the Zenith decision and the passage of the Radio Act of 1927, 200 new broadcasting stations went on the air, and an uncountable number shifted frequencies, power, and hours at will. In most of the country the reception of a consistent broadcast signal was impossible, particularly in heavily populated areas. (New York City had thirty-eight stations, and Chicago had forty.) Purchases of sets and parts, which had totalled $430 million in 1925, and $506 million in 1926, dropped to $425.6 million in 1927.

The public also responded accordingly. Individuals and organizations, particularly businesses, nationwide demanded legislative remedy. President Calvin Coolidge told Congress in December 1926: "The whole service of this most important function has drifted into such chaos as seems likely, if not remedied, to destroy its great value."[9]

Congress approved legislation on February 23, 1927, effective immediately. Although the response was swift, the legislation was neither hastily drawn nor hastily passed. Radio bills had been considered since 1923. The foremost leader and legislative authority was Wallace White, of Maine, who, first as representative and then as senator, had attended the Washington radio conferences and drawn up bills embodying their recommendations. The recommendations of the 1925 conference were embodied in a bill that eventually became the Radio Act of 1927. The conference recommended legislation that would give the federal government authority to control radio traffic by issuing, denying, and revoking licenses, and by specifying the frequencies, power, and hours of broadcast stations. This authority did not extend to "mere matters of station management, not affecting service or creating interference," nor was there authority to censor what was broadcast. This was the kernel of the legislation President Coolidge proposed and Congress passed. The only basic idea in the act not already recommended by the fourth conference was that of a regulatory commission, which was, after the first year, to recede to a lesser position, while most of the regulatory power was to be exercised by the Secretary of Commerce.

THE RADIO ACT OF 1927

The following is a summary of the main items of the Radio Act of 1927 and their significance for the future development of a national noncommercial broadcasting system.

1. *The philosophy that the public has the right to service was substituted for the philosophy that any American citizen or corporation wanting to transmit by radio has a right to do so.*

"Service," however, was not defined, except as the ability to receive radio signals without interference. Nor were any standards set for the regulatory agency to define service except in such technical terms.

2. *The electromagnetic spectrum is regarded as a natural resource belonging to the people, and therefore a private person cannot "own" a channel and can use one for private purposes only if such use also serves the public interest.*

3. *To be eligible to use a frequency a licensee must meet certain tests.*

These two items must be considered together because the conditions of use and the tests of the users determine whether the electromagnetic spectrum is really to be a "natural resource belonging to the people." Experience was to demonstrate that the electromagnetic spectrum was a hybrid, but much more private property than a natural resource belonging to the people, and that the qualifying tests the users were required to meet had little relevance to their ability or intent to serve the public interest.

Illustrations of the statement above can be found in the records of the renewal of licenses and the transfer of stations (and licenses) by sale and purchase. The doctrine established in 1925 by the Department of Commerce "that the license ran to the apparatus" was continued, with the result that the purchase price of a station became many times the value of the apparatus because the license came with the apparatus. Thus, in fact, if not in law, private persons could and did own channels.

4. *"In considering applications for licenses and renewals of licenses . . . the licensing authority shall make such a distribution of license bands or frequencies of wave lenghts, periods of time for operation, and of power among the different states and communities as to give fair, efficient, and equitable radio services to each of the same."*

When the Federal Communications Commission did finally reserve channels for noncommercial stations, first in FM radio and later in television, it did so for the entire country, thereby providing the opportunity for a *national* educational broadcasting system.

5. *No license may be issued to any person or corporation guilty of unlawful monopoly or unfair methods of competition; all laws in all fields relating to such practices are applicable also in radio communications.*

This concern to give all individuals the maximum degree of freedom of choice in all aspects of life and to preserve the conditions of competition in the intellectual, cultural, and economic market place was another powerful influence in the later establishment of a national noncommercial system of broadcasting.

6. *The licensing authority has no power to censor radio communications or to interfere with the right of free speech, except obscene, indecent, or profane language.*

This is a guarantee against censorship by government, but there is no such guarantee against private censorship in various ways by the owners and operators of the commercial stations. The desire to extend the right of free expression and reception beyond the limits of the commercial system of broadcasting was yet another factor in the establishment of a noncommercial system of broadcasting.

7. *A licensee is not obligated to permit any candidate for a public office to broadcast over its station, whether on free or purchased time, but if it permits one to do so it must afford equal opportunities to all other offical candidates for the same office and has no power of censorship over the material they broadcast.*

Under this provision a station could treat all candidates equally by giving none of them access to its air waves, and many commercial stations followed this policy. Thus many candidates had no opportunity to reach the voters by radio, and the voters had no opportunity to hear them. Later, one of the arguments for the establishment of a noncommercial system would be that stations were needed that would provide opportunities affirmatively by giving equal opportunity to all official candidates.

8. *The government has broad discretionary powers to regulate radio communications, limited by the "public interest, convenience or necessity."*

This phrase, or slight variants of it, is repeated in every section of the 1927 act pertaining to the basic authority of the regulatory commission. " 'Public interest, convenience, or necessity' means about as little as any phrase that the drafters of the Act could have used and still comply with the constitutional requirement that there be some standard to guide the administrative wisdom of the licensing authority."[10] Congress delegated judgment concerning what is in the "public interest" almost entirely to the commercial owners and operators of stations. But the law was broad enough to permit the regulatory authority eventually to make decisions that encouraged the development of a supplementary broadcasting system in which noncommercial institutions could share in determining what is in the "public interest."

9. *The government's regulatory powers must be used with regard to due process of law and may be appealed to a court of law.*

Three other observations should be made about the act as a whole. The only reference to networks in the act is a direction that the regulatory commission shall have "authority to make special regulations applicable to radio stations engaged in chain broadcasting," which gives the commission only indirect authority over the networks through the stations. The word *advertising* does not appear in the Radio Act of 1927; however,

Section 19 requires that broadcast matter which is paid for be identified as such and attributed to the payer. Finally, the word *education* does not appear in the act. When this omission was questioned during congressional hearings and debates, the supporters of the bills answered that education was included in the category of "public interest, convenience, or necessity."

The Radio Act of 1927 vested regulatory authority in a five-member Federal Radio Commission (FRC), appointed by the President and approved by the Senate. The legislation intended that once the FRC brought order to the air-waves chaos, its powers would then be transferred to the Secretary of Commerce, who could refer the revocation of licenses back to the FRC. The FRC's job, however, proved harder than was anticipated. Congress extended the FRC's regulatory authority twice temporarily and on December 18, 1929, made it permanent. The FRC thus became the direct ancestor of the Federal Communications Commission, which was established in 1934.

TRAFFIC CONTROL AND CONTENT

The Radio Act of 1927 authorized the Federal Radio Commission to regulate the traffic of the air waves. The standard that Congress set to check the FRC's power—the "public interest"—inescapably involves judgments of the contents of the traffic.

The authority of the regulatory agency—the FRC and then the FCC—to control traffic is unquestioned. The authority of the regulatory agency to influence the contents of the traffic, however, has been challenged from the beginning. At first any attempt by the FRC to eliminate even the most obviously deceptive advertising and personal vilification was challenged in the courts as a violation of free speech. The courts later upheld the FRC doctrine that broadcasters voluntarily subject themselves to certain restrictions on freedom of speech because the air waves are limited. The FRC's first decision not to renew a license because of past program and advertising content was against John Brinkley, of KFKB, Milford, Kansas—a precedent set in 1930, upheld by the U.S. court of appeals in 1931, but not often followed by the FRC or FCC. However, the application of such negative restraint upon broadcasters is one thing, and the requirement that broadcasters carry certain types of content is quite another. When the regulatory agency (FRC or FCC) has attempted to apply an affirmative test, the industry has usually defeated the attempt, often with the help of Congress. The inability of the regulatory agency to influence the contents of the commercial traffic later led to the development of a national noncommercial broadcasting system.

The following three cases document the inability of the regulatory agency to regulate the content of the traffic of radio broadcasting.

The licenses of the three 50,000-watt stations owned by G. E. Richards (WJR, Detroit; WGAR, Cleveland; and KMPC, Hollywood) were regularly renewed despite charges by groups of listeners that some of their programming was false, vilifying, and partisan. Hearings on these charges, finally begun in 1950, resulted in an examiner's recommendation that the licenses not be renewed. Richards died in the meantime, but the FCC renewed the licenses to his widow, upon her written assurances that news slanting would be discontinued. Thus, a private property in "public" channels was extended through inheritance.

In 1945 the Federal Communications Commission approved the transfer of the Crosley apparatus and license of WLW, Cincinnati, to the Aviation Corporation (Avco) despite proof that its officers knew nothing about the obligations to the public they were seeking to undertake. This led the FCC to adopt the "Avco rule," requiring owners to publicize their intention to sell their stations, thereby soliciting buyers to make competitive bids, with the FCC choosing the applicant best qualified to serve the public interest. The FCC applied the rule only a few times, usually deciding for the purchaser that the seller preferred, and then it repealed the rule in 1949. (In 1958 Congress amended the Communications Act of 1934 to forbid the FCC to consider any transferee other then the one to whom the licensee wanted to sell.)

Since 1939 the FCC had been considering adopting rules for stations regarding program service, and with widespread public judgment that the quality of radio programming was deteriorating as the end of World War II approached, the Commission was criticized by some members of Congress for not having set criteria by which to judge whether or not licenses should be renewed. Commissioner Clifford J. Durr had begun to refrain from voting on license renewals when he felt there was no basis for judging past performance. The information he asked for and received concerning the records of promises that certain licensees had made to the FCC compared to their later performances led to a month-long study of promises and performances, the results of which the FCC adopted and published in 1946, titled *Public Service Responsibility of Broadcast Licensees.*

This report, called the "Blue Book" because of the color of its cover, said that the licensee of a broadcasting station has a primary responsibility for determining program service but that the Commission has a statutory duty to concern itself with performance when passing upon the application for renewal by a licensee. While noting some "socially valuable" programming on a number of stations, the report documented that despite enormous profits the quality of the programming over most stations had sharply deteriorated; and that, although the networks were broadcasting some excellent series, most affiliate stations did not carry them. Therefore, the FCC stated, in considering renewals it would weigh a station's performance against criteria distilled from statements by industry leaders and the code of the National Association of Broadcasters: (1) carrying sustaining programs to provide a balanced program structure; (2) carrying local live-talent programs; (3) carrying programs dealing with important public issues; and (4) eliminating advertising excesses. To gather data concerning these factors, the FCC designed a new form for application renewal and shortly thereafter held up the renewal of several licensees because of poor performance. Reaction from the industry and Congress was so swift and hostile, however, that the FCC did not deny renewal to a single station on these grounds. These defeats of the Federal Communications Commission by the industry were almost simultaneous with the FCC proposal to reserve television channels for educational stations.

U.S. EDUCATIONAL BROADCASTING
UNTIL 1948

AFTER THE DEVELOPMENT of the overwhelmingly commercial broadcasting system that had taken place in the United States by 1950, how did a
handful of noncommercial educational stations backed by educational
associations win a chance to develop a national noncommercial educational broadcasting system?

The most important clue to an answer is found, not in the history of
the educational stations alone, but even more in the tradition of public
service of American land-grant colleges and state universities, which
owned most of the thirty-eight educational AM stations that survived
through 1936 and began to develop educational FM stations after World
War II. These colleges and universities operated their stations as part of
their mission to provide educational services to the American people.

The American state university, beginning with the University of
Virginia in 1819, was dedicated to the idea that the opportunities for
higher education should be open to all who could benefit from them. By
1860 there were twenty-one such universities in the United States. Their
number was increased and their services were expanded by the Morrill
(land-grant college) Act of 1862, and in 1887 the Hatch Act made federal
money available for agricultural experiment stations, designed both to
expand and to disseminate scientific knowledge of agriculture. A third
step was taken in 1914 when the Smith-Lever Act established the Cooperative Agricultural and Home Economics Service—a three-way collaboration of local agencies and organizations, the state land-grant college,
and a special unit of the U.S. Department of Agriculture. Many land-

grant colleges had begun extension services before 1914, as had many state universities. In 1915 the National University Extension Association was organized and held its first conference with twenty-two member institutions, stating as its purpose "to carry light and opportunity to every human being in all parts of the nation."

Thus a tradition of extension services to the people existed in American public colleges and universities before the Secretary of Commerce began to issue licenses to the new classification of broadcasting stations early in 1921. Many of these public colleges and universities conceived of broadcasting as an additional means of providing service to the people, particularly in rural areas. From their beginnings these stations rendered services important to the people and provided one of the bases for the national system of educational broadcasting.

EDUCATIONAL STATIONS
UNDER THE FEDERAL RADIO COMMISSION

By 1925 the commercial radio stations had begun to find in the sale of time for advertising an enduring answer to the problem of financial support, while the educational stations had not. When the Secretary of Commerce adopted policies that created trafficking in licenses in 1925, the number of noncommercial stations began to decline. In 1926 when the impetus for networks to get local affiliates and for local stations to acquire network affiliation was added the decline quickened.

The Radio Act of 1927 had been written according to the recommendations of the industry made in the four radio conferences. The members of the Federal Radio Commission were appointed by President Coolidge at the recommendation of Secretary Hoover, who believed that the commercial industry would serve the "public interest." The commission had latitude in interpreting its mandate to give service equitable to all parts of the country and to eliminate the "chaos of the air." And whereas the *contents* of radio programming did not influence the FRC's reallocation of frequencies, assignments of power and hours, and the license grants, the *statistics* of programming did. It was hard for the FRC not to favor a commercial station's 5,000 hours of programming, which might well include 1,000 hours of network programming featuring first-rate "live" orchestras and nationally prominent speakers, over an educational station's 500 hours of programming, much of which was the broadcast of local athletic events and recorded music.

Between 1926 and 1931 many changes in transmitting equipment occurred. The FRC adopted stringent engineering standards aimed at reducing interference and improving signal quality. Some of the educational stations could not afford the new equipment, and few were able to get the money to make the changes as quickly as the FRC required.

In the early years the FRC members tried to make all administrative decisions themselves and usually decided contested issues on the basis of legal arguments and facts—often presented for the industry by lawyers or members of Congress and not often by spokesmen for the educational stations. Beginning in 1930, the FRC lightened its work load by delegating the authority to conduct initial hearings to hearing examiners. This procedure entailed the costs of preparation, travel, and legal counsel, which few of the educational stations could afford.

THE EFFECTS OF THE DEPRESSION

During the Depression, beginning in the fall of 1929, commercial revenues from advertising increased, whereas educational stations either closed or reduced their budgets. In the five-year period through mid-1935 local commercial station revenues had more than tripled and network revenues had increased by more than half.[1] There are no comparable statistics for the financing of educational stations as a group, but the three public institutions of higher education in Alabama, for example, gave up their station, WAPI, in 1932 to help pay faculty salaries.

Educational stations also felt political pressures. President M. G. Powell of the University of Florida, whose station, WRUF, went on the air in 1928, wrote: "The greatest handicap that an educational station of this nature has to meet is the selfish onslaught made by other radio stations in various communities of the state before the legislature, stations bringing great political power to bear upon the representatives to close up a station of this nature because it takes away the local radio listeners when an educational station's programs are of popular appeal."[2] Educational stations also suffered from frequent shifts in their frequencies, power, or hours made by the FRC. Commercial stations made money, convertible into political power; educational stations cost money. If their programming was not popular enough to attract sizable audiences, they were hard to justify politically; if it was popular, it provoked political opposition.

MANIFESTATIONS OF CONCERN

Just before the Depression some influential persons, organizations, and institutions were moved to action by the concern that the opportunities of radio broadcasting were being lost and its powers misused.

On May 24, 1929, Secretary of the Interior Ray Lyman Wilbur called a meeting of fifteen persons, including the U.S. Commissioner of Education, two FRC members, the vice-president of the National Broadcasting Company, the president of the Columbia Broadcasting System, a representative of the Western Electric Company, and six educators. The Secretary began: "We now face the question of what we shall do with radio in connection with public education. That includes not only school room teaching but adult education, and what we shall do with the latter in developing a better citizenship."[3]

This broad concept of public education governed all later developments in educational radio. The group accepted the goal that "the most searching scientific study should be made as to the best way in which radio can find its place in education," but its members differed on the question of whether the advancement of education by radio was adequately provided for by commercial broadcasting and the Federal Radio Commission. Secretary Wilbur and FRC Chairman Ira E. Robinson did not think so. Robinson was blunt: "Frankly, I say to these commercial people—the Columbia and National Broadcasting companies—I accuse them of being commercial. Shall we leave these matters of the educational use of radio to the commercial enterprises—and if perhaps not to the great broadcasting chains, then to the local stations? Shall there not be some head to direct a local or a national chain in these matters?"

Wilbur and Robinson were ready to consider some kind of a national radio university, operating over a number of frequencies reserved for education. FRC Commissioner Eugene O. Sykes and the network officials thought that commercial stations and networks were doing "promising" work under the current arrangements and were willing to do much more, given cooperation by the U.S. Office of Education. The meeting ended with agreement that Wilbur should appoint a committee of educators, broadcasters, and others to investigate the use of radio for educational purposes.

The Wilbur Committee (ACER)

Wilbur's Advisory Committee on Education by Radio, a sixteen-member group supported by the Payne Fund, the J. C. Penney Foundation, and the Carnegie Corporation of New York, held its first meeting on June 19, 1929. Its director was Dr. Levering Tyson, who, as field representative for the American Association for Adult Education, had just completed an extensive study of college and university broadcasting.[4] By the end of the year Tyson had convened representatives of the American Association for Adult Education to discuss cooperation with the commercial networks and stations—a move which resulted in the formation of the National Advisory Council on Radio in Education (NACRE). Meanwhile, Armstrong Perry, radio advisor to the U.S. Commissioner of Education, argued that the actions of commercial radio and the FRC required new safeguards for educational radio, resulting in the formation of the National Committee on Education by Radio (NCER).

The National Advisory Council on Radio in Education (NACRE)

Tyson's movement of cooperation with commercial networks and stations was well underway several months before the Wilbur committee made its recommendations to the Secretary of the Interior on February 15, 1930.[5] Two of the recommendations were to form an advisory committee representing educational institutions, the radio industry, and the general public; and to seek funds to develop broadcasts in school subjects. To implement these and related recommendations, NACRE, funded by the Carnegie Corporation of New York and John D. Rockefeller, Jr., came into formal being on July 1, 1930. Its hope was that as soon as educators developed excellent programming, networks and local stations would give it good places and times on the air. NBC's promise was quoted in NACRE's publications: "When they are ready we will place our facilities at their disposal without charge." The objectives of the council were to develop and encourage the development of programs, to do research, and to help place educational programming on the air. At its height the council was composed of sixty-three U.S. and forty-four foreign organizations. It held annual meetings from 1931 through 1935, bringing together authorities in the field to give papers on major problems in education by radio and receiving progress reports from its active committees, which numbered almost a dozen. The proceedings were published in an annual volume.[6]

The National Committee on Education by Radio (NCER)

Another group in the Wilbur committee was convinced that more than a cooperative approach was needed to safeguard and advance educational stations. Consequently, U.S. Commissioner of Education William J. Cooper called an emergency conference on October 13, 1930, to which he invited representatives of education, educational broadcasting, and commercial broadcasting. He opened the conference by expressing an anxiety he shared with many others: "Before education knows what it wants to do, commercial stations will have practically monopolized the channels open for radio broadcasting, and that expressed fear was one reason I thought it well that we should come together."[7] Those who agreed with Cooper resolved that he should appoint a committee representing national educational associations; that broadcasting originating in educational institutions should be protected and promoted; and that Congress should enact legislation "which will permanently and exclusively assign to educational institutions and government educational agencies a minimum of 15 percent of all radio broadcasting channels which are or may become available to the United States."

With a small grant from the Payne Fund, Cooper organized the committee, which first met in Washington, D.C., on December 30, 1930. Its members were from the National Education Association, the National Association of State University Presidents, the National Council of State Superintendents, the Association of College and University Broadcasting Stations, the National University Extension Association, the National Catholic Education Association, the American Council on Education, the Jesuit Education Association, and the Association of Land-Grant Colleges and Universities. The members were officially designated to represent their organizations, making the committee "an organization of organizations"—the first to champion the cause of autonomous educational broadcasting.

At its first meeting the organizing group adopted the name the National Committee on Education by Radio (NCER) and formulated its program, contingent on funds. A grant of $200,000 for five years was secured by February 1931 from the Payne Fund, and the program was followed through 1935. The purpose of the committee was:

> To secure to the people of the United States the use of radio for educational purposes by protecting the rights of educational broadcasting, by promoting and coordinating experiments in the use of radio in school and adult education, by maintaining a service bureau to assist educational stations in securing licenses and in other technical procedures, by exchange of information through a weekly bulletin, and by serving as a clearing house for the encouragement of research in education by radio.[8]

Notably absent in that statement of purpose is the goal of supporting legislation to reserve for educational institutions and government educational agencies a minimum of 15 percent of all radio broadcasting channels—one of the recommendations of the Cooper conference. A bill to this purpose was introduced in the Senate in January 1931, and again in 1932 and 1933, by Ohio Senator Simeon D. Fess, but it was never reported out of committee. The NCER endorsed the Fess bill but recognized that not only would the legislative route be a long one at best and that the NCER was not designed to wield power with Congress, but that educators were divided on the issue, and there was much work to do even to protect the channels that existed. NCER rendered vital service during the crucial period of 1931–35 on an annual budget averaging $40,000 and with a staff of two full-time men (Armstrong Perry, director of the Service Bureau, and Tracy F. Tyler, secretary and research director) and two part-time men. The chief activities were a weekly bulletin, "Education by Radio"; a service bureau, both in Washington and in the field; and a clearinghouse for research and experimentation.

To protect college and university stations the service bureau examined all FRC reports for applications that might affect the interests of educational stations. In February 1931, when applications threatened possible encroachment upon the facilities, frequencies, power, or hours of twenty-eight educational stations, the bureau notified and offered help to all, eleven of which requested and received it. Some threatening applications were withdrawn, some hearings were canceled, and some hearings resulted in decisions favorable to educational stations. The number of threatening applications had fallen to thirteen in January 1932, and remained lower thereafter.

Perry and Tyler made two extensive trips from coast to coast during 1931, visiting with the operators of educational stations and the officials of their institutions. In 1932 Tyler directed an appraisal of radio stations operated by land-grant colleges and universities. Thus in various ways the committee gave important direct services to scores of educational stations.

KOAC, owned and operated by Oregon State College, is an example of a station that NCER aided. Operating at 550 kc., using only about five hours daily and shutting down on weekends and during vacations, it was in danger of losing its license. After three years of aid from NCER, KOAC, besides keeping its license and increasing its budget, had converted the college officials to a firm belief in its importance; had opened its facilities to other colleges and educational agencies; had expanded its programming to a twelve-hour schedule around the calendar; and had given the state legislature and the general public an awareness of its worth.

To increase knowledge about educational broadcasting, the committee, despite its slight budget and small staff, began fact-finding concerning educational broadcasting under the direction of Tracy F. Tyler.

The bulletin "Education by Radio" published information about radio activities. For example, the issue for February 26, 1931, contained a table showing all educational stations in the United States, their locations, ownerships, frequencies, hourly schedules of operation, and quota units (a measurement the FRC used to assure equitable service to all parts of the country). This list was the first comprehensive data published on educational stations as a group. The March issues of "Education by Radio" presented tables showing all the actual broadcasts of an educational character made during the week of January 11, 1931, classified according to source. The tables also specified the broadcast hours of both educational and commercial stations. The April 2 issue gave a four-page table showing the quota units each state was given by the FRC and the quota units actually being used in each state.

The most ambitious fact-finding project resulted in *An Appraisal of Radio Broadcasting in the Land-Grant Colleges and State Universities.*[9] This book is a detailed picture of the broadcasting done during the first half of 1932 by seventy-one land-grant colleges and separate state universities in all forty-eight states, over either their own stations, commercial stations, or both. Forty-five broadcasting stations were owned and operated by educational institutions; twenty-four of these were licensed to land-grant colleges and state universities. The following summary, focusing on the twenty-four, gives a picture of the educational broadcasting stations of 1932.

Of the stations reporting data in 1932, the average cost per institution invested in equipment was $31,306. The average annual maintenance cost was $1,271. The annual operating expenses for the radio services, of which salaries were the chief item, was about $10,000. There were few full-time workers, and most of the personnel had duties other than broadcasting. For their radio programming duties faculty members received no consideration in money, reduced teaching load, or more rapid advancement in professional rank. There was almost no research. The principal source of income was from state appropriations not specifically designated for radio purposes, with appropriations specifically designated for radio coming second. The faculty committee system was the most common arrangement for administering the station.

The NCER initiated, lobbied for, and publicly supported a bill sponsored by Representative Hampton P. Fulmer of North Carolina to establish a commission, representing both Congress and the public, with an authorization of $25,000 to make a thorough study of American radio practices as well as those of foreign systems. Like the Fess bill, the Fulmer bill never got out of committee. The kind of study it proposed, however, was sorely needed because neither the executive nor the legislative branch of the federal government had solid factual grounds for planning broadcast policy.

As the committee approached the end of its five-year grant period it decided to sponsor a national meeting to review the social impact of radio broadcasting and perhaps to make recommendations for the new communications bill that President Franklin D. Roosevelt was drafting. The First National Conference on the Use of Radio as a Cultural Agency[10] was attended by delegates from educational stations, many universities and educational organizations, and several government agencies. Discussions focused on what could be done to improve radio broadcasting. A general report was drawn up by a committee chaired by Arthur G. Crane in May 1934 titled "Fundamental Principles Which Should Underlie American Radio Policy." Among the eight principles presented were: "Responsible groups, even the minorities, should not be debarred from broadcasting privileges"; "positive, wholesome broadcasts for youth at home and in the schools should be provided"; "discussion of controversial issues of general public concern should be encouraged"; and adequate financial support must be provided for these objectives. The NCER presented this statement of principles to the House committee considering the communications bill that Roosevelt submitted and later to the Federal Communications Commission during its hearings mandated by the Communications Act of 1934 to study the proposal to reserve radio channels for educational stations.

The Institute for Education by Radio (IER)

Another manifestation of concern was the formation of the Institute for Education by Radio in 1930. The IER (IERT after television was added to its name in 1951) was an annual conference sponsored by Ohio State University to provide a common ground where educators, commercial broadcasters, and others could discuss the problems of educational broadcasting in an atmosphere that did not favor any interest, policy, or opinion. When the Payne Fund made a grant to the Bureau of Educational Research, Ohio State University, in 1929 for the development of a radio department, Professor W. W. Charters, director of the bureau, decided that the money should be used to establish a national forum to clarify the objectives and to advance the techniques of education by radio. Charters and Mrs. Frances Payne Bingham Bolton formally founded the IER, which was held in Columbus each year from 1930 through 1953, except 1945.

The program for the first institute stated the following objectives: "(1) to provide the leaders in educational broadcasting with an opportunity to become acquainted with each other; (2) to pool existing information about the problems of educational broadcasting; (3) through the publication of the proceedings, to make this information available for general use; and (4) to develop a program for cooperative fact-finding and research."[11]

The institute fostered and recorded the development of a body of theory, information, and techniques of educational broadcasting, beginning with the period between 1930, when concern over the fate of educational broadcasting assumed organized forms, and 1934, when Congress decided that the newly created Federal Communications Commission should study the proposal to reserve AM channels for educational stations.

Discussions of Educational Broadcasting, 1930–34

During this period the issue that dominated the institute's discussions was the relationship of radio in education to existing educational institutions and practices. Because there was little theory, information, and experimentation concerning education by radio, U.S. Commissioner of Education William Cooper told the 1931 institute that his office was beginning to gather and systematize information. The 1931 institute set up a research committee to systematize the reporting of research.[12]

Discussion during this period centered on the following questions.

1. *Was radio to be a tool primarily for formal education or for educational and cultural service to the general public?* Most of the research and experimentation reported in the institute proceedings for the period concerned radio as a tool for education, but most of the educational programming was intended for the general public. The entertainment and cultural programs of the educational stations that were most popular were those that had local appeal. The educational stations, however, had no means for syndication of those informational and cultural programs with potential regional or national appeal.

2. *As a tool for formal education, was radio to be a supplement to existing institutions and methods or a force for radical change?* Early research in education by radio suggested that radio by itself was better suited to arouse interest and increase motivation to learn than it was to impart systematic instruction. At the first institute W. W. Charters sketched the handicaps to radio as an instructional tool by itself.[13] The fear that automation would produce unemployment was particularly

keen during the Depression. Moreover, the budgets assigned to educational stations were determined by administrators who regarded radio as supplementary, and the programming for instructional purposes was in the hands of educators who were traditional in their ways. The main spokesman opposed to radio as a supplement was Levering Tyson. He believed that radio exposed the worst methods of traditional education and should be used to change, rather than to reinforce them:

> The radio, as a modern wonder, has unlimbered the mind and has thrown the intellect into the limbo of freedom of choice. . . . Useless formalism in education is breaking down. The public and the educators are certain that education means more than it formerly did in the school, the college, or the university. I believe sincerely that in the past decade, along with the reawakening of the adult public as indicated by the interest in what is known as adult education, radio broadcasting has been a powerful factor —more influential than is commonly supposed.[14]

3. *Could radio as an instrument for educational and cultural service to the general public attract and hold the interests of sizable audiences without sacrificing the integrity of its purpose?* John Elwood, vice-president and educational director of NBC, thought not. "The group of 'little serious thinkers' is small," he said, concluding, "A leading writer has stated that 'information, in order to be popularly received, must be sugar-coated.' There is undoubtedly much truth in that statement, especially if we are considering a large proportion of those reached through a medium of universal distribution."[15]

P. O. Davis, general manager of educational station WAPI, Birmingham, thought that if it was possible to make sound educational programming attractive to large audiences, educators would have to change their attitudes and invest much more money: "They must remember that they are broadcasting to serve the listener, and if they do not catch and hold his attention, they are cluttering up the air and giving nothing in return. Successful broadcasting is an expensive business. Very few educators have grasped this fact. Many are still willing to assign their broadcasting to someone who is already carrying a full load, and, too frequently, one who has no special qualifications for arranging and presenting programs."[16]

Another major issue debated at the institute between 1930 and 1934 was whether educational broadcasting stations should receive reserved channels. At the 1934 institute Judith Waller, educational director of the NBC-Central Division, and Armstrong Perry, director of the Service Bureau of the National Committee on Educational Radio, differed on

whether channels should be reserved but agreed that school administrators were the chief obstacle to more effective use and better support of
educational broadcasting.

T. M. Beaird, executive secretary of the Association of College and
University Broadcasting Stations, thought that educational broadcasters
themselves were a more formidable obstacle: "After all is said and done,
we might summarize the whole situation by saying that in many cases we
are reluctant to ask for additional money, even though we know we will
get it, because of the pertinent question of the hour which seems to be,
when we are speaking of this infant radio, 'Where do we go from
here?' "[17]

THE COMMUNICATIONS ACT OF 1934

The mood of the New Deal and the knowledge that Franklin D. Roosevelt intended to change the Radio Act of 1927 excited hopes and fears
within broadcasting. Perhaps his actions would be as drastic as the Canadian Radio Broadcasting Act of 1932, which provided for the creation of
the Canadian Radio Broadcasting Commission to establish a mixed
public-private broadcasting system. Or perhaps the New Deal might only
be the reservations of channels proposed in the Fess bill again being considered in the 1933 Senate. Roosevelt's plans, however, had nothing to
do with radio[18] and everything to do with telephone and telegraph. He
wanted federal jurisdiction in the field of communications under a single
act and regulatory agency.

Regulation of the telephone and telegraph industries under the 1910
law was unsatisfactory. State commissions were powerless to regulate
wire communications extending beyond state and national boundaries.
Moreover, the telephone industry increasingly used radio, and the radio
industry increasingly used telephone and cable, particularly in network
operations.

The Administration Bill

During the summer of 1933 Roosevelt appointed an interdepart-
mental government committee, chaired by Secretary of Commerce Daniel C. Roper, to study the problem and recommend a national communications policy. The committee recommended that a new federal commission
be created to which all existing authority over both wire and wireless
communications would be transferred. In 1934 Roosevelt submitted this

recommendation to Congress. The resultant administration bill was a combination of the Radio Act of 1927 and provisions for federal jurisdiction over interstate and foreign wire communications. It would have passed quickly if an amendment had not been proposed in the Senate.

The Wagner-Hatfield Amendment

Senators Robert F. Wagner from New York and Henry D. Hatfield from West Virginia proposed an amendment[19] to have the Federal Communications Commission cancel all assignments of frequencies, power, and time within ninety days and then "reserve and allocate only to educational, religious, agricultural, labor, cooperative, and similar nonprofit-making associations, one-fourth of all the radio broadcasting facilities within its jurisdiction." These reservations and allocations were to be "equally as desirable as those assigned to profit-making persons, firms, or corporations." Moreover, the nonprofit licensees could "sell such part of the allotted time as will make the station self-supporting."

This proposal squarely met two major issues: whether the air waves really belonged to the people, as the Radio Act of 1927 proclaimed in principle; and whether nonprofit stations were to be dependent upon noncommercial sources for their support.

The proponents of the amendment were disorganized and often contradicted one another, the opponents well-organized and consistent in their arguments. The opposition was led by Senator Clarence C. Dill, who found the most vulnerable point in the amendment to be the proposal to permit nonprofit stations to sell time. There was, the opponents argued, too much commercialism on radio already; there was no safeguard against nonprofit stations making profits beyond self-support; and such competition would push many commercial stations into bankruptcy. The administration was impatient because the amendment was holding up its bill. Finally, Dill proposed another amendment: "The Commission shall study the proposal that Congress by statute allocate fixed percentages of radio broadcasting facilities to particular types or kinds of nonprofit activities, and shall report to Congress, not later than February 1, 1935, its recommendations together with the reasons for the same." This amendment passed. The Wagner-Hatfield amendment was then defeated.

The study-report amendment was included as Section 307 (c) of the administration bill, which was quickly passed. The Communications Act of 1934, approved on June 19, became effective when the new Federal Communications Commission took office on July 1. The seven commissioners are appointed by the President with the advice and consent of the Senate for a period of seven years, with one member designated by the President as chairman. No more than four members may be of the same political party, and the commission must make an annual report to Congress.

Thus the Communications Act of 1934 became the basic law governing both wire and wireless communications. With respect to wireless communications, it was a re-enactment of the Radio Act of 1927 with only one substantial change: Section 303 (g) specifically called upon the FCC to "study new uses for radio, provide for experimental uses of frequencies, and generally encourage the larger and more effective use of radio in the public interest."

THE FCC HEARINGS AND REPORT ON RESERVED CHANNELS

The Broadcast Division of the FCC, in compliance with the law, held public hearings from October 1–20, and from November 7–12, 1934. FCC *Files* record almost fourteen thousand pages of testimony and several thousand pages of exhibits from 134 witnesses.[20] The representatives of commercial stations and networks argued against the provision and were joined by spokesmen for many nonprofit agencies, including some educators.

Of those who favored the proposal, or at least its intent, none could speak on behalf of nonprofit organizations and institutions as a group. The spokesmen for the NCER included Joy Elmer Morgan, representing the National Education Association; Arthur G. Crane, representing the National Association of State Universities; Henry Lee Ewbank, representing the Wisconsin State Radio Council; and staff members Tracy Tyler and Armstrong Perry. But they did not take a clear stand for reserved channels. Rather they asked that control "by the people's agency" give existing educational stations the fullest possible protection and encouragement, and recognize that the extension of such facilities was desirable and should be made possible as new frequencies opened up.

Father Cornelius Deeney, on behalf of the Jesuit Education Association, testified that commercial radio was indecent and irresponsible in many respects and that channel reservations for nonprofit organizations would create more responsible radio. Floyd W. Reeves, personnel director of the Tennessee Valley Authority (TVA), advocated government ownership, operation, and control of a national educational radio service, but Arthur E. Morgan, chairman of the board of TVA, said that the position was not TVA's official policy.

The testimonies of John W. Studebaker and Robert M. Hutchins deserve note for the role these men were to play in future developments. Studebaker, U.S. Commissioner of Education, was later to head the official government attempt to bring about cooperation between educators and broadcasters, and to take the lead in getting new frequencies reserved. Hutchins, president of the University of Chicago, which was cooperating with NBC in broadcasting "The University of Chicago Round Table," was later to be an associate director of the Ford Foundation. Studebaker said he was appearing neither as a proponent nor as an opponent of reserved channels but as one favoring a solution to broadcasting problems through research: "It is our belief that many of the most important problems involved in educational broadcasting can never be solved by legislation but must be worked out by scientific research and cooperative experimentation." Hutchins said, "Education must have guaranteed time; it must have good time; it must also have more time." Then he stated: "The charges that can be substantiated are these: the claims of minorities have been disregarded, the best hours have been given to advertising programs, the hours assigned to education have been shifted without notice, censorship has been imposed, experimentation has been almost nonexistent, and the financial support of educational broadcasting has been limited and erratic."

The commercial industry—stations, networks, and manufacturers of radio equipment—was well prepared, having been warned by Henry A. Bellows, of the National Association of Broadcasters' legislative committee: "This, after all, is the New Deal. . . . The broadcast industry has got to justify its existence but it has got to do a great deal more than that. It has got to prove that its operation is in the public interest, that any material change in the method of that operation would hurt the public."[21] The industry made a strong case against reserved channels and an effective defense of commercial broadcasting by introducing witnesses and evidence from nonprofit groups favoring the system.

Philip G. Loucks, managing director of the NAB, submitted sworn statements from radio stations affirming their cooperative efforts with educational and religious organizations, and he marshaled witnesses from schools and churches who said commercial stations were broadcasting excellent programs in their interests. William S. Paley, president of the Columbia Broadcasting System, said his network broadcast commercial programs only 30 percent of the total schedule; almost 70 percent of the time was devoted to educational public service and religious programs. Merlin H. Aylesworth, president of the National Broadcasting Company, testified that 20 percent of NBC's programs had educational purpose and another 30 percent had educational value. Frank M. Russell, vice-president of NBC, stated that the government was "the greatest user of the American system of broadcasting for educational purposes"; he submitted data that during the year ending September 1, 1934, NBC had carried 871 broadcasts by government officials, totaling 250 hours, including 25 broadcasts by the President and 93 by cabinet officials and members of the House and Senate. The commercial broadcasters referred to, or actually produced portions of, programs of educational value, among them the CBS "American School of the Air," the NBC "University of Chicago Round Table," and NBC's "Amos'n'Andy." Barnouw points out that the commercial broadcasters were "citing examples everyone knew or had heard of. Those who argued for something else—for reserved channels for education, for example—had no such advantage. . . . Thus protesting educators were in effect talking about an abstraction, an idea. Commercial broadcasters were talking about a reality that was becoming a part of the nation's daily life."[22]

The Federal Communications Commission submitted its report to Congress on January 22, 1935, recommending that "at this time no fixed percentages of radio broadcast facilities be allocated by statute" to nonprofit persons, programs, or activities. The reasons given were: (1) there was no need for a change in the existing law to accomplish the purposes of the proposal; (2) flexibility in the provisions of the law was essential; (3) the provision for specialized broadcasts could not be made consistent with fair and equitable services throughout the country; (4) no feasible plan for a definite allocation of facilities to nonprofit organizations had been presented; and (5) there was no evidence of demand for the proposed allocations. "It would appear that the interests of the nonprofit organizations may be better served by the use of existing facilities, thus giving them access to costly and efficient equipment and to established audiences. . . . In order for nonprofit organizations to obtain the maximum service possible, cooperation in good faith by the broadcasters is required. Such cooperation should, therefore, be under the direction and supervision of the Commission."

The Commission presented its plans for specific action: (1) a national conference for planning mutual cooperation; (2) active encouragement of the technique of presenting educational programs attractively—specifically the building of helpful radio programs through cooperation with the U.S. Office of Education and other governmental agencies; and (3) informal preliminary hearings to reduce the occasions when educational institutions need defend their assignments.

Following through on such plans, the FCC Broadcast Division called a meeting in Washington, D.C., of broadcasters and educators on May 15 and 16, 1935. The same exchange between some educators and some broadcasters took place, and again the group of educators showed their internal dissension. But at the end of the conference some educators and broadcasters had established the Federal Radio Education Committee (FREC) under the chairmanship of Dr. John W. Studebaker, U.S. Commissioner of Education.

DISCUSSIONS OF EDUCATIONAL BROADCASTING, 1935

A week after the May 15–16 FCC meeting the National Advisory Council on Radio in Education and the Institute for Education by Radio held their annual conferences jointly in Columbus. It was the last meeting of NACRE and the last year of the grant the National Committee on Education by Radio had received from the Payne Fund. This meeting marked the growth of the IER into a forum that was fully national and that attracted leading figures from many fields. It was also the first national forum after the crucial decision that neither Congress nor the FCC would reserve channels for noncommercial purposes had been made.

The 1935 institute was a platform for ambitious ideas and plans. Most notably, A. G. Crane, president of the University of Wyoming and a member of NCER, presented "A Plan for an American System of Radio Broadcasting to Serve the Welfare of the American People," which he had given just eight days before at the meeting called by the FCC. It proposed the establishment of a federally funded national system of regional and state radio councils "to supplement but not to supplant the present system, and to make available to American listeners programs free from advertising and presenting entertainment and information."[23]

Despite the fact that noncommercial stations had not received reserved channels, the circumstances of educational broadcasting had improved between 1929 and 1935. The first organization of national organizations to promote educational broadcasting had been formed. The rate of decline of educational stations had been slowed, and the surviving stations were becoming stronger and better organized. Educators and educational broadcasters had learned some basic lessons: they needed to achieve and maintain a unity among themselves; they needed to enlist allies from the larger society; and an essential part of educational broadcasting is effective participation in the political process. At the same time the issue of the educational and cultural role of radio had been raised to the point of national attention, and the commercial industry had gone on record with promises. The FCC had made a formal pledge to Congress "actively to assist in the determination of the rightful place of broadcasting in education and to see that it is used in that place." The Office of Education had assumed a formal responsibility to assist. All had, in effect, given hostages to assure the protection of educational broadcasting.

Before 1935 the question whether the commercial broadcasting system in the United States could and would adequately serve the educational and cultural interests of the American people had never been explicitly posed. But between 1934 and 1935 it was posed and answered in the affirmative. The answer—a policy of cooperation—would soon be put to a test.

COOPERATIVE ACTIVITIES

"Cooperation in good faith" officially began with the conference the FCC held on May 15 and 16, 1935, and similar efforts were later made by the Federal Radio Education Committee (FREC), the U.S. Office of Education's Federal Radio Project, the National Committee on Education by Radio (NCER), and the broadcasting industry.

The Federal Radio Education Committee (FREC)

Formed as a result of the May 1935 meeting and chaired by Commissioner of Education John W. Studebaker, FREC held its first meeting on February 17-18, 1936. It was made up of almost forty leaders in education (representatives of educational stations, NACRE, NCER, and individual educators) and commercial broadcasters (both NBC and CBS, and some individual stations). They were pledged: (1) to eliminate controversy and misunderstanding between groups of educators, and between the industry and educators; and (2) to promote actual cooperative arrangements between educators and commercial broadcasters, nationally, regionally, and locally.[24]

FREC sponsored two National Conferences on Educational Broadcasting, one in Washington, D.C., in 1936, and the other in Chicago in 1937,[25] but its real contribution to educational broadcasting was fact-finding and research. Two FREC research projects financed by the Rockefeller Foundation's General Education Board greatly influenced future research in the field. One, the Evaluation of School Broadcasts, analyzed the educational values of radio in schools and classrooms, studied the social and psychological effects of radio listening upon children and young people, and aided teachers and broadcasters by disseminating the results. This study, directed by I. Keith Tyler, was conducted by the Bureau of Educational Research, Ohio State University, between 1937 and 1943. The other project, research "to study what radio means in the lives of the listeners," brought about the establishment of the Office of Radio Research, Columbia University, in 1937; directed by Paul F. Lazarsfeld, its activities led directly into much research supported during World War II by the Office of War Information.

FREC also appointed subcommittees, although money for publication of their reports was not available until 1939. Pamphlets and bulletins were published regularly beginning that year and continuing into the television age of 1950.[26]

The Federal Radio Project

The chairman of FREC, Commissioner Studebaker, got New Deal emergency funds—$70,000 in 1935, and $130,000 in 1936—to support programs such as the Radio Script Exchange, to establish facilities for teaching educators how to use radio, and to produce radio programs for network broadcast.

The Radio Script Exchange developed collection and distribution of radio scripts usable by commercial as well as noncommercial stations that the committee (NCER) had begun for noncommercial stations. Workshops in Washington, D.C., and New York City furthered the pioneering work that had been done at the University of Iowa and Ohio State University; courses and workshops to prepare educators to use radio effectively spread rapidly among American Universities. The many radio series that the Office of Education's Federal Radio Project produced or caused to be produced, in cooperation with NBC-Blue, NBC-Red, and CBS, included such series as "The World Is Yours," "Answer Me This," and "Let Freedom Ring."[27]

Although FREC superseded the National Advisory Council on Radio in Education after 1935, several books were later written by persons who had participated in NACRE activities. One of these can be regarded as an authoritative assessment of how well the policy of cooperation in the broadcasting of instructional programs worked on a national level. Thomas Reed, chairman of the NACRE Committee on Civic Education by Radio, presented a harsh indictment of NBC's educational programming practices. He concluded: "Educational broadcasting has become the poor relation of commercial broadcasting, and the pauperization of the former has increased in direct proportion to the growing affluence of the latter. . . . Imagine the devastating effect of the usefulness of radio in education when classes which have begun listening to a series in good faith are cut off because the time is sold."[28]

The Rocky Mountain Radio Council

In January 1935, when the FCC recommended against reserved channels, the National Committee on Education by Radio (NCER) undertook a new program which it operated during the final year of its first grant and the five years of a second smaller grant from the Payne Fund. All the activities of the previous period were continued on a reduced scale. As the higher radio frequencies were opened, from 1936 through 1941 the committee supported the reservation for educational stations of some of the bands that eventually became FM. The distinctive part of NCER's new program, however, was the Radio Council Plan—a modification of the previous plan which had been publicized by A. G. Crane. Regional or state councils were to become voluntary program-organizing and program-building agencies for the marshaling of educational forces. Nonprofit organizations would unite into councils to survey needs and resources, plan programs, and make the programs available to radio stations (commercial as well as noncommercial).

The most successful effort was the development of the Rocky Mountain Radio Council, which broadcast its first program on December 23, 1939. The twenty-seven-member council included twelve colleges and universities, the state education departments of Colorado and Wyoming, the Denver public schools, the Denver public library, and associations of women, physicians, farmers, and educators. Financial support came from the Rockefeller-based General Education Board, the Payne Fund, the NCER, the Boettcher Foundation of Colorado, and contributions by members; other support came in the form of facilities or services from the University of Colorado, the Colorado State Department of Education, and members of the council. Robert B. Hudson, who had been specially trained for the job under a Rockefeller fellowship, was director. Between December 23, 1939, and July 31, 1940, a test period, the agency produced 222 radio programs, developed in cooperation with 28 divisions in 16 educational and civic organizations and broadcast by 20 radio stations in Colorado and Wyoming.

Telephone surveys indicated that 17 percent of the radio sets in use in Denver were tuned in for one council program; and in Grand Junction 62.5 percent for a second and 82 percent for a third. Hudson wrote in his

1940 report that in every survey council programs attracted a higher percentage of the potential audience than any educational broadcasts over a national network. Regional programming over local stations found a particularly favorable response in these two states, where network programs were not receivable in large areas and where a sense of regional identity was keen.[29]

Although the Rocky Mountain Radio Council activities were even more successful in 1941 and reached peak performance during World War II, the council did not make the transition to educational television. However, the need for broadcasting stations—television even more than radio—to assess local needs and use local resources and to give many people and groups opportunity to participate would remain one of the most important problems for stations to solve.

Contributions by Networks

NBC and CBS created educational units in 1930, and during the next two decades both broadcast important cultural and educational series. CBS broadcast Walter Damrosch's "Music Appreciation Hour" from 1928 to 1942. In the first half of the thirties CBS started the "American School of the Air" and NBC had the "University of the Air." NBC also began "America's Town Meeting of the Air" and carried "The University of Chicago Round Table," and CBS began "The People's Platform" and "Invitation to Learning."

None of these programs continued through World War II or much thereafter. The formal course format never attracted large audiences; the discussion-debate format was not as attractive to the American people in the postwar years as before, even on radio and less so on television. Regardless of the reasons for their ending, for almost two decades network programs had provided the American people with vigorous, fair, and thoughtful exploration of issues.

The question of how well a policy of cooperation between educators and commercial broadcasters would serve the educational and cultural needs of the American people disappeared from national attention between 1935 and 1950. When the FCC reserved some high-frequency radio channels for educational stations, there was not much of a stir. The American people were impatient for television. The FCC and the broadcasting industry were engaged in a fierce struggle for power, and both were concerned with what uses would be made of the higher bands of the electromagnetic spectrum that the FCC was opening.

OVERVIEW: FCC'S EFFORTS TO BALANCE CONTROL
AND DIVERSIFY PROGRAMMING

The FCC's reservation of some radio channels for educational stations was only a small part of its efforts to balance control and diversify programming in American broadcasting. One significant event was the FCC's regulation of network-station relationships. During an investigation of the telephone industry in 1936, many members of Congress called for a probe into monopolistic practices by the radio networks. Following a complaint by the Mutual Broadcasting System (a network, founded in 1934, owned by the independent member stations), in 1938 the FCC began an investigation of radio network business practices. In 1941 the Commission published its *Report of Chain Broadcasting* and later the same year its *Chain Broadcasting Regulations.* These regulations brought about changes in network practices through the FCC's authority to deny licenses to individual stations. Three of the most important changes resulting were NBC's sale of the Blue Network in 1943 to Edward Noble, who changed its name to the American Broadcasting Company (ABC); the loosening of network-affiliate contracts to strengthen the affiliated stations' control of programming; and a limit to the number of stations a network might own. These regulations were opposed in court by both NBC and CBS, but they were upheld by the Supreme Court on May 10, 1943.

Two other events, described in the previous chapter, were significant because they revealed that in the ceaseless struggle between the FCC and the broadcast industry, the balance of power began to shift back in favor of the industry about 1945. One was the FCC's attempt to establish criteria to test promises against performances in deciding whether to renew a station's license. The criteria were set forth in *Public Service Responsibilities of Broadcast Licensees*—the "Blue Book"—but the industry soundly defeated this attempt. The other event was the industry's defeat of the FCC in the "Avco ruling," in which the Commission unsuccessfully tried to require the owner of a station up for sale to solicit competitive bids, from which the Commission would choose the applicant judged best qualified to serve the public interest.

OVERVIEW: THE EMERGENCE OF FM AND TELEVISION

The reservation of radio channels for educational stations was only a small part of the struggle over the uses of the frequencies higher than 25 mc. (megacycles, or millions of cycles). The anticipation was that these frequencies would be used for television. However, the FCC's problem of how to allocate these frequencies was unexpectedly complicated in the mid-1930s by Edwin H. Armstrong's solution of the technical difficulties blocking the development of FM broadcasting. Thus the allocation of frequencies and the licensing of stations for FM radio came into conflict with the demands for television on two fronts—space in the spectrum and resources for research and development.

The FCC faced two sets of questions: what channels to allocate for FM and what for TV and where to place them?; and what standards to require for television and when to set them? On April 30, 1941, the Commission adopted the standards recommended by the industry-wide National Television System Committee. It allocated to television eighteen VHF channels, each 6 mc. wide, between 50 and 294 mc.; and on these channels it authorized full commercial operations. World War II, however, halted production of transmitters and sets before commercial television operations could get under way, although during the war many technical advances were made in both TV and FM. On June 27, 1945, the Commission allocated the 88–108 mc. band as the "permanent home" of FM radio. Of the one hundred channels thereby made available, the first twenty were reserved for educational stations, and the rest were authorized for commercial operations.

The FCC did not authorize full commercial operations in television again until March 18, 1947, when it decided on twelve VHF channels and reaffirmed the standards of 525 lines per inch, FM sound, and monochrome. These decisions started a race for licenses. Within a year the FCC saw that the table of allocations was causing much interference in the reception of TV signals, that the twelve VHF channels would be far from enough to meet the demand, and that the UHF and color questions needed further study. On September 29, 1948, therefore, the FCC stopped processing applications for television stations for a while beyond the 108 licenses it had granted. (The 100th license was granted to Iowa State College.)

OVERVIEW: COMMERCIAL RADIO PROGRAMMING, 1935–50

The high quality of some commercial radio programming was one of the reasons the FCC gave in 1935 for recommending against reserved channels for educational stations. The programming between then and 1950, when the issue of reserved channels for television was raised, can be divided into three periods—from 1935 until the start of World War II, the war years, and the postwar years until 1950.

From 1935 until the start of the war, the programming of American radio was marked by increasing commercialization. Many local stations and all the networks turned programming responsibilities over to sponsors and advertising agencies, and audience ratings became increasingly important.

World War II was a greenhouse period for American commercial radio. The loss of foreign markets made the domestic market all-important, and the shortage of newsprint turned much advertising from newspapers toward radio. Advertising agencies set up the War Advertising Council, which, in cooperation with the Office of War Information, distributed war-related messages and services to the various media. The federal government permitted businesses to charge advertising costs as expenses against the excess-profits tax, which went up to 90 percent. Even businesses and industries that had nothing to sell were glad, in some cases at the cost of only 10 percent, to keep their names before the American people by sponsoring prestige radio programs. The result was that during most of World War II radio programming was more varied and of a higher quality than before or since.

There were at least three reasons why the end of the war brought a sharp decline in the quality of commercial programming. One, the networks and some local stations were using the huge profits of radio to subsidize their entrance into television instead of paying for new or expensive radio programming. Two, the increase in the number of radio stations, particularly in the FM band, which was foreseeable when the war ended, made radio executives prepare for sharpened competition for radio advertising. Finally, when it was clear that the war was going to be won, national unity dissipated, and prestige programs became less important. The quality of commercial radio programs declined before the end of the war, and the lower quality of programming carried over into early television. The low quality of early television programming, as described in the first chapter, would be a weighty factor in the FCC's decision to reserve TV channels for educational stations.

EDUCATORS AND RESERVED RADIO CHANNELS, 1938–48

The U.S. Office of Education gave leadership to educational groups in securing reserved radio channels for educational stations between 1936 and 1945. U.S. Commissioner of Education John W. Studebaker first recommended that the FCC reserve frequencies for education in June 1936—a year after the meeting that founded the Federal Radio Education Committee. In subsequent FCC hearings his office mobilized more than 300 educators to support the request for reserved channels in the new higher frequencies that technology had opened.

On January 26, 1938, the FCC announced the allocation of the band between 41 and 42 mc. for educational broadcasting and the creation of a new "noncommercial" educational station classification. This action was not only the first reservation of frequencies for special audiences, it was also the first distinction between "noncommercial" and "nonprofit" stations (noncommercial stations could not sell time).

There was no chance to explore the possibilities of AM broadcasting in the higher frequencies that the FCC had reserved because in 1940 the FCC asked for opinions concerning the allocation of channels for FM radio. At hearings in March Howard Evans, executive secretary of the National Committee on Education by Radio, speaking also for the NAEB, asked the FCC to make each reserved channel 200 kc. wide to enable educational stations to make several uses of FM sound—two or more monaural signals at the same time, which would permit both local broadcasting and simultaneous broadcasting for networks; stereophonic broadcasts; and facsimile (slow-scan television). The FCC did not request that the educators restate their case for reservations, which they had made in earlier hearings, and commercial broadcasters did not oppose the reservations. On May 22, 1940, the FCC allocated forty channels, between 42 and 50 mc., for FM, reserving the first five for noncommercial stations, and opening the rest for commercial stations. By the time World War II halted further developments, almost thirty commercial FM stations and five noncommercial FM stations were broadcasting. The educational stations were WBEZ, Chicago; WBOE, Cleveland; WNYE, New York City; KALW, San Francisco (all four boards of education); and WILL, the University of Illinois.

During the war the FCC halted new construction permits for FM radio stations but received applications for postwar operations. Applications for the reserved channels were so few, however, that FCC Chairman James L. Fly, in a speech to the May 1943 IER, warned educators that they would lose the reservations if they did not use them: "Those choice channels were not set aside for *absentees*. . . . The Commission . . . has now done everything in its power to redress the balance of the old standard broadcast band."[30] By September (in addition to the 5 educational stations on the air, 4 under delayed construction, and 2 with construction permits) 8 applications were pending, 16 incomplete applications had been received, and more than 160 other educational institutions had requested application forms.[31]

At FCC hearings for postwar allocations of FM frequencies in 1944 Studebaker again requested more reservations. His request, he said, was based "not on conjecture or on wishful thinking . . . but, instead, on concrete evidence."[32] FM networks were being planned in twenty-eight states, he reported, and school systems in six other states were developing plans for local stations. He requested an "irreducible minimum" of fifteen consecutive FM channels, each 200 kc. wide, immediately adjacent to or continuous with the commercial FM band, and relay transmitter links to facilitate regional and national networks. He concluded, almost as an afterthought: "In addition, I urge the reservation of at least two television broadcast channels." Representatives of the American Council on Education, the National Association of Educational Broadcasters, the National Education Association, the National Association of State Universities, and the Association of Land-Grant Colleges and Universities also supported the request for more FM reservations. The spokesman for the latter two associations, Howard L. Bevis, president of Ohio State University, added that the FCC should "keep in mind the needs and resources of educational institutions as television developed."[33]

On June 27, 1945, the FCC allocated and reserved for noncommercial educational stations the first twenty of the one hundred FM channels between 88 and 108 kc. It said that, although little evidence had been given in the 1944 hearings warranting a reservation of television channels for education, the issue could be raised again.

Another factor in the 1945 reservations does not appear in the transcripts of the hearings: the reservation of channels for educational stations was more acceptable to commercial broadcasters than other proposals by the FCC. During the 1944–45 dialogue between the FCC and the industry the Commission had proposed that as AM licensees developed FM broadcasting, they devote two hours each day to new and original programming on FM, but the industry unanimously opposed this. The Commission then proposed to reserve twenty FM channels from immediate assignment, but again the industry opposed this. The FCC finally proposed that twenty FM channels be reserved from immediate assignment "except for educational broadcasting," and the industry did not oppose. Thus the FM reservations in 1945 were possible because of a balance of power agreement between the FCC and the broadcasting industry.[34] Fly's 1943 warning that educators would have to use or lose the reserved channels was still valid. Reserved channels could be taken away one by one if commercial broadcasters could prove that they were not being used more easily than a block of twenty channels indefinitely reserved could be pried loose from the FCC.

After 1945 the growth of educational FM stations was steady but disappointing. To encourage development, on September 27, 1948, the Commission authorized educational FM stations to operate with a power of 10 watts or less, for which equipment and operating costs are low. The number of educational FM stations on the air increased from 48 at the end of 1949, to 292 by September 1, 1966. Yet of the twenty-eight states that in 1944 John Studebaker said were planning networks, by 1967 only the one in Wisconsin had become a reality.[35]

Why has educational FM developed so slowly? Why, despite this fact, have the reservations not been lost? The answers to these two questions are related. Noncommercial FM was slow to take off because commercial FM was slow to do so. Noncommercial FM needed commercial FM to lead the way. Yet, if commercial FM had done so, the channels reserved for noncommercial stations might have been lost, and certainly they would have been challenged. The fact is that in the United States (in contrast with, say, Great Britain) receiving sets were developed, produced, and purchased mainly for commercial broadcasting.

Two days after the FCC authorized educational FM stations to operate with a power of 10 watts or less in the hope of encouraging educational institutions to apply for the twenty reserved channels, the FCC suspended processing applications for commercial TV stations because there were so many applications for so few allocated channels. What chance would educational institutions have to get television channels reserved for educational stations after the freeze on licensing was lifted?

This question brings us up to the period covered in the first chapter of this history. We are now ready to go on with the story from March 22, 1951—the day the Federal Communications Commission announced its proposal to reserve 209 television channels for noncommercial educational stations.

BUILDING THE BASE OF NATIONAL ETV, 1951–1956

On MARCH 22, 1951, when the Federal Communications Commission made public the "Third Notice of Proposed Rule Making," which included reserving VHF and UHF television channels for educational stations, the members of the previous Ad Hoc Committee on Educational Television met to consider whether to form a "continuing organization to promote educational television" (ETV). The Commission took three steps. It received statements from interested parties for a year. Then in April 1952, it made reservations in a way that could be interpreted as being for one year only. Finally, in May 1953, it declared that the channels were reserved "indefinitely." Each step was a test of the educators' desire and ability to take advantage of the opportunity to establish a national educational television system. Recognizing that they were being tested, the educators and educational broadcasters pressed forward, guided and supported in a series of well-coordinated activities from early 1951 through 1956 by the Fund for Adult Education and financed by the Ford Foundation.

"THIRD NOTICE OF PROPOSED RULE MAKING"

The FCC proposed a national allocations table of 1,965 VHF and UHF assignments in 1,256 communities, of which 209 channels would be reserved for noncommercial educational stations. The Commission said the nation needed educational stations and educators needed extra time to activate them—"long enough to give educational interests a reasonable opportunity to do the preparatory work that is necessary to get authorization for stations" but "not so long that frequencies remain unused for excessively long periods of time." It said it would keep an eye on the situation. It stressed that the reservations of the TV channels would not be in a single block as they were in FM radio but community by community, according to the following formula:

> In all communities having three or more assignments (whether VHF or UHF) one channel has been reserved for a noncommercial station. Where a community has fewer than three assignments, no reservation has been made except in those communities which are primarily educational centers, where reservations have been made even where only one or two channels have been assigned. As between VHF and UHF, a UHF channel has been reserved where there are fewer than three VHF assignments, except for those communities which are primarily educational centers, where a VHF channel has been reserved. Where three or more VHF channels are assigned to a community, a VHF channel has been reserved except in the communities where all VHF assignments have been taken up. In those cases, a UHF channel has been reserved.[1]

The Commission gave all interested parties a year in which to file statements.

Comments by individual commissioners indicated that the proposal was provisional upon educators' performance. Webster and Sterling feared that the reservations might limit channel activation. Coy doubted that they were wise because of "a startling lack of data concerning the willingness and readiness of educational institutions . . . to use television as an educational tool." On the other hand, Hennock objected: the number of reservations was not large enough for a nationwide educational service; some large metropolitan areas received only UHF reservations; educational reservations should not be singled out for periodic review; and the record of radio broadcasting justified more educational TV reservations. Again she recommended that educators receive 25 percent of all available television allocations.

The Joint Committee on Educational Television (JCET)

It was by no means certain at the March 22, 1951, meeting that the Ad Hoc Joint Committee on Educational Television would form a permanent organization to promote educational television. What had been an advocacy of reserved channels for only two months in Washington, D.C., would become long-term and strenuous activity to develop ETV stations over the entire country. A new joint permanent organization would be a huge commitment not only of the associations but also of the member institutions. Because it represented the stations, the National Association of Educational Broadcasters would be a keystone in any new organization. None knew so well as its officers that many of the member stations were reluctant and ill-prepared to enter television. Despite all this, the persons meeting in the office of Arthur S. Adams, who had recently become president of the American Council on Education, still shared the values, vision, and goals that had inspired them during the recent FCC hearings. Moreover, they had sound reason to anticipate that substantial money would be available. George Probst, Richard Hull, and Robert Hudson had met in February 1951, with C. Scott Fletcher, who was president-designate of the not-yet-established Fund for Adult Education. He had assured them that he could arrange for a discretionary grant of $15,000 from the Ford Foundation and indicated that a body effectively uniting the field of education in behalf of ETV might receive substantial support. When the meeting ended on March 23, the group had agreed to establish the JCET as a permanent organization. The formal agreement asked the American Council on Education to solicit, receive, and disperse funds for the committee's operations. The Ford Foundation, under new leadership and with a new set of objectives, was the main source of potential funds.

THE FORD FOUNDATION, HOFFMAN REGIME

In 1948, preparing for the receipt of many stocks in the Ford Motor Company, the Ford Foundation (which previously had handled only the philanthropies of the Ford family) appointed a study committee, which recommended that the foundation act to achieve five objectives: (1) to contribute to the establishment of peace; (2) to strengthen democracy; (3) to strengthen the economy; (4) to strengthen, improve, and expand education; and (5) to increase knowledge of individual behavior and human relations (soon shortened to the "behavioral sciences"). In 1950 the trustees adopted these objectives as policy.

The first president of the Ford Foundation on its new scale was Paul G. Hoffman. Two of the four associate directors were Robert M. Hutchins and Chester C. Davis. Hoffman, who had been president of the Studebaker Corporation from 1935 to 1948, was administrator of the Economic Cooperation Administration (an outcome of the "Marshall Plan") from 1948 to 1950. Hutchins, who had been president of the University of Chicago from 1929 to 1951, was long famous as a critic and would-be reformer of both American education and communications. Davis had been administrator of the Agricultural Adjustment Administration from 1933 to 1936, a governor of the Federal Reserve System from 1936 to 1941, and president of the Federal Reserve Board of St. Louis from 1941 to 1951.

These men, who were used to dealing with large affairs, were not awed by the size of the Ford Foundation but, on the contrary, attracted by the opportunity to do much with relatively little money. An anecdote may convey the mood of the early days. Early in 1951 Chester Davis, Scott Fletcher, and I had a leisurely dinner discussing my joining the Fund for Adult Education. At its end Davis said to me, matter-of-factly, "The Ford Foundation could, if it so decided, spend all its capital in a single year on a single venture. If you had half a billion dollars to help establish peace, what would you do? We'd like to have your ideas by tomorrow morning."

The foundation under Hoffman established several subsidiary foundations to work in special fields. Hoffman believed that "to get results quickly and on a large scale, the Foundation would have to subcontract, bringing in, if possible, existing organizations to do part of the work, but, if necessary, creating new organizations, because what we wanted was brainpower." In the area of education the foundation established two subsidiary foundations in April 1951: The Fund for the Advancement of Education (TFAE), "an independent organization concerned with problems and opportunities in formal education from elementary grades through college levels"; and the Fund for Adult Education (FAE),[2] "an independent organization, which will take as its area of activity that part of the educational process which begins when formal schooling is finished." The directors of the FAE conceived "its special task as that of supporting programs of liberal adult education which will contribute to the development of mature, wise, and responsible citizens who can participate intelligently in a free society." They also decided "a program of liberal adult education must employ the mass media of communications as well as all the traditional channels of adult education."

In 1951 the Ford Foundation had to decide what to do with the many requests for money it received concerning educational radio and television. Several of these were large: for example, requests from Harvard University for $4 million and from Massachusetts Institute of Technology for $5 million to found ETV stations; from the NAEB a request for $4 million to support headquarters and a tape network; from George Probst a plan for an educational network of sixty radio and television stations costing $25 million to build and $12 million a year for central production; and a suggestion that the foundation buy the struggling ABC network for educational television outlets and program development.

The foundation did not want to handle these requests itself because it had decided to subcontract through subsidiary foundations. It had planned to establish a subsidiary foundation in the field of the mass media, but the plan did not work out. The Television-Radio Workshop, established in October 1951, was producing program series presented over CBS with commercial sponsorship. The Fund for the Advancement of Education, which was concerned with formal schooling, was not interested at that time in the use of educational technology. So there remained the Fund for Adult Education. President Fletcher and his board *were* interested in helping develop educational television and radio. Hoffman asked Fletcher to work out a plan of matching grants to stations that would be within manageable scope and in this way try "to make educational television a reality." FAE accepted the assignment.

The movement to establish a system of noncommercial educational television in the United States began in a general climate of fear and suspicion that had begun to develop even before World War II was finished. The United States began its policy of containing the Soviet Union with military aid to Greece and Turkey in 1947. The Chinese Nationalist government retreated to Formosa from the Chinese communist forces in 1948. The USSR exploded its first fission bomb in 1949, and many Americans believed that traitors had given away the "secret." The Korean war started in June 1950, and in October of that year China entered the war against the forces of the United States and the United Nations. Senator Joseph R. McCarthy began his accusations of treason within the U.S. government in a speech on February 9, 1950, and inevitably fear and suspicion focused on the mass media because of its influence upon public opinion. In January 1950, *Red Channels: The Report of Communist Influence in Radio and Television* was published. In such a climate the goals of the Ford Foundation—"to contribute to the establishment of peace"; "to strengthen democracy"; "to help develop mature, wise, and responsible citizens"; and "to make educational television a reality"—were bold enterprises.

In 1952 the House of Representatives appointed the Select Committee to Investigate Tax-Exempt Foundations and Comparable Organizations, whose main target was the Ford Foundation. Its chairman was a Republican from Tennessee, Representative B. Carroll Reece, long-time champion of commercial broadcasters and bullier of the FCC. Among the persons whom Reece and other members of his committee found "questionable" were several connected with organizations given grants by the Fund for Adult Education and even two directors of the Fund. I add a personal example of the atmosphere: in mid-1952, as then Midwestern representative of the Fund, upon the invitation of the executive committee of the American Legion, I spent a full day in Indianapolis answering its questions. The committee asked about the entire range of the Fund's activities, but its focus was on support to ETV. My answers apparently satisfied the committee.

THE FUND FOR ADULT EDUCATION

The directors of the Fund were men and women of the highest achievements in varied fields, both in their careers and in public service. Without exception they saw in the potential of ETV an opportunity to further the objectives that the Fund was established.[3] The president of the Fund during its entire existence (1951–61) was C. Scott Fletcher.

Fletcher was born in Sydney, Australia, the son, grandson, and great-grandson of educators. After a twenty-year worldwide career with the Studebaker Corporation, Fletcher entered public service during World War II, directing fund-raising for China War Relief and then serving as director of the Committee for Economic Development. He was president of Encyclopedia Britannica Films from 1946 to 1951. Hoffman, Hutchins, and Davis chose this unconventional man to head the Fund for Adult Education because they believed that adult education needed, even more than money, fresh ideas, new directions, and focused drive. Fletcher conceived his particular role as that of a matchmaker—bringing together the dynamics of business enterprise and the ideal of lifelong liberal education. Alluding to the fact that his forefathers had been educators, he once said, "When I joined Encyclopedia Britannica Films, three generations of Fletchers stopped twirling in their graves."

The Concept, the Task, and the Method

The Fund had undertaken to "make educational television a reality." Its concept was a system of independent, interrelated stations—enough in all parts of the country eventually to reach the entire population. Each station would be locally controlled and a source of programming—both to serve the needs of each community and draw upon its resources, and to guard against the abuses and limitations of centralization. Each station would be able both to contribute to and to draw upon a common pool of good programs. All stations would be tied together by a national center that would facilitate the voluntary exchange of programs, information, and ideas, and obtain and distribute programs from sources other than the stations.

The Fund defined three tasks: first, to persuade the FCC to reserve channels for educational stations, that is, to make the proposed reservations an actuality; second, to stimulate educational institutions and community organizations to apply for licenses on the reserved channels, to construct and equip the stations, and to employ and (in many cases) find and train the needed staff; and, third, to create a national educational television center for the exchange of programs and the providing of services. The Fund had formulated a general approach to these tasks before April 11, 1952, when the FCC issued its "Sixth Report and Order" reserving 242 channels (at least for a year). The Fund's role in laying the base for a system of educational television in the United States between 1951 and 1956 is, to borrow a remark Sir John Reith made about the British Broadcasting Corporation, "a striking example of the advantages that are gained through being able to be definite—it may appear arbitrary —in the pursuit of a line of policy capably and deliberately chosen."

The directors of the Fund formally stated its method of operation: "The fundamental approach of the Fund is to seek out, encourage, strengthen, develop, and expand appropriate agencies already existing. New operations and agencies will nevertheless be created when investigation proves them necessary." The Fund sometimes took a third, informal approach to get certain operations performed under the auspices but not under the actual control of agencies and resources already existing. Disappointment and friction were inevitable when the Fund decided to give a grant to one existing agency rather than to another or to create a new agency instead of working through an existing one. Nevertheless, through the Fund the loose alliance of many people, in many roles and places, who built the base for ETV demonstrated, in Walter Emery's words, "the ability of dedicated persons to resolve their differences for the greater public good."

The remainder of this chapter gives sequential accounts of the FAE's three tasks: (1) securing the reservations of channels (until late 1956, when the Ford Foundation took over support of that function); (2) activating the stations (until 1961, when the Fund made its last grant for station assistance and when Congress was ready to pass the Educational Television Facilities Act); and (3) establishing the Educational Television and Radio Center (until mid-1958, when there was an important change in the center's policies).

SECURING THE RESERVATION OF CHANNELS: TASK NUMBER ONE

All interested parties were given a year from March 21, 1951, to file statements about the FCC's proposal to reserve 209 television channels. During the year opposing and supporting statements along with suggestions for modifications were filed. Opponents included the National Association of Radio and Television Broadcasters (as the National Association of Broadcasters called itself briefly), Allen B. DuMont Laboratories, the Tribune Company, and CBS. Some statements challenged the Commission's authority to make reservations. Others objected to specific reservations. For example, CBS challenged reservations in Boston, Chicago, and San Francisco because it wanted these channels for itself. The Joint Committee on Educational Television and many individual educational institutions and civic nonprofit organizations filed in support of the reservations. Although plans for activating stations and for establishing a center for program exchange were being made, the task upon which everything else depended was to persuade the FCC to translate its proposal into an "Order." A large part of this task fell to the JCET, which held its initial formal meeting as a permanent body on April 23, 1951.

The Joint Committee on Educational Television (JCET)

The members of the JCET were: Chairman Edgar Fuller, executive secretary of the National Council of Chief State School Officers; David Henry, president of Wayne State University, representing the American Council on Education; Franklin Dunham, chief of radio-television of the U.S. Office of Education, representing the Association for Education by Radio-Television; Belmont Farley, director of the press-radio relations division of the National Education Association; James Denison, of Michigan State University, representing the Association of Land-Grant Colleges and Universities; I. Keith Tyler, of Ohio State University, representing the National Association of State Universities; and Seymour Siegel, of WNYC, New York City, representing the National Association of Educational Broadcasters.

Richard Hull observed that the formalization of the first specialized educational television agency brought together "through its constituent member organizations [themselves representative of other educational agencies] the full spectrum of U.S. education in support of ETV."

Through the American Council on Education, the JCET had by April 23, 1951, received a $90,000 grant from the Fund for Adult Education —the Fund's first grant. Ralph Steetle, from WLSU, Louisiana State

University, became executive director after Hull returned to WOI TV to supervise a project of experimental ETV program production.

The main functions of the JCET were to get the proposed reservations officially made and to give legal assistance and information on engineering and construction to persons that wanted to apply for the reserved channels. The first big job was to get institutions and individuals to support or seek addition to the reservations proposed in the Third Notice. Between September 4 and October 22, 1951, 838 statements or exhibits of support or requests for additional reservations were filed with the FCC by colleges, universities, public school systems, state departments of education, and voluntary organizations. Information was also filed by the NAEB based upon monitoring studies of commercial television programming demonstrating the need for an educational television service in Los Angeles and Chicago. The reports and exhibits (or lack thereof) in behalf of reservations in particular communities, especially those assigned VHF reservations, made a difference in the FCC's decisions, as was demonstrated by the "Sixth Order and Report."[4]

"Sixth Order and Report"

The FCC reported that it would resume the licensing of television stations on June 2, 1952, mixing both UHF and VHF channels in the same communities ("intermixture")—the assignment plan for UHF channels was "coordinated with and made complementary to" the assignment plan for VHF channels. The Commission said this was the only means "of providing television service to all the people."[5] For educational stations it had reserved 242 channels—80 VHF and 162 UHF.[6] The FCC repeated that the reservations were to be "long enough to give . . . reasonable opportunity" but "not so long that the frequencies remain unused for excessively long periods of time." It demonstrated that the time for reservations of VHF channels would be shorter than for UHF channels by deleting the four VHF reservations in Indianapolis, Kansas City, Mo., and Omaha, where educational interests did not respond or responded favoring commercial channels, and another in Columbia, where the University of Missouri would not accept a "noncommercial" status. But, in general, the Commission said, "We consider that the record shows the desire and ability of education to make a substantial contribution to the use of television. . . . It is much easier for those seeking to construct educational television stations to raise funds and to get other necessary support if the channels are definitely available." Both the deletions of four reserved VHF channels and the increased total of reserved channels attested that the Commission had been influenced by the statements filed and by the failure to file statements in behalf of educational television during the previous year.

The reservations were qualified, however, both in space and time. The FCC made no reservations in the "closed" cities (where all VHF channels had been already licensed, including New York, Los Angeles, Washington, Philadelphia, Detroit, Cleveland, and Buffalo). In these the Commission echoed the cant of the old Federal Radio Commission: "Educational interests can apply just like any other interest when the license term expires." The Commission said it would not consider any petition to change the reservations for one year, until June 2, 1953.

The Year of Grace

Within two weeks of the Sixth Order, FCC Chairman Paul Walker told the Television Programs Institute at Pennsylvania State College: "These precious television assignments cannot be preserved for you indefinitely. They may not even be reserved for you beyond one year unless you can give the Commission concrete, convincing evidence of the validity of your intent. . . . Time began to run out the minute this Report was issued. . . . I fear you will find this year of grace the shortest year of your lives."[7]

This year was probably the most strenuous test that has ever been made of the ability of those concerned with education to move with speed, balance, and imagination. The Fund for Adult Education was ready to give guidance and financial support to the movement, provided the reservations were made firm. The directors had approved Fletcher's basic approach in principle before the Sixth Order of April 11, 1952. With the Sixth Order, the first task was to get the reservations made permanent (or, at least, for an "indefinite" period). To do so the Fund dealt directly with the FCC. The main events between the FCC's provisional reservations in April 1952, and its firm reservations of channels in May 1953, occurred through an informal but close relationship between the two organizations. The Commission needed assurance that the reserved channels would be used; the FAE needed assurance that the reservations would be made firm.

In May 1952, FCC Chairman Walker gave the Fund's directors a report of the urgent need for educational institutions (alone or in cooperation, established or newly created) to apply for licenses and to activate stations. At that same board meeting President Fletcher explained to

Walker the Fund's plan: to stimulate applications, to aid station activation financially, and to establish a national program exchange center. After the meeting with Walker the Fund quickly requested and received a special grant of $4,750,000 from the Ford Foundation to advance educational television.

On April 21–24, 1952, only ten days after the Sixth Order, the Television Programs Institute had been held at Pennsylvania State College. Although it was sponsored by the American Council on Education, it was engineered by the Fund. The FAE was also the main financial backer but insisted that funds also come from other sources in order to demonstrate a broader base of support. These other sources were the Alfred P. Sloan Foundation and the Payne Fund. Those attending defined needs and goals and made plans. This national meeting was rapidly followed by a steady series of similar regional and state action conferences.

On October 29, 1952, Fletcher met with the full FCC at a dinner in Washington arranged by the JCET and outlined the details and developments of the Fund's plan: to stimulate license applications through further support to the JCET and the formation of a national citizens committee; to aid station construction with a program of matching grants; and to create a national center for program exchange, procurement, and distribution which was nearly ready for incorporation. These activities, he said, depended upon firm reservations of channels, with which he would "guarantee" that twenty or thirty ETV stations would be on the air within two or three years.[8] Fletcher then asked the Commission to give informal assurance, which it did, that the reservations would be affirmed so the Fund could proceed with the execution of its plan.

By the end of 1952 the Fund had given an additional $326,400 for the JCET; had brought into being the National Citizens Committee for Educational Television with $355,000 for support through the American Council on Education; had begun its program of offering matching grants-in-aid for station construction; and had founded the Educational Television and Radio Center. By December 1952, twenty-two educational institutions had filed requests with the FCC for construction permits.

The climax of the year of grace came at the First National Conference on Educational Television in Washington, D.C., on May 4, 1953, sponsored by the JCET and the National Citizens Committee for Educational Television (NCCET). Twenty-nine speakers from twenty-one states reported progress made since April 15, 1952.[9] And a week later the FCC released an explanation that, although petitions to delete or change the reserved channels would be received beginning June 2, 1953, the assignments were reserved indefinitely, except where individual assignments were successfully challenged by other applicants.

Protecting the Reservations, 1953–56

The strongest challenge to an assigned channel was evidence that the reserved assignment was being wasted. The best way to secure the reservation against challenge was to activate a station on the reserved channel. The JCET and the NCCET worked jointly towards the end of station activation—the former focusing on educational institutions, the latter on new, cooperative-community organizations. The JCET kept the educators' case before the FCC, as well as encouraging and aiding educational institutions by giving help in planning, information about procedures, and advice on legal, technical, and financial matters. NCCET publicized ETV nationally, mobilized voluntary associations at all levels, and organized local support, particularly of business, industrial, and lay leaders in the larger cities.

From 1953 to 1955 the FCC rejected all petitions for deletion of reserved television channels, created sixteen new assignments for educational stations, seven of them VHF, and waived a substantial portion of the financial qualifications in approving applications from educators. In 1955, however, the situation changed—not because hostility to ETV increased but because demand for VHF channels increased, particularly from commercial broadcasters with UHF channels. UHF wasn't working well either in transmission or reception, therefore, the mixture of VHF and UHF stations in the same communities wasn't working well. On March 31, 1955, the FCC issued a "Notice of Proposed Rule-Making" for the "deintermixture" (separation of UHF and VHF assignments) of channels in five areas. The whole basis underlying the allocations in the Sixth Report was being re-examined and with it the principle of VHF educational reservations.

On June 2, 1955, the FCC instituted the first rule-making proceeding regarding a deletion of a VHF reservation. Rib Mountain Television, Inc., operator of KGTV, UHF, Channel 23, Des Moines, wanted the license to VHF Channel 11, proposing that Channel 23 be reserved for education. The weakness of those who opposed the shift (the JCET and some Iowa educators) was that Des Moines had no organization ready to occupy the reserved Channel 11. The FCC denied the Rib Mountain petition by a 4–3 vote. In July 1956, however, the FCC ordered the shift of reserved VHF Channel 3 to UHF Channel 48 in College Station, Texas, because there was no evidence that any educational institution would activate the VHF channel in the foreseeable future. Soon thereafter, Eugene, Oregon, lost reserved VHF Channel 9 for the same reason. Thus there was a continuing need for the JCET to help preserve reserved channels by aiding educational institutions to activate stations. Paul Walker's warning, "Those precious television assignments cannot be preserved for you indefinitely," was advance notice of a real danger.

ACTIVATING THE CHANNELS: TASK NUMBER TWO

Having begun the first task of obtaining and protecting the reserved channels, the Fund for Adult Education turned to the second—getting stations on the channels. The goal was to establish "educational television stations in many parts of the country; each supported by its educational sponsor and responsible to the whole community; each with a broadly representative governing or advisory board, or both, each not just an 'outlet' but a source of programming as well. Tying them all together, a national center . . . for the voluntary exchange of programs, ideas, and information in order to multiply resources, set standards, and stimulate constructive competition."[10] When Fletcher approached the Ford Foundation with the idea of a special grant to help bring some thirty ETV stations into being, Henry Ford told him he thought that a large grant should be made to bring into being one big model station. Fletcher later convinced him that the Fund's plan was preferable because the FCC wanted a system of stations with nationwide educational and community support.

The task of getting channels activated involved bringing about a national climate favorable to the idea of ETV and encouraging the move to activate channels in the communities where channels had been reserved. To accomplish this task the Fund for Adult Education gave financial support to three existing organizations and created two new ones. It used also the informal approach of getting existing organizations to give auspices to new activities that the Fund thought necessary.

The ACE ETV Committee

Led by Arthur S. Adams, the American Council on Education formed the Educational Television Committee, which was given financial aid by the Fund. The committee dealt with matters "over and above the Council's participation in the JCET" and began a series of interuniversity conferences and publications to stimulate educational institutions to activate stations. But its first action was on the national level—to convene the Penn State Conference.

The Television Programs Institute

The Television Programs Institute at Pennsylvania State College, April 21–24, 1952, was called by the American Council on Education at the inducement of the Fund for Adult Education. It was financed by the FAE and also—to demonstrate that the ETV movement had support from other sources—by the Alfred P. Sloan Foundation and the Payne Fund. The 116 participants included officials from colleges and universities; representatives from professional schools; state and local school superintendents; and representatives from the FCC, the U.S. Office of Education, the television industry, and several foundations other than FAE, among them the Carnegie Corporation, the Mellon Trust, and the Twentieth Century Fund.

The meeting began ten days after the FCC issued the Sixth Report reserving, at least provisionally, 242 channels for educational stations. The objective was to plan the establishment and operation of ETV stations. There were prepared presentations, structured discussions, exhibits of equipment, and demonstrations of programs. Significant developments were made in proposals and plans for a national citizens committee to supplement the JCET, for a scheme of financial aid for bringing stations into being, and for a national center for the exchange and distribution of programs.[11] After the institute similar policy and action meetings were held in many regions and states. A JCET list of reports on state actions concerning ETV during 1952 and 1953 includes "no report" from only ten states.[12]

The National Citizens Committee for Educational Television (NCCET)

In July 1952, Fletcher expressed his conviction that the ETV movement needed a "strong, separate, independent organization to literally promote the idea of ETV nationally and in communities which were logical station points." In October a planning group was formed that included Raymond Wittcoff, a young businessman in St. Louis and chairman of that city's Mayor's Committee on ETV, and Edgar Fuller. The National Citizens Committee for Educational Television (NCCET) was established in November 1952, sponsored by the ACE and supported by the FAE. The original members of the NCCET were Raymond Wittcoff, Edgar Fuller, Telford Taylor, James Quigg Newton (mayor of Denver), Leland

Hazard (Pittsburgh Plate Glass Company), John Ivey, Jr. (Southern Regional Education Board), Kenneth Bartlett (Syracuse University), Ralph Steetle, and Irving Salomon (a retired businessman). Honorary co-chairmen were Milton Eisenhower, president of Pennsylvania State College, and Marion Folsom, director, Eastman Kodak Company.

Executive Director Robert R. Mullen, formerly chief of information of the Economic Cooperation Administration under Hoffman, commented on the NCCET: "This citizen participation was not there in the history of AM. Nor was it there in the movement to establish stations in the 20 channels reserved for educators in the FM band. This new fact in broadcasting is peculiar to the rise of educational television and is, I believe, a most hopeful augury of success in this exciting venture."[13]

To acquaint "business, professional and civic leaders and organizations with the problem" and to encourage them "to support the educators in their efforts to build and operate the stations," the NCCET undertook two jobs. The first was field service, with staff members working out of offices in New York, Washington, Chicago, Los Angeles, and San Francisco. The second job was to establish the NCCET Advisory Council. At its height in 1956 the Advisory Council numbered 106 organizations, including the U.S. Chamber of Commerce, the AFL-CIO, the National Council of Churches, the NAACP, and local chapters of the Junior League, PTA, and the League of Women Voters. The formation of community ETV stations—owned and operated by nonprofit corporations composed of private citizens—was largely due to the leadership provided by laymen who were stimulated and aided by the NCCET.[14]

The Joint Committee on Educational Television (JCET)

The committee's second function (its first was lobbying with the FCC) was field work—to give legal assistance and information on engineering and construction to institutions and communities considering applying, constructing, and activating stations. Lobbying with the FCC and assisting stations were integral functions because the best way to persuade the FCC to maintain or add reserved channels was to prove that they were going to be used. Challenges in such cities as Boston, Chicago, San Francisco, and, later, Des Moines, New Orleans, Birmingham, Toledo, and Milwaukee could be defeated only by action within these communities. John W. Powell commented in 1961: "There is hardly any ETV station in existence that does not owe its initial progress to the personal advice and help of the JCET staff during the early and critical stages."[15]

The National Association of Educational Broadcasters (NAEB)

The NAEB was a member of the JCET, of course. It was supervising experimental radio programming that demonstrated the ability of educational broadcasters to combine sound scholarship with popular appeal, which had important implications for television programming. With financial support from the Fund, the NAEB also served as consultant to the more than one hundred educational radio stations in the United States and ran workshops and conferences for the professional development of the persons who would manage, operate, and program the forthcoming ETV stations.[16]

The FAE's Program of Matching Grants to Stations

Just as the Fund for Adult Education dealt directly with the FCC to help secure the reservation of television channels, so did it deal directly with educational institutions and community corporations to help activate the stations. The objective was to develop a core of about thirty stations. Key questions were: Which communities? How to select them? How much financial aid to offer? On what conditions? A step toward getting answers was to investigate the resources of the communities with reserved channels to determine which had the greatest potential and importance for ETV. Under the auspices of the American Council on Education and financed by the Fund, Robert Hudson, between May 15 and July 15, 1952, investigated promising communities following a priority list drawn up in collaboration with the JCET and the ACE. He looked for both a demonstrated interest in establishing a station and a known program of action. After visiting most of the major communities where there was a likelihood of initiating an ETV station, he submitted a list and report on twenty-one metropolitan areas and fifteen educational centers, plus ten cities in New York, where the state board of regents was proposing a state network.[17]

On the basis of Hudson's report to the ACE and the FAE of his "Study of Community Readiness for Educational Television," in the fall of 1952 the Fund began offering grants-in-aid to university and metropolitan centers where channels had been reserved. The basic principle behind the offers of grants was that each "would mean the difference between the presence or absence of an educational television station in the community" and each would be "large enough to have an effect while avoiding any tendency to retard local initiative." On the basis of the best engineering advice available the general formula was to offer $100,000 to each university or public school center and $150,000 to each metropolitan center. Among the conditions of the offer were these stipulations: that each university or community corporation double the amount of the grant in cash or value of equipment; that the Fund's grant be used for equipment only, with specific quality standards; that title to the equipment remain with the Fund for eight years (to provide for transfer if a station failed—a provision later followed by the Ford Foundation and the federal ETV facilities program); that the station agree to affiliation with the Educational Television and Radio Center for the exchange of programs and have kinescope recording equipment so as to be able to contribute programs; and that a reasonable proportion of the station's programming be for the education of adults in the liberal arts and sciences. All conditions were precisely drawn up in a "Letter of Agreement."[18]

The grants proceeded in stages. The first step was a visit by a Fund staff member to make a tentative offer. This was usually taken by one of the Fund's three regional representatives—G. H. Griffiths (Western); R. J. Blakely (Central); and Delbert Clark, later John Osman (Eastern); or by Ann Spinney (who with Fletcher and Griffiths made up FAE's "ETV team"). Some of these overtures did not lead to anything, at least at the time. An anecdote may illustrate the different responses to the Fund's offer of an amount designed to "have an effect" and at the same time stimulate local initiative. My first visit to a potential recipient of a grant was in 1952 to the men who were then heading the ETV movement in Chicago, both officials of the educational institutions that had taken the lead. When I pridefully announced, "We are prepared to offer you aid in the amount of $150,000," I was answered with surprised, scornful laughter. A year later, however, when the initiative had been taken by the Chicago Educational Television Association, whose president was Edward L. Ryerson, chairman of Inland Steel Company, the Fund offer was quickly accepted. WTTW TV, Channel 11, began operating in September 1955.

To some recipients the conditions of the grants seemed unnecessarily cumbersome because the technical considerations behind them were not obvious. On the other hand, unusual circumstances sometimes required the Fund to be flexible. A case in point is East Lansing, Michigan. Michigan State University, highly advanced in all aspects of educational television, had applied to the FCC for the only channel in that area available to it—nonreserved UHF Channel 60. Not satisfied with UHF, it was trying to work out a joint application for nonreserved VHF Channel 10 with a commercial television corporation. The FAE's "Letter of Agreement" did not cover such circumstances. Sitting beside John Hannah, president of the university, who was impatient with what he considered red tape, I called Fletcher in Pasadena, explained the situation, and received immediate assurance that the contingency would be accommodated. Another organization that did not fit was the Pacifica Foundation. As licensee and operator of KPFA, Berkeley, the foundation was a broadcasting venture in noncommercial educational FM radio for adults, supported by listener contributions and subscriptions. The Fund early gave grants to aid this station, both as an experiment in radio and as an experiment in the financing of broadcasting through contributions from audiences.

In total, from 1953 to 1961, the Fund contributed almost $4 million for station equipment to thirty-three ETV stations; a few grants of less than $100,000 were made when the money began to run out, and grants of less than that amount were also made to a few stations for kinescope recording units. The FAE's grants to aid station activation laid the base upon which the Educational Television Facilities Act of 1962 would build.

The Beginnings of the Stations

By mid-1955 sixteen channels reserved for ETV stations had been activated. Their existence and the exchange, procurement, and distribution of programs through the Educational Television and Radio Center made it easier to activate other reserved channels. The following brief accounts tell the story of the beginnings of twelve of the first sixteen ETV stations.[19] The stations in Houston and Los Angeles are selected because they were the first two. Others are included either because they became especially important to the entire ETV system or because they represent examples of the four types of ETV licensees—universities, community corporations, state agencies, and school boards.

KUHT, 8 VHF, Houston, May 25, 1953

W. W. Kemmerer, president of the University of Houston, and John C. Schwarzwalder, manager of KUHT FM, persuaded the chairman of the university board of regents to support the venture into ETV. Members of the Houston public schools organized a television council to represent both the schools and the community, and ETV was built into the teaching structure of the university. The license, initially given jointly to the university and the public schools, was later held exclusively by the university.

KTHE, 28 UHF, Los Angeles, November 29, 1953

This station, licensed to the University of Southern California, was on the air only until September 11, 1954, when it went off permanently—the only educational television station to fail during the first twenty years. It could not build an audience on a UHF channel in a seven-station VHF market. The sole support of the station was a grant from the Allan Hancock Foundation, and funds were cut off when Hancock resigned as head of the foundation. (Note, however, that Channel 28, Los Angeles, was reactivated on September 28, 1964, licensed to Community Television of Southern California.)

WQED, 13 VHF, Pittsburgh, April 1, 1954

The establishment of ETV was part of the city and countywide drive spurred by the Greater Allegheny Conference on Community Development to rejuvenate the area. Mayor David E. Lawrence, friend and political colleague of Frieda Hennock, called the first ETV meetings in Pittsburgh. ETV became a project of one of the conference committees, chaired by Leland Hazard, vice-president of Pittsburgh Plate Glass Company, which helped by the JCET and urged by the NCCET began the movement to establish a station. The Arbuckle-Jamison Foundation, the A. W. Mellion Educational and Charitable Trust, Westinghouse Electric Company, and the Pittsburgh Plate Glass Company all gave money, equipment, or facilities. The Metropolitan Pittsburgh Educational Television Coporation filed for a construction permit in 1953.

KQED, 9 VHF, San Francisco, June 10, 1954

Early interest in ETV in San Francisco began primarily as a public school and vocational school service. Successive meetings of the Western Radio-Television Conference, strenuous efforts by the JCET and the NCCET, and especially the State ETV Conference called by Governor Earl Warren broadened the concept and led to the formation of the Bay Area ETV Association. Business and industry were not much involved. Almost one-fifth of the initial capital came from donations by individuals, with the rest coming from the Rosenwald Foundation. KIPX, the local CBS outlet, and the San Francisco public schools made transmitter and studio properties available through lease arrangements.

KETC, 9 VHF, St. Louis, September 20, 1954

Mayor Joseph Darst officially began the movement toward an ETV station in St. Louis by appointing the Mayor's Committee on ETV. Leadership was soon assumed by Raymond Wittcoff, who worked closely with the JCET and the NCCET. The St. Louis ETV Commission was created, and the efforts of citizens groups, business, industry, and educational leaders raised nearly $1 million before the station's opening broadcast. Arthur Baer, president of Stix, Baer, and Fuller department store, financed a new building, St. Louis University gave land for the building, and many firms contributed on the basis of $1 per employee. More than twenty-five school systems in the area agreed to make payments in consideration for programs intended for school use at the rate of $1 per student per year. PTA women collected more than $100,000 in one evening. The St. Louis ETV Commission applied for a license in January 1953.

KUON, 12 VHF, Lincoln, November 1, 1954

This station had the unconventional origin of being a gift from an out-of-state commercial company. In 1954 the Fetzer Broadcasting Company of Kalamazoo, Michigan, purchased two commercial TV stations in Lincoln, Channels 10 and 12. The FCC approved the transfer of WOLN TV, then operating on Channel 12, to Channel 10 and the gift of Channel 12 to the regents of the University of Nebraska. (Jack McBride was the key figure within the university.) KUON is now the flagship station of the Nebraska ETV Commission, licensee of a network throughout Nebraska.

WCIQ, 7 VHF, Munford, January 7, 1955; WBIQ, 10 VHF, Birmingham, April 28, 1955; and WDIQ, 2 VHF, Dozier, August 8, 1956

These three channels are key components in the first state ETV network under an agency especially established for the purpose by a state legislature. The Alabama Educational Television Commission was created by the Alabama legislature in 1953 under a bill personally planned and directed by Governor Gordon Pearsons. Graydon Ausmus, director of the University of Alabama's radio station, WUOA , and then president of the NAEB, was the leader of the ETV interests.

WGBH, 2 VHF, Boston, May 2, 1955

The WGBH Educational Foundation was incorporated in 1951—an outgrowth of the Lowell Cooperative Broadcasting Council's program activities, first over commercial stations and then with its own WGBH FM. Parker Wheatley, general manager of WGBH FM, and his associate

Hartford Gunn promoted the idea and planned the operations; Ralph Lowell, trustee of the Lowell Institute, made those plans a reality.[20]

WILL, 12 VHF, Champaign-Urbana, August 1, 1955

The University of Illinois' application, filed in May 1953, under the leadership of President George Stoddard and Dean Wilbur Schramm, continued that institution's long-time involvement in educational broadcasting. The commercial Illinois Association of Broadcasters delayed activation of the channel for at least a year by opposition in the legislature and then a challenge in the courts.

WTHS and WPBT, 2 VHF, Miami, August 12, 1955

The Dade County-Miami situation and the history of the activation of Channel 2 defy simple exposition.[21] Vernon Bronson, acting for the Dade County school board, applied to the FCC for a construction permit in 1952. After the station went on the air Bronson turned to the organization of a community corporation because there was little tax support for anything except instructional television. Channel 2, Miami, is licensed (for time-sharing) to WTHS, School Board of Dade County, and WPBT, Community Television Foundation of South Florida.

The stories of the beginnings of these twelve stations give a fair impression of the varieties and complexities of the local communities and of the intricate interplay of national and local leadership, agencies, and resources, including commercial television companies.

Many commercial interests gave various kinds of help (equipment, service, and money) to numerous ETV stations for several reasons, and this significantly large help was in some cases crucial to ETV stations' activation, survival, or both.[22]

PROGRAMMING FOR THE STATIONS: TASK NUMBER THREE

The main obstacle that deterred many universities and communities from activating stations on reserved channels was the fear that they would not have enough programs to meet the day-by-day demands of broadcasting. The Fund for Adult Education took early steps to ensure that the ETV stations would have access to programs from many sources.

Beginning in 1951, the Fund made grants for experimental and demonstration productions in radio and television. Fletcher relied on the advice of George Probst, Robert Hudson, Seymour Siegel, Richard Hull,

Harold McCarty, and Parker Wheatley and later requested that the NAEB appoint these six men as the Adult Education Committee so they would have some official status within the association.

FAE grants for the NAEB (through the Lowell Institute Cooperative Broadcasting Council, to keep the production in the hands of persons Fletcher trusted) resulted in five series of radio programs that set new standards of excellence for educational radio. The most notable were "The Ways of Mankind," written under the direction of anthropologist Walter Goldschmidt, produced and recorded by the Canadian Broadcasting Corporation (CBC); and "The Jeffersonian Heritage," edited by historian Dumas Malone and narrated by Claude Rains, who portrayed Jefferson. The NAEB appointed William G. Harley director of the project, and Probst was in charge of the production. Much was riding on this project, for although the Ford Foundation and the Fund for Adult Education were enthusiastic about the potential of educational television and radio, they were skeptical that educational broadcasters could produce programs that were both educational and interesting. The two series won high popular and critical acclaim, demonstrating that educational broadcasters in cooperation with subject matter specialists could produce programs of the highest quality, provided they were given adequate funding and worked together cooperatively.

Also beginning in 1951, the Fund made grants to WOI TV, Iowa State College, for ETV programming because it was the only TV station then operated by an educational institution. Although the first programs were experimental, later ones were fed into the Educational Television and Radio Center (ETRC). The station hired writer Robert Lewis Shayon and film producer Charles Guggenheim, who had to learn educational television while producing programs. One of their first productions was "The Whole Town's Talking"—a series of discussions of problems in a small Iowa town. The Fund made another grant to WOI TV to buy a kinescope recording unit and improve the quality of that method of recording programs. Before videotape recording developed in the late fifties, the "kine"—a recording of a program made from the television tube— was the only method of duplication other than film. Improved skills and techniques learned at WOI TV and passed on to other stations significantly raised the picture quality of locally produced programs.

Founding the Educational Television and Radio Center (ETRC)

To test some ideas he thought should underlie an exchange center, Fletcher called a meeting on July 9, 1952. Persons from outside the Fund were Hudson, Probst, Wheatley, Steetle, Wittcoff, Adams, Stoddard, and Harold Lasswell (professor of law and political science, Yale University).

They agreed with the principles that the center should be a body representative *of* broad areas, not a delegate body *from* specific organizations or associations; that the fear of a "central agency's developing dictatorial ambitions" should be allayed in appearance as well as in fact; and that swift action was urgently needed. They stressed that the center should be a new body, not an existing one such as the NAEB; that it should not itself engage in program production; and, to speed up the process, that Fletcher should be acting president until the board chose a permanent president. The Fund board approved Fletcher's plans two days later, and he immediately formed an organizational committee for the center, composed of himself, George Stoddard, Harold Lasswell, Robert Calkins (president of the Brookings Institution), and Ralph Lowell (trustee of the Lowell Institute). He then met with a key group of the NAEB to discuss the ideas that had been stated in the proposal "Educational Television Programs, Inc."[23] Hudson wrote a twenty-four-page memorandum, "The Educational Radio and Television Program and Exchange Center," dated November 15, which became the working paper in the establishment of the center. The Educational Television and Radio Center (ETRC) was incorporated on November 21, 1952, and on December 5 the board of directors of the center first met. The men on the twelve-member board from 1952 through 1958 fulfilled Fletcher's idea of having "top figures in scholarship, education, social science, communications, arts, business management, and program production" involved in the ETRC—thereby encouraging support from many fields.

The Educational Television and Radio Center, 1952–58

The center's goals, formally stated in the bylaws, were broad, but its operating objective was almost solely to give program service to educational television stations. The Fund made an operational grant to the center of over $1 million through 1956, and a programming grant of $3 million from mid-1953 through 1956. The programming grant provided that at least $2.5 million be used "for facilitating the production and exchange of programs in the four subject areas . . . international affairs, national or political affairs, economic affairs, and the humanities." This provision was to ensure that the developing ETV system serve the needs of mature individuals as persons and citizens, not just the needs of educational institutions schooling children and youth or offering vocational and avocational training to adults. The provision left only $500,000 for programs for other general audiences (e.g., children) or for special purposes (e.g., instruction in schools), but the center was deliberately designed to include the full potential of educational television and to appeal to many sources of support for many purposes.

The operating policies of the center were to provide a film and kinescope network that would supply regularly scheduled programs to affiliated stations (that is, it would not be simply an exchange library from which the stations could draw programs at will); that it would not neglect either the quality or the quantity of the programs needed by the stations; and that it would employ others to produce television and radio programs (that is, the center would not itself engage in production).[24]

The educational philosophy that guided the programming service was: "Foremost . . . an educational television program must in fact be educational; . . . it must effect changes in the viewer of an educational nature." The goal, therefore, was to achieve desired effects from programs rather than to attract large audiences, although "numbers of viewers are important in a pragmatic sense." Effective educational broadcasting, reasoned the ETRC, can be fully exploited in several ways, including by acquiring programs in a series and by reinforcing "other educational experiences" associated with them. The center intended that its programs should "supplement and enrich local program activities, not take the place of them."[25]

The board selected as president of the center the man nominated by Chairman George Stoddard, Harry Newburn, president of the University of Oregon. Before he assumed the presidency of the center, Newburn took part in the Lincoln Lodge Seminar where the center's philosophy was thoroughly explored,[26] and he had the benefit of the Gunflint Lodge Conference where the interim plans for the center were evaluated.[27]

The center established headquarters at Ann Arbor, Michigan—Newburn's preference—in the fall of 1953, with Robert Hudson as program coordinator. Newburn's personnel policy was to have as small a staff as possible, leaving the maximum amount of money for programming. He hired consultants for special purposes.

ETRC Television Activities

The center started occasional programming service on January 1, 1954, to the two stations then on the air. On May 18, 1954, it began regular shipments of programs to the four stations then broadcasting at the rate of four and three-quarters hours per week. The rate rose to five hours per week in 1955, five and three-quarters in 1956, seven and one-half in 1957, and was seven and one-quarter hours in 1958, a temporary dip. Meanwhile, the number of stations on the air constantly increased: from nine at the end of 1954, to seventeen at the end of 1955, twenty-two at the end of 1956, twenty-seven at the end of 1957, and thirty-six at the end of 1958. All were affiliated with the center; the stations all needed programs, and affiliation was one of the conditions of the Fund's grants-in-aid.

By the end of 1954 the center devised the "block system" whereby stations were divided into scheduling blocks of four or five stations each. While the stations in Block One were being sent program-set A, the stations in Block Two were being sent program-set B, and so on. When the stations in Block One had returned program-set A to the center (usually after three weeks), it would be cleaned, inspected, and sent to the stations in Block Two, and so on. The center was servicing seventeen stations in three blocks by the end of 1955, and the number of blocks had increased to five in late 1956 and six in 1957.

The "Flexible Service" plan, which began in 1958, was the inclusion in each week's programs of one and one-half hours of programs chosen by each station from the center's pool. The plan was the addition of a library service component to the regular service; it was made possible because the center's resources of programs had increased, both of old ones suitable for reruns and of new ones of greater variety and higher quality. In June 1958 the center began distributing a "special" once a month.

A study of the ETV stations on the air in mid-1956 shows that ETRC programs averaged 25 percent of all programs broadcast, with a range of from 12 to 75 percent; and that they averaged 75 percent of all nonlocal programs broadcast, with a range from 41 to 100 percent.

In addition to the services to ETV stations described above, there was also "Extended Service"—designed to gain outlets through commercial stations in areas that lacked ETV stations, with conditions such as clearance, priority for ETV stations, and no commercial sponsorship. By 1957 more than 682 programs from 51 series had been broadcast over 21 commercial stations in 15 states; all these figures rose sharply during 1957.

ETRC Radio Activities

The ETRC included radio in its title, statement of purposes, and promotion, but radio took a definite second place to television. Early in 1954 the center announced that grants-in-aid would be made for the production of radio programs for national distribution, with plans worked out by the NAEB Advisory Committee and the grants administered by the NAEB. In addition, the center occasionally made a direct grant for a production. The existing NAEB tape network distributed the programs to the stations. In 1954 seven universities and the Lowell Institute Cooperative Broadcasting Council received a total of $42,000 in grants-in-aid. The number of recipients and the total of grants remained about the same during 1955 and 1956. In April 1957, the center announced a new plan to make available $100,000 for each of the next three years for both the radio grants administered by the NAEB and the grants made directly by the center for commissioned programs.

Related Activities

Publicity and Promotion. Until 1956, the main responsibility for national publicity and promotion of ETV was assigned to the National Citizens Committee for Educational Television (NCCET). At the end of 1955, because of the agreement that the Ford Foundation would assume concern for ETV, the Fund ended the existence of the NCCET, and its functions were taken over by the center, a reorganized JCET (renamed the Joint *Council* on Educational Television—same initials), and the National Association of Educational Broadcasters. In December 1955, the Ford Foundation made a grant of about $90,000 to the center to perform some of what had been the NCCET's activities. These included relations with the 106-member Advisory Council, which was the main channel for national publicity about ETV. The center was not able to achieve the concentrated impact of publicity and promotion that the NCCET under Mullen had achieved.

Consultation and Training. In performing this function many of the center's activities were aimed at improving the quality of the kinescope recordings by the stations. With a special grant of $27,000 from the Fund for this purpose, in January 1954 the center started consultant service to each ETV station or nonstation production unit (university center or independent producer) before it began any production for exchange or contract. It also had expert consultants review monthly kinescope samples from the stations. The center produced and distributed the "Production Handbook" and held sessions on technical standards at meetings of the affiliates as well as a week-long seminar in St. Louis in 1957 for the engineers of five new stations. Finally, the center provided a kinescope series of four half-hour training programs for each station.

Nonbroadcast Use of Programs. The center's purposes included the use of television and radio material in ways other than broadcasting. In September 1954, the board authorized Newburn to contract "to sell and rent those programs cleared for nonbroadcast use and which are in demand by schools, discussion groups, and other such agencies." In February 1955, the center contracted with Indiana University to establish the National Educational Television (NET) Film Service, which the university hired Edwin Cohen to undertake. The NET Film Service reviewed all ETRC programs, selected suitable ones, and duplicated and distributed them to audiovisual (AV) centers throughout the country (most of them at universities), which served as retail distributors. By mid-1957 twenty-seven retail AV centers were participating, and the estimated number of persons who had viewed NET programs in nonbroadcast use was nearly nine million.

Development. A goal of the center was to win continuing financial support from the broadest possible range of interests. Yet it remained almost wholly dependent upon Fund support through 1956. During the formative years there were good reasons for not seeking broader support: ETV was still an idea, not yet a product, and a drive by the center might compete with local educational stations' quests for support. However, two years after the Ford Foundation had become the all but sole supporter of the center, the foundation gave it a special grant of $98,000 for a development program. The board quickly announced a four-point program: to engage fund-raising counsel for stations; to survey selected ETV communities to determine the availability of support; to survey stations' accounting procedures; and to explore possible support for the center's own program services. The development scheme did not get up steam until late 1958.

Research. Another of the center's purposes was to "engage in, support, and otherwise assist research" in the educational uses and effects of broadcasting, particularly television. Yet in 1955 I. Keith Tyler concluded: "So far . . . the Center has barely begun any systematic research." The center's meager support of research could be explained in part by shortage of funds; in all, during Newburn's term only about $105,000 was spent on forty-nine separate studies.[28] But the center under Newburn was not research minded, even about its own operations. Tyler observed also that the center did not itself engage in or use the results of research to determine the needs of the stations for programming, the impact of the programs, or, above all, the effectiveness of its own relations with the stations and other organizations.

Problems

Procurement and Development of Programs. Since the center's board had ruled out its engaging in production, it acquired programs: (1) produced by affiliated stations ("exchange programs"); (2) from existing film material (including kinescope recordings); and (3) produced under contract. The high hopes for programs by exchange were not fulfilled at first; the advantage of exchange was economy, the disadvantage was usually poor quality. Programs from existing film material were mostly either inappropriate or involved legal snags, such as copyrights. Programs produced by contract were usually better but always more expensive. Sources from other countries were cultivated but did not begin to yield important results until the fall of 1958. The percentage of programs procured by acquisition and contract was high until 1956, but declined as exchange programs increased and improved. Newburn favored getting programs from affiliated stations, either by exchange or contract, both to save money and to "build the stations' muscles." He also favored contract programs from nonstation university centers. The affiliated stations and nonstation university centers produced programs of highly uneven quality, from excellent to unusable. Five of the large-city community corporation stations (KETC, St. Louis; KQED, San Francisco; WGBH, Boston; WQED, Pittsburgh; and WTTW, Chicago) produced three-fourths of all station-produced programs through 1958. The nonstation University of Michigan ranked with the "Big Five" as one of the six largest producers.

Selection. The center's selection of programs involved decisions concerning both content and quality. Regarding content, a program or series had to be judged appropriate both to the wishes of the stations and to the balance and variety that the center sought to achieve. Regarding quality, a program or series had to be judged by several standards, such as artistic worth and technical excellence. In selection the center was in two binds. The first was the Fund for Adult Education's stipulation that five-sixths of its $3 million grant for programming be spent on "international affairs, national or political affairs, economic affairs, and the humanities." The second bind was Newburn's favor toward programming in categories borrowed from academic disciplines. The result was a rather arithmetic "balance" in many subject fields that was increasingly unsatisfactory to the stations. The Ford Foundation's basic grant ($6,263,300 from January 1, 1957, through 1959 for both administration and programming) was without conditions concerning subject matter, which allowed a wide scope in programming. However, it was at a rate only about 50 percent higher for a period during which costs for duplicating and distributing to a rapidly increasing number of stations were rising sharply.

Distribution. The center's distribution problem was simply that, lacking interconnection (wired or wireless, for instant or delayed broadcast), it had to rely on films and kinescopes mailed set by set to each individual station, with periodic recall for cleaning and repair. An exception during the Newburn administration was the ETRC-NBC venture in which the center and the National Broadcasting Company cooperatively sponsored and produced fifteen series in 1957 and 1958 that were broadcast to most of the ETV stations by special circuits on the NBC lines.[29]

Publicity and Promotion. One of the center's handicaps was its inability to give concentrated national publicity and promotion to programs that were broadcast locally at various times. The publicity and promotion given simultaneously all over the country to the cooperative ETRC-NBC series in 1957–58, which were broadcast over network lines, emphasized, by contrast, the inadequate publicity and promotion given to filmed series sent by mail and broadcast by block-scheduling. Another handicap was that about half of the ETV stations and almost two-thirds of the reserved channels were UHF and therefore at heavy disadvantage. Finally, ETV had no stations during this period in either New York City or in Washington, D.C.

Money. The center's chief problem was that the money it had was only a small fraction of what it needed to do the job it was created to do. Almost all the center's income through 1956 came from the FAE and after that from the Ford Foundation.[30] Since the center's primary purpose was to provide programs on the screen, the significant figure is the price the center was able to spend on each hour of programming. Between mid-1954 and the end of 1958 the center procured, duplicated, and distributed almost 1,500 hours of programming, making the average expenditure per hour of programming less than $3,500. By comparison, in 1958 for "See It Now" CBS had a budget of $90,000 per program hour,[31] and in 1959 NBC's "Bonanza" cost nearly $200,000 per hour.[32] The Carnegie Commission on Educational Television was to base its 1966 recommendations for public television on the cost figure of an average rate of $45,000 per hour for national programming.

Trends in Relationships

To achieve its broad educational goals, the center needed good relationships with several national associations and agencies. To achieve its sharp operational objective of serving educational television stations, the center needed good relationships with the increasing number of affiliated stations.

Relationships with National Organizations. The 1955 decision that responsibility for support to educational television would shift from the Fund for Adult Education to the Ford Foundation brought about the end of the National Citizens Committee for Educational Television and rearrangement of the Joint *Committee* into the Joint *Council* on Educational Television, with a broader membership base and a narrower function.[33] Supported by the Ford Foundation, the JCET's goal remained to guard and promote the utilization of the channels reserved for educational stations. There was no overlap of functions between the center and the JCET. But the differences between the ETRC and the NAEB were more complex and delicate. One difference was history. The NAEB had been formed in 1925, and in 1930 had made the first formal request for reserved broadcasting channels. It called the 1950 meeting that founded the Joint Committee on Educational Television, which won the reserved television channels. Some of its leaders had designed the plan that in many respects was the blueprint for the center, and they had wanted to be the builders of the new exchange and programming center. The NAEB, with a growing membership, would continue to exist regardless of decisions by foundations. In contrast, the ETRC was a legal creation of the FAE, had been providing regular services only since May 1954, and could be ended by a foundation decision as abruptly as it had been begun.

Another difference was the divergent but overlapping concerns of the two organizations. The NAEB was primarily committed to radio but increasingly concerned with television; the ETRC was primarily committed to television but could become increasingly concerned with radio. Obviously, if the center chose to become a national network, with all the ancillary functions entailed, and if the NAEB developed into a strong trade and professional association, then a collision would be hard to avoid. By 1956, with a larger grant for 1957–59, and with special grants for promotion, publicity, and development activities—all from the Ford Foundation

—the center was moving toward a more ambitious role, and the NAEB had made long strides toward becoming a more effective association.[34]

Relationships with Affiliated Stations. The stations could not maintain sustained programming without the aid of a national programming service. The center's primary purpose was to provide such a service for wide audiences through the affiliated stations. However, without general agreement between the center and the stations about the programs being distributed, the audiences, and the intended effects, the programs would not be widely used and the justification of the center would disappear. As the number of stations increased—from nine by 1955, to thirty-six by 1959—the problem of general agreement also increased. It was compounded by the fact that the stations were of four different types which differed in philosophy, goals, and audiences. As of mid-1958 fourteen stations were owned by nonprofit community corporations; thirteen by colleges and universities; five by public school systems (local or state); and five by state authorities legislatively created for this special purpose. Moreover, the station managers' views concerning the role of the center ranged from its being a library only to its being a network.

The center had two major means for maintaining communication with the stations. One was having program associates in the field; the other was holding periodic meetings with the affiliates. Neither worked well. The program associates were primarily interested in programs being produced for exchange or by contract. The meetings with the affiliated stations were infrequent and usually taken up with details rather than questions of philosophy, goals, and roles.

At the third affiliates' meeting, on April 16, 1956, held in conjunction with the Institute for Education by Radio-Television in Columbus, the affiliates organized their own committee of six representatives of the station managers. The members were John F. White, WQED, Pittsburgh; James Robertson, WTTW, Chicago; Hartford Gunn, WGBH, Boston; William Harley, WHA, Madison; Loren Stone, KCTS, Seattle; and Earl Wynn, WUNC Chapel Hill. The formation of the Affiliates Committee was a formalization of the station managers' dissatisfaction with the center that had been growing for at least a year. The committee gradually pressed harder for changes in guiding philosophy, operating policies, and finally in the center's presidency—changes that would make the programming better and respond to the ETV stations' needs. In 1967 Gerard L. Appy wrote: ". . . the greatest successes and the most serious difficulties in NET-affiliate relationships have been rooted in the same items that were of concern during the 1954–58 period."[35]

The Affiliates Committee met with Newburn in February 1958, to help prepare the agenda for a special three-day session of the center's top staff and all station directors at Edgewater Park, Mississippi, March 6–8, 1958, "to discuss in considerable depth the broad aspects of television in education." At the March meeting everything went wrong, and soon thereafter Newburn announced his resignation effective at the end of his five-year contract, September 15, 1958, and his intent to return to university administration (as he had earlier said he wanted to do).

In the summer of 1958 the center board asked the Affiliates Committee for recommendations to be passed on to the new president when he was selected. One was that the center create a station relations department. During the following decade the Affiliates Committee (later called the Affiliates Council) remained in existence, representing the stations with the ETRC, as it evolved first into the National Educational Television and Radio Center (NETRC) and then into National Educational Television (NET). The committee members, elected by all the station managers, served three-year staggered terms.

The formation of the Affiliates Committee was also a reaction against the NAEB, which some of the community-corporation stations had not even joined. Richard Hull wrote in 1957: "In effect, this group constituted a new organization which had 'spiritually seceded' from both the NAEB and the ETRC, and were in a frame of mind to present 'demands' for services to both organizations or to consider forming a national structure of their own."

The development of an effective mechanism to exert "station power" was, sooner or later, inherent in the healthy development of a balanced local-national system of educational television. This new organization was more than a protest and a reaction. It was an indication of the growing strength and autonomy of the stations and a demonstration that they could work together to further their common interests. The seeds of the NAEB's reorganization in 1963, with the consequent foundings of the Educational Television Service (ETS), National Educational Radio (NER), and the establishment of the Public Broadcasting Service (PBS) after the Public Broadcasting Act of 1967, lay in the founding of the Affiliates Committee.

ASSESSMENTS

Would enough communities activate the reserved ETV channels to preserve the reservations? Would a station going on the air stay on? Those were the questions facing educational television in 1951, and the Educational Television and Radio Center between 1952 and 1959 made a critical difference in the way they were answered. While specific flaws may be attributed to Newburn's "university president" style of administration—such as his neglecting broadcasting quality for academic quality—the ETRC's basic policies were thoughtfully set and his selection carefully made by the center's board, which had been deliberately fashioned by the FAE as part of a larger design to achieve both national and local influence for educational television.

The founding of a national system of educational broadcasting has been frequently likened to the founding of land-grant colleges in the United States, and properly so, because both were new social inventions. But the differences between the two foundings have rarely been spelled out. When we consider them, the founding of a system of noncommercial broadcasting appears to be the greater achievement. In the founding of land-grant colleges there was no deadline to meet, the individual colleges did not need a *system* of colleges for each to survive, and the waste of the land grants was shocking.[36] In contrast, ETV stations faced a tight deadline, they had to be developed as a system, and there was no waste of the channels and little waste of the tangible resources.

The founding of a nationwide educational television system has been likened also to the founding of public libraries by grants-in-aid from Andrew Carnegie, who gave over $40 million for public library buildings in the United States alone. This, too, was the creation of a new public institution. Carnegie insisted that the local communities commit themselves by making the grants contingent upon the local assumption of responsibility for continuing support. The wisdom of Carnegie's policy of stimulating rather than supplanting local leadership is attested by its success,[37] and so was the wisdom of the Fund for Adult Education in following a similar policy.

Against huge odds, between 1950 and 1952 a substantial number of reservations of television channels had been won for educational stations, and between 1952 and 1953 these reservations had been made secure in every community where they could reasonably be defended. Between 1952 and 1958 the base for building a nationwide system of ETV stations had been laid. In terms of the past, much had been done. In terms of the requirements for the future, much more needed to be done.

In his "Status Report—1957," Richard Hull wrote, "Since it first appeared in 1950, the term 'educational television' had become ambiguous, creating confusion and difficulty. As a crusader's cry it was excellent; as a basis for formulating television policy in education it was

almost useless."[38] He thought that confusion about and failure to distinguish between ETV "as a point-to-point communications device for the
systematic instruction of captive audiences within the framework of formal education and as a broadcast facility for free-choice audiences of
adults and out-of-school children" was the root of policy problems at
both the local and national levels. He concluded:

> If ETV is to fulfill its promise for U.S. education and the American
> public, policies must be formulated and appropriate facilities acquired to
> permit an optimum development of both its major applications.
> Each aspect of ETV should complement, not compete with the other.
> Neither is alternative to the other in a plan of continuing education which
> goes beyond the high school and the university. Chances for broadcast
> ETV success are limited in time, but opportunities for success of point-to-
> point ETV are not.

Hull then made a series of recommendations, the last of which was for:

> a sober and conscientious rethinking of ETV in terms of what its future de-
> velopments and directions can be and should be. The Ford Foundation, the
> Fund for Adult Education, the Fund for the Advancement of Education,
> and the Kellogg Foundation now have the opportunity—if not the obligation
> —to do this.
> Such deliberations, scheduled as quickly as possible, should involve
> consultation with ETV agencies and ETV leaders, the foundations and
> funds noted above, and—at some stage—other foundations as well.
> Study should be carried on within the known framework of more
> than three decades of effort in educational communications.
> This kind of effort is fundamental to a decision in any foundation to
> stop, continue, or increase financial support for ETV. A terminal decision
> cannot now be made in conscience (nor a decision to continue support be
> made in logic) without such an exploration.

When the Ford Foundation took over responsibility for educational
television, the question was: Would ETV receive the same kind of
prompt attention to the ends and means within a broad and related context that the Fund for Adult Education had given it in 1951?

5

JERRYBUILDING ON THE BASE, 1956–1963

In his "Status Report—1957" Richard Hull diagnosed the problem of making policy for educational television as the failure to distinguish between broadcasting for adults and out-of-school children and broadcasting for students in formal instruction. To realize the optimum development of both, he recommended that the major foundations, educators, and educational broadcasters cooperate in a systematic rethinking of ETV within a concept of lifelong learning.

No such rethinking was done. Other foundations shunned the field because the Ford Foundation was doing so much in it. The Ford Foundation itself was reorganized in a compartmentalized way that precluded coherent planning and action.[1] The foundation increased aid to educational television for general audiences, and both it and The Fund for the Advancement of Education gave strong support to instructional television, but not within an overall plan. The federal government entered the field with large programs of aid to research and experimentation and to equip ETV stations. The result was many activities that were often unrelated one to another.

Nevertheless, on all fronts and at all levels there were many significant advances. Since there was no single thread to follow during this period, unlike the period from 1951 through 1956, this chapter is organized into eight sections: (1) the Ford Foundation; (2) the educational stations (television and radio); (3) national organizations; (4) the rift between ETV as an alternative service and instructional television; (5) instruc-

tional television; (6) ETV as an alternative service; (7) Congressional
Acts of 1962; and (8) opening opportunities and persistent problems.

THE FORD FOUNDATION

In 1953 Paul Hoffman resigned as president of the Ford Foundation,
and with him went the overall plan that the foundation had adopted
from the 1949 study report as well as the policy of decentralization
through subsidiary foundations. During the interim presidency of
Rowan Gaither (1953–56) the foundation began to liquidate its subsidiaries. In 1955 the Fund for Adult Education (FAE) received a five-year
grant that proved to be its last; it dissolved in 1961. In 1956 a new arrangement was made under which The Fund for the Advancement of
Education (TFAE), with a final grant, became simultaneously a subsidiary foundation and the Education Division of the Ford Foundation;
TFAE was formally ended in 1967. Beginning in 1955 and continuing
through the presidency of Henry Heald (1956–66), the foundation assumed direct support of educational television for general audiences, and
both the foundation and TFAE became much more interested than they
previously had been in television for instruction.

The foundation's taking over direct support of educational television for general audiences was the result of the experiences of "Omnibus," of the Television-Radio Workshop, which the foundation had
established in 1951 and ended in 1956.

> Although conceived as an agency to improve the educational use of
> television and radio within the normal practices of *commercial* broadcasting,
> the experience of the [Television-Radio] Workshop was a significant factor
> in the Foundation's decision to support *non-commercial* educational televi-
> sion. The Workshop produced several program series between 1951 and
> 1956, the most ambitious and well-known of which was "Omnibus." . . .
> The idea behind "Omnibus" was that quality programming could be
> made sufficiently attractive to compete for audience attention against other
> commercial television programming. Qualitatively "Omnibus" was suc-
> cessful; it was awarded numerous citations for excellence and developed
> several production techniques that became standard procedure throughout
> the industry. By 1956, however, the competition among the networks for
> larger Sunday audiences and higher advertising revenue had increased to
> the point that no network felt it could afford to assign a portion of its Sun-
> day schedule to a program with limited audience appeal. With no network
> to distribute the program, "Omnibus" and the [Television-Radio] Work-
> shop were discontinued.

The "Omnibus" experience thus demonstrated that commercial television did not provide a dependable vehicle for high-quality cultural and informational programming on a continuing basis. In order for such programming to survive on television, an alternative avenue for presentation was required.[2]

Note that in a different form and a shorter time the "Omnibus" experiment repeated the unsuccessful educational-commercial broadcasting experience in "cooperation" between 1935 and 1950. By 1951 it had become clear to the FCC that it should reserve channels because educational television stations were necessary. By 1955 it had become clear to the Ford Foundation that it should support "an alternative avenue" for presenting high quality cultural and informational programming on television.

EDUCATIONAL TELEVISION STATIONS

The number of ETV stations increased from twenty-two to seventy-six between the end of 1956 and the end of 1962.[3] These figures conceal four factors that should be noted: the new availability of magnetic-tape picture recording, the depletion of grants to aid station activation, the handicap of UHF stations, and the differences in types of ETV stations.

Videotape recording (VTR)—magnetic-tape picture recordings— was much superior to kinescope recording. When the Ampex Corporation first marketed VTR in 1956, the Ford Foundation moved quickly to promote its adoption in ETV, acting through the National Educational Television and Radio Center (NETRC). (The center had added a word to its title and a letter to its initials soon after White became its second president in mid-1958.) John White announced at an affiliates meeting on June 25, 1959, that the Ford Foundation, through the center, would give a videotape recorder to each qualified ETV station then in operation. Moreover, Minnesota Mining and Manufacturing Company gave more than $250,000 worth of videotape to the stations. When NETRC placed the first big order with Ampex, the company gave the center five VTR machines, thereby enabling four "slave" machines to reproduce from one "master"; by mid-1962 the NETRC had nine VTRs. In December 1960, again through the center, the Ford Foundation offered VTR machines to the next twenty-five ETV stations coming on the air by the end of 1962 (later extended to the following October). Minnesota Mining and Manufacturing Company offered another $250,000 worth of tape to the stations. VTR strengthened ETV. Activation of channels was accelerated (ten stations came on the air in 1961 and fourteen more in 1962). More stations could contribute more and technically better programs. The NETRC could more easily duplicate and distribute the increasing number of programs to the increasing number of stations. Special instructional libraries for exchange and distribution could be established because the quality of reproduction was now acceptably high, and state and regional ETV networks became more practicable and attractive.

The grants of VTRs could speed up already-begun activation of reserved channels, but they were not enough to make the critical difference between activation and nonactivation. By 1956 most of the Fund for Adult Education's money to aid station activation had been granted or committed. Early in 1959 NAEB President William Harley said that no more than forty to fifty stations were likely to be constructed and remain in operation unless the federal government aided station activation.

Neither VTRs nor grants-in-aid, however, could alter the technical handicaps that all UHF stations suffered. Both in transmission and reception UHF was inferior to VHF. Relatively few sets could receive UHF; converters for VHF sets to receive UHF signals were expensive and crude. All-channel sets dwindled to a low of 5.5 percent of new sets manufactured in 1961.[4] Commercial UHF stations, which reached a high of 125 in 1954, declined to 75 by the end of 1960, and as a group UHF stations consistently lost money.[5] The future of ETV was heavily dependent upon the future of UHF because more than two-thirds of the reserved channels were UHF; and in seven of the first metropolitan areas and ten of the first twenty metropolitan areas the reservations were UHF. Despite such difficulties, the number of UHF ETV stations slowly grew. By the end of 1958 there were seven UHF ETV stations and twenty-seven VHF stations; by the end of 1962 there were twenty-six UHF ETV stations and forty-nine VHF ETV stations. In many communities UHF ETV stations were in effect closed-circuit operations between the stations and the schools. This fact determined that their basic financing would be used mainly, if not exclusively, for instruction.

The fourth factor—the differences between the four types of ETV stations—persisted and grew in importance. These differences reflect the differences in institutional ownership and support. The school station tends to neglect broadcasting for general audiences; the state-agency station tends to shun controversy; the university station tends to broadcast for an elite audience; and the community corporation station tends to let the budget answer questions about audience and purpose.[6]

Probably the most important difference is the one between stations owned and supported by educational institutions or agencies, on the one hand, and those owned and operated by community corporations, on the other hand. The ratio of the number of community stations to the total number of ETV stations fell as university, school-system, and state-agency stations were activated. Yet the community stations' audiences were larger, and a handful of them had greater resources to produce programs for national distribution.

Four New Big City Stations

The activation of ETV stations in several large cities greatly increased the audiences, tapped much larger sources of financial support (particularly from the audiences), made many more program production resources available to all the affiliated stations, and gave the national ETV system on the spot coverage from major sources of news and public affairs, particularly New York City and Washington, D.C.

WTTW, VHF, Channel 11, Chicago, went on the air September 5, 1955, owned and operated by the Chicago Educational Television Association and with the leadership of Edward L. Ryerson, chairman of the board of Inland Steel. The philosophy of WTTW was that it should not be dependent on tax funds, should have community roots of its own, and should perform the widest possible community service, including broadcasting for instruction under contract. By the end of 1963 three more major metropolitan areas were able to receive educational television programming.

The most important addition was the transfer of VHF Channel 13—a Newark station with studios in New York City—from the commercial National Telefilm Association (NTA) to noncommercial Educational Television for the Metropolitan Area (ETMA).[7] The FCC had reserved no VHF channel in that area because all seven available had been activated before the 1948 freeze. After the National Telefilm Association announced in February 1961, that it would accept bids for the station, ETMA's offer was lower than offers by two commercial groups. FCC Chairman Newton N. Minow (recently appointed by President John Kennedy) was eager to bring about a noncommercial VHF station in that area, but by that time Congress had prohibited the FCC from considering any applicant other than the one to whom the licensee wanted to sell. Knowing that NTA wanted a quick sale, Minow persuaded the FCC to schedule hearings on the proposal to make available for educational broadcasting VHF channels in the Los Angeles and New York City areas. The other bidders withdrew their offers. On June 30, 1961, NTA signed a contract with ETMA, subject to FCC approval. Then entered Robert

Meyner, governor of New Jersey, who petitioned the FCC to deny the transfer because it would deprive New Jersey of its only VHF channel (even though NTA was transmitting from Manhattan). On October 26, the FCC approved the transfer. In the U.S. Court of Appeals Meyner won a stay, which threatened the deal. Norman Cousins, board member of both ETMA and NETRC, arranged a meeting between Meyner and ETMA, where on December 2 assurance that New Jersey's programming needs would be met and other accommodations were worked out. On September 9, 1962, Channel 13, relettered WNDT (later to be WNET) went on the air, licensed to ETMA.[8] ETV now had both an outlet to the most populous area in the country and a production-broadcasting center in the city with the most programming resources.

WETA, UHF, Channel 26, Washington, D.C., went on the air October 2, 1961, with a history beginning in March 1953, when the Greater Washington Educational Television Association (GWETA) was incorporated. Effective broadcasting over a commercial station to elementary schools of a science series for one-half hour each school day from September 1958 to June 1961 gave impetus to the activation of reserved UHF Channel 26. Although the initial purpose was to provide more television courses for in-school use, cultural and public affairs programs were broadcast during the evenings from the date of activation. Thus ETV gained both an outlet and a source of programming in the national capital.

WHYY, VHF, Channel 12, Wilmington, Delaware, went on the air September 12, 1963, licensed to noncommercial WHYY, Inc., Philadelphia. This event tied together two strings.

One was the history of the Philadelphia Metropolitan Educational Television and Radio Corporation—owner and operator of WHYY FM and WHYY TV, UHF, Channel 35, Philadelphia. WHYY 35 went on the air September 16, 1957, with a compromise between leaders. Some wanted the station to do predominantly adult and cultural programming, and others wanted it to bring into noncommercial television the outstanding instructional broadcasting of the Philadelphia Board of Education's Division of Radio and Television, long directed by Martha Gabel and broadcast over commercial radio and television stations. WHYY 35 was handicapped because it was UHF in the VHF Philadelphia market. WHYY, Inc., looked for a VHF channel so it could fulfill the conditions of the compromise agreement. A VHF channel seemed available, which brings us to the second thread in the story.

Channel 12, Wilmington, the only VHF station allocated geographically to Delaware, was licensed to the Storer Broadcasting Company of Miami, which owned and operated WVUE TV in Wilmington. This independent commercial station could not compete successfully for revenue in the Philadelphia-Camden-Baltimore-Wilmington areas served by other VHF stations in Philadelphia and Baltimore that were affiliated with all three commercial networks. The Storer Company shut down WVUE TV on September 12, 1958, offering it and the license for sale, asking $2 million. Five years later it relinquished its license to Channel 12 because it could not get the asking price. Noncommercial WHYY, Inc., and four commercial companies applied for the license. The Republican governor of Delaware, the mayor of Wilmington, and Wilmington business interests opposed the licensing of WHYY, Inc., because they feared both that a future business opportunity would be lost and that the licensing of Channel 12 to WHYY, Inc., in Philadelphia would be followed by a change in the geographical allocation, thereby leaving Delaware with no VHF channel. In November 1960, Elbert Carvel was elected governor of Delaware. A Kennedy Democrat, Carvel immediately announced that he supported the proposal for the educational use of Channel 12. In 1963 the FCC also favored WHYY. The corporation agreed to maintain offices and studios in Wilmington, to provide a news service of primary interest to Wilmington and Delaware residents, and to permit the Wilmington schools to use free of charge for one year the instructional broadcasting that would be provided on a fee basis to Philadelphia and other Delaware Valley school systems.[9] To knot the two threads the call letters WHYY were transferred to Channel 12, WHYY's Channel 35 kept the same call letters, and its FM station was given the call letters WUHY FM.

State and Regional ETV Networks

The ability of one station to transmit to and receive from one or more other stations enables them to broadcast the same programs simultaneously or to record and store the programs for later or repeated broadcasts. Wireless transmission is much cheaper than transmission by long-distance lines or cables. Wireless interconnection of broadcasting stations became technically feasible with the development of microwave relay directional transmission in 1945. (Microwaves are on the order of 1,000 megacycles—above TV frequencies in the electromagnetic spectrum; in directional transmission they are focused from one facility to another, then amplified and relayed to still another, which, because the waves travel in line of sight, must be no more than about thirty miles away.) Wireless ETV networks, within and between states and regions, became economically feasible as the number of ETV stations increased during the mid-1950s. Alabama began ETV network broadcasting in 1957, and Oklahoma followed in 1959. In September 1959, the NAEB and the U.S. Office of Education held a national conference in Washington, D.C., on the feasibility of state and regional networks for both radio and television; the meeting was funded under Title VII of the National Defense Education Act.[10] By 1963 ETV networks governed by state agencies were operating in Alabama, Oklahoma, Puerto Rico, Arizona, South Carolina, and Oregon; many other states were implementing or planning networks.

Regional networks linked not only individual stations but also state and regional networks. The Eastern Educational Television Network (EEN) began in Mittersill, N. H., at a 1959 meeting of representatives of the two ETV stations then broadcasting in New England (WGBH TV, Boston; and WENH TV, Durham, N.H.), the Massachusetts and New Hampshire state departments of education, and the Ford Foundation, which gave $40,000 for the EEN's activation. The thirteen original members of the network were ETV stations, universities, state departments of education, the Canadian Broadcasting Corporation, and the NETRC. The region originally included New England, New York, New Jersey, Pennsylvania, Delaware, Maryland, and the District of Columbia. During 1961 EEN's budget was $23,000, and its member stations grew to five in five states. During 1963 the budget reached $45,000, and stations had increased to eleven in eight states. After the initial Ford grant, EEN supported its operations with dues and contributed programs and services. It sought to establish two-way physical interconnection of all stations throughout the region, while relying also upon mailed kinescopes and videotape recordings. In 1961 it contracted with the U.S. Office of Education (under Title VII of the NDEA) to establish the Northeastern Regional Instructional Television Library project. "The network has developed slowly and naturally out of recognized mutual need. . . . The most important advantage of the interconnection may lie in its potential to stimulate creative and experimental television programming."[11] Hartford N. Gunn, Jr., vice-president of WGBH, Boston, served as president of the EEN from 1960 until 1965.

Midwest Educational Television, Inc. (MET) was incorporated in December 1960, following the first studies of interconnection, which were financed by the Hill Foundation of Minneapolis through the NAEB. MET's objective was to facilitate the sharing of educational resources throughout the Upper Midwest. It sought to do so by operating and maintaining a privately-owned interconnection system—the first full-time interconnected regional ETV network in the nation—that began quickly to link up all ETV stations in Minnesota, North Dakota, and South Dakota; and by acting as an agent in production and broadcasting contracts and projects to make programs available to the entire region. Most of the early production was done at KTCA TV, St. Paul-Minneapolis. The guiding force behind MET was John Schwarzwalder.

Unresolved Issues

Plans for ETV station associations and networks during the period began in other regions—the central Midwest, the South, the Rocky Mountain area, and the far West. The future of regional television networks, however, was tangled in two unresolved issues: (1) the relationship between television broadcasting for general audiences and television broadcasting for instruction; and (2) the relationship between stations (and state and regional networks of stations) and the National Educational Television and Radio Center.

There was conflict between the NETRC's primary concern of broadcasting for general audiences and the public school and state television agencies' primary concern for instructional television. In the fall of 1971, when there were sixteen state broadcasting authorities with a total of sixty-three television stations, John P. Witherspoon described a situation that had existed for more than a decade:

> In all cases, one of the chief reasons for the creation of a statewide system of public television is instructional television (ITV), designed for use at various levels, whether elementary, secondary, or college, or—and this is an increasingly important area of programming—in-service training that ranges from high-school equivalency programs to broadcasting for medical doctors. Most public television systems broadcast approximately one-third ITV programming and two-thirds general public television programming. . . . The uniqueness of a state network can be found in its ability to create programs—both ITV and general broadcasts—which can expressly fill the needs of a particular State.[12]

NETRC President John White saw no competition or conflict between his center and the state and regional networks.[13] But John Schwarzwalder, founder of MET, saw the growth of local interconnected ETV networks as eroding the reasons for NETRC's being, or at least as changing its function. In fact the stations needed programs from both the national center and the state and regional networks. Nevertheless, there was conflict. One reason was money, since the stations paid dues to the NETRC and also to the regional networks. Another reason was that the local stations had no direct voice in the decisions that NETRC made about programming, whereas they did have a direct voice in the programming decisions by the state and regional networks.

EDUCATIONAL RADIO STATIONS

Despite being overshadowed by educational television, educational radio grew. AM stations, thirty-eight by the end of 1936, declined to twenty-seven at the end of 1963, but some of these stations shifted to FM, and others added FM. The number of FM educational stations on the air, 10 at the end of 1946, increased steadily to 237 by the end of 1963. This increase was disappointing, but it was enough to retain the twenty channels that had been reserved in 1945 and to lay the base for what might someday be a national system. The main reason that the FM reservations were not activated in greater numbers is that commercial FM stations did not pave the way by developing markets for FM sets very fast. Commercial FM broadcasting slumped between 1948 and 1956 because broadcasters were protecting their investments in AM radio, and many were using their resources to enter television. Therefore, they did not challenge the channels reserved for educational FM stations even though most of them were not being used.

Almost all the twenty-seven AM educational stations operating in 1963 were owned and operated by universities and colleges. About two-thirds of the FM educational stations were licensed to universities and colleges, about one-fourth to local school districts and systems, and the rest to state agencies, high schools, and other nonprofit institutions. The measures the FCC took to encourage FM educational stations restricted many of them, at least at first, to instructional broadcasting only. In 1948 the Commission authorized FM educational stations to operate on very low power (10 watts); in 1951 it authorized remote control operations (transmitting facilities without stations) of very low power, no minimum antenna height, and no minimum hours on the air. Throughout the 1950s and 1960s about 45 percent of all educational FM stations operated at 10 watts, with coverage of from only three to ten miles. A detailed survey of educational radio was not available before 1967, but even before then it was obvious that educational radio stations were unevenly distributed geographically, generally lowly regarded by educational administrators, underfinanced, understaffed, and they engaged in little promotion or research into educational methods and broadcasting techniques. Educational radio did, however, have some exemplary models.

The Wisconsin State Broadcasting Service was throughout the 1960s the only statewide educational radio network in the United States. As soon as the FCC reserved FM channels, in 1945 the state legislature established the State Radio Council, with authority and resources to plan and set up an educational broadcasting network. The council consisted of representatives of the university; the state board of regents; the governor's office; the state superintendent of public instruction; and the board of vocational, technical, and adult education; and three citizen members. Station WHA FM was inaugurated on March 30, 1947. By mid-1965 the network was completed. It consisted of two AM stations (WHA, Madison; and WLBL, Auburndale) and nine FM stations with a broadcasting range of 95 percent of the population of the state.

The Pacifica Foundation stations—KPFA and KPFD, Berkeley; KPFK, Los Angeles; KPFT, Houston; WABI, New York City; and WPFW, Washington, D.C. (all FM)—are outstanding in their freedom, depth, and range of services; in their successful reliance for operating expenses upon subscriptions to program guides, contributions, and volunteers in operating and programming; and in the size of their audiences. Following published schedules of news, commentary, interviews, local public affairs and community service programs, and poetry and drama (often experimental or avant-garde), the stations are on the air sixteen hours a day or more. Their coverage areas in the two West Coast cities contain more than 13 million people and in the New York City area more than 14 million. The originator of the Pacifica Foundation was Lewis Hill.

When one listens to the Pacifica stations, one is aware of how comparatively bland are the programs of the stations dependent upon means of support other than the listeners and contributors. When one reviews the ordeals of the Pacifica stations, one understands why the others *are* cautious. All Pacifica stations are subjected to continual opposition in their communities. KPFT, Houston, was bombed out twice during 1970. The Pacifica Foundation suffered from a long and brutal inquisition by a Senate subcommittee. The FCC held up the renewal of Pacifica's licenses for several months in 1963, ostensibly on the grounds of alleged obscene, indecent, or profane language. In one of its finest hours the Commission finally renewed the licenses. Chairman E. William Henry justified the renewal as being in accord with the statutory charge to promote "the larger and more effective use of radio in the public interest." He wrote, "We recognize that . . . such provocative programming as here involved may offend some listeners. But this does not mean that those offended have the right, through the Commission's licensing power, to rule such programming off the air-waves. Were this the case, only the wholly inoffensive, the bland, could gain access to the radio microphone or the TV camera."[14]

An anecdote may illustrate how the pressures to be cautious concerning broadcasting can touch foundations. During the 1950s the Fund for Adult Education had a scholarship-fellowship-internship program in the field of the mass media, which I directed. Many of our best candidates and recipients were connected one way or another with KPFA. Most of these, in varying degrees, were "controversial." After spending a full day with one particularly provocative applicant, I concluded that he was not a Communist. I recommended him to the Fund's selection committee, which, fully informed, awarded him a grant. Some time in 1959 Henry Heald, president of the Ford Foundation, made his first telephone call in months to FAE President C. Scott Fletcher, who had been waiting to hear whether the foundation was going to make another grant to the Fund. Without giving names, Heald simply said there had been complaints from San Francisco that the Fund had given a fellowship to a "communist." He did not want information or discussion.

Station WAMC FM, Albany, New York, licensed to the Albany Medical College of Union University, and managed in the early years by Alfred P. Fredette, is an example of the effective use of educational radio by special groups to reach special groups. The college started in 1955 to use two-way radio communication in the amateur band for postgraduate medical education because most physicians cannot attend formal lectures. It began operating WAMC in 1958, with FM tuners and remote transmitters in participating hospitals providing two-way communication. Physicians gathered in hospitals at set times (often lunch hours) to hear lectures, see slides, and ask questions. The first year Albany Medical College invited the faculties of medical schools in other areas of the Northeast to take part. Transmitters in Boston; Burlington, Vermont; and New Haven enabled professors to originate programs from the medical schools there. Programs gradually originated from other places, some as distant as Pittsburgh, Philadelphia, and Columbus, by combining telephone and radio. By the end of 1963 sixty hospitals in seven states were participating in the Albany Medical College program, with support from hospitals, foundation grants, and government grants or contracts. (In 1961 the University of North Carolina School of Medicine started two-way radio conferences of physicians over the university station WUNC FM, Chapel Hill, and Ohio State University College of Medicine began a similar program in 1962 over WOSU FM.)

The Broadcasting Foundation of America

The two main sources of syndicated programs for educational radio stations during the period 1958 through 1963 were the National Association of Educational Broadcasters and the Broadcasting Foundation of America (BFA). In Europe for the NAEB, George Probst and Seymour Siegel made contacts with radio producers that led in 1955 to the founding of the BFA—primarily an exchange and clearance center for acquiring radio programs from foreign sources and distributing them to both commercial and noncommercial stations in the United States. With a grant from the Rockefeller Foundation, in 1957 the BFA surveyed resources for an exchange of cultural broadcasts between the United States and France, Italy, Greece, Turkey, and Great Britain; each of these other nations agreed to meet the costs of producing oral and musical programs for radio stations in this country especially for the BFA. Soon many nations on several continents were lined up, and the Ford Foundation gave a grant for a tape duplication and distribution center in New York. By late 1959 the BFA was making almost eighteen hours per week of foreign musical, cultural, and social programs available to more than two hundred commercial and noncommercial stations in the United States. On February 19, 1960, the BFA merged with the National Educational Television and Radio Center to become the center's International Exchange Division, both in radio and television, while maintaining its separate identity as a radio unit. This arrangement ended in 1963, after which the BFA operated independently again.

The Educational Radio Network

The struggle of educational radio to avoid being neglected in the excitement over ETV was helped by two NAEB seminars, both at the University of Wisconsin, one in the spring of 1959, the other in the summer of 1960. The first, in cooperation with the NETRC, was conducted for radio station managers by the NAEB Radio Planning Committee.[15] The managers concluded that efforts should continue to develop live state and regional radio networks. The second seminar was held specifically on this point, with the conclusion that while the ultimate goal was a national live radio network, intermediate goals were live regional and state networks.[16]

The first live regional network came about, however, with the help of the NETRC, whose foundation money brought rapid results. After discussions between NETRC and NAEB broke down concerning, among other things, the center's proposal to take over the tape network, the center met in late 1960 with a select group of radio station managers to consider ways it might most effectively aid educational radio. The managers said that the main need was live interconnection and that first steps could be taken immediately. The center commissioned a study of the technical aspects of a live network along the East Coast. At the same time WGBH FM, Boston, with Ford money, was laying the groundwork for the network. On April 3, 1961, at a meeting of seventeen educational radio station managers and representatives of the NETRC, the Educational Radio Network (ERN) was established, partly financed by the NETRC as a pilot program. By November 1961, six FM educational radio stations were interconnected by a combination of long-distance wires and microwave relays. Immediately after a major grant to the center from the Ford Foundation in July 1962, the NETRC proposed to assume financial support for the ERN, and the ERN accepted. The arrangement was experimental for eighteen months. NETRC President John White said the center would then either get into radio all the way or get out altogether. At the end of the eighteen months, the center withdrew from radio, ending the interconnection of the ERN.

NATIONAL AGENCIES

The National Television and Radio Center (NETRC)

When, early in 1959, the board of the Educational Television and Radio Center voted to add to its title the word *National,* it signified that the center had embarked on a new course of large-scale planning and bold action. The ground to do so had been cleared by Newburn's resignation as president.

The ETRC board's first major decision after accepting the resignation (effective September 15, 1958) was to move the center's headquarters to New York City. Its second was to ask the Affiliates Committee to recommend changes in policy. Its third was to agree on the criteria for a new president—a person who, besides being an educator, could raise the quality of the broadcast programs, improve relations with the affiliated stations, and broaden financial support. The choice (nominated by Leland Hazard, businessman president of the Pittsburgh community ETV station, WQED) was John F. White. He knew colleges and universities from his experience as admissions counselor at Lawrence College, as dean of students and director of development at Illinois Institute of

Technology, and as vice-president of Western Reserve University. At Western Reserve he had initiated the nation's first full-credit college course on TV. He had managed WQED, Pittsburgh. He was a founder and member of the Affiliates Committee. He was a friend of Henry Heald, president of the Ford Foundation, under whom he had served at IIT.

When White took office on October 1, 1958, the Ford Foundation grant had only fifteen months to go. Within two weeks, at the regular affiliates meeting, he sketched his plans: to create three new vice-presidential positions; to establish a station-relations department; to hire program staff on a permanent basis; to locate the major part of the center's activities in New York City; to investigate the possibility of a Washington office; and aggressively to seek non-Fund funds.

White acted swiftly. E. James Robertson became head of the newly created stations relations department, Robert B. Hudson was named vice-president for programming,[17] and Warren A. Kraetzer was appointed to fill the new vice-presidency for promotion and development. On January 24, 1959, the board officially changed the agency's name to *National* Educational Television and Radio Center (NETRC). The same day the center officially requested a $5 million five-year "terminal" grant from the Ford Foundation. White began to enlarge his staff with full-time persons who had professional television experience.

Crucial to a shift in the center's policy of procuring programs was the affiliates meeting March 9–10, 1959, to which the directors had been asked to bring programs suitable for exchange. Of nearly two hundred submissions only seven resulted in distributed series. After this revealing test the center turned to contract and acquisition. Exchange programs distributed by NETRC fell from about 38 percent of the total in 1960, to about 11 percent in 1962. Programs obtained from all stations by all methods fell from about 73 percent of the total in 1960, to about 40 percent in 1962.

Some of the station managers opposed and others defended the center's new policy of separating the objective of acquiring the highest quality programs affordable regardless of source from the objective of building the stations' ability to produce programs. But the weakness of the position of those who opposed the separation of the objectives was that, while they all liked to get money for contracts to produce programs for exchange, they usually did not like the programs other stations submitted. The center's policy of getting the highest quality of programs affordable from whatever source caused tensions between the center and the stations, among the stations, and within the Affiliates Committee.

The rift steadily widened between the NETRC, a rootless national agency, and the stations rooted in the communities.

On April 2, 1959, a new "terminal" grant from the Ford Foundation was announced, and the NET National Conference was held. Of the grant for a five-year period, beginning in 1960, Henry Heald said: "The Center and the local stations are relying to an increasing extent, and eventually must totally rely, upon a broad base of support. . . . The Foundation's terminal $5,000,000 is designed to give the National Educational and Radio Center maximum opportunity and incentive to develop such support."[18] That same day representatives of the 106 organizations of the Advisory Council, members of Congress, FCC commissioners, government officials, and leaders in the field of educational broadcasting attended the NET National Conference in Washington, D.C., whose theme was "Forecast of the Future." In his formal address White predicted that within five years the center would be recognized as the nation's "fourth network."[19] At the end of the five years the center was to be free of financial reliance upon the Ford Foundation.

At a staff retreat August 4–5, 1959, the center decided on the "go-for-broke" policy—to spend money for programs that would attract more money for next year's budget. Almost all of the center's activities[20] from April 1959 until July 1963 were moves to make itself the "Fourth Network."

By July 1959, the center had moved most of its operations to New York City and had joined the European Broadcasting Union (EBU)—a cooperative programming exchange. With a special Ford grant of $500,000, in February 1960, it took over the Broadcasting Foundation of America, which became the center's international exchange division in both television and radio. In November of that year the center helped found the International Television Federation (Intertel)—a cooperative television programming venture by the Australian Broadcasting Corporation, Associated Rediffusion of Great Britain, the Canadian Broadcasting Corporation, Westinghouse Broadcasting Corporation, and NETRC.

The center established an office in Washington, D.C., early in 1961 as part of an agreement with the Joint Council on Educational Television and the National Association of Educational Broadcasters. NETRC and NAEB took over the previous action functions of the JCET, which became the Joint Council on Educational *Broadcasting* (JCEB). The JCEB, with six organization members, devoted itself to formulating policy statements on matters affecting the use of both radio and television in education; David Steward was director.[21] The NETRC office in Washington, staffed by Steward and Cyril Braun, gave engineering, legal, and information services—the station activation function of the former JCET. The NAEB, which had moved to Washington in 1960, took responsibility for legislative and government relations in matters affecting educational broadcasting—the lobbying function of the former JCET but broadened to include radio. John White for NETRC and William Harley for NAEB agreed upon a general division of functions, but overlaps and differing interpretations produced friction. Of the four agencies in 1954—the NAEB, the ETRC, the NCCET, and the JCET—only the NETRC and the NAEB were still operating in the field by 1961, both had offices in Washington, and the lines of demarcation of function were fuzzy.

The center became vigorous in activating stations, particularly of WNDT, Channel 13, New York City; WETA, Channel 26, Washington, D.C.; and WHYY, Channel 12, Wilmington-Philadelphia. Its administration of the Ford grants to stations for videotape recording machines in 1961 and 1962 was a strong stimulus. There was no overlap of functions between the NETRC and the NAEB in station activation, but there were friction points in Washington and beyond, nationally in radio and internationally in both radio and television. In 1960 the center had proposed taking over the tape network, but negotiations broke down. In 1961 the NETRC helped start the Educational Radio Network. What had begun primarily as a television program exchange center was seeking to become a national television and radio network and was colliding with a national membership association becoming more effective in radio and television.

The center was continually improving and expanding its primary service of programming. The quality of programs, both substantively, professionally, and technically, was rising, although still not satisfactory to the stations or audiences because of underfinancing. The mechanics of distribution and communication were better—thanks to VTR and good administration—and regular distribution increased to ten hours per week by 1962, including reruns and "flexible service."

The most dramatic introduction was the beginning of "prime time" scheduling. Since White had taken office, center officials had discussed a distribution plan that would guarantee all stations specific programs the same evening. At the March 1960 affiliates meeting all the managers, except John Schwarzwalder of Minneapolis (who soon ended KTCA's affiliation) requested the center to present possible approaches. The prime time scheduling plan went into operation in September 1961. Because of videotape recording it was possible to get duplicates of the same program to all stations simultaneously. Each station agreed to schedule a designated NET program between 7:30 and 10:00 P.M. each Monday, Wednes-

day, and Friday. The programs were intended to be showcase examples
of ETV. Each of the three evening slots was given a rubric title under
which loosely related programs could be included. Monday night was
called "Television International" (later "Perspectives"); Wednesday
night, "Significant Persons" (later "The Light Show"); and Friday night,
"Festival of the Arts." The prime time plan permitted national promotion and publicity, which, with the improved quality of the programs, increased audiences. NET programming had not yet reached the vigor and
bite to become "controversial." It did, however, reach occasional points
of excellence in cultural programs, such as the fifteen-part BBC series
"An Age of Kings," which was broadcast weekly beginning October 15,
1961.[22]

Late in 1961 the center decided to include instructional TV. Plans
were altered, however, when money became available through the U.S.
Office of Education and the Ford Foundation. Two projects were added
to the center. One, at the end of 1961, was the National Instructional
Television Library (NITL), with the first installment of a $750,000 three-
year contract with the U.S. Office of Education. It was directed by Edwin Cohen, who had headed the NET Film Service at Indiana University
and had come to the center as program associate in 1958. The other project was the Learning Resources Institute (LRI), established by the Ford
Foundation in 1959. NITL was attached to the center under terms of an
agreement signed on June 15, 1961.

Not all the managers of the affiliated stations accepted White's
premise that a national ETV service should be modeled after a commercial network. But the managers were divided on every major issue. Two
years after taking office, White challenged the managers: "If you don't
want the kind of leadership we have sought to render, all you have to do
is say so and this Center or any other nationally representative group will
disappear; for, as I have said so often, we are *you* and no more than
you."[23] In another two years White was more pointed: "As I consider the
concerns voiced by those who fear a strong Center, I cannot help recall-
ing that just four very short years ago, we who were then the affiliates
were deeply concerned about the weakness of the Center and the threat
of failure. Now the tables, for a few at least, are turned."[24] No one could
speak for all the affiliates, but, despite disagreements among themselves,
they wanted a voice in the center's decision-making.

The center's drive to broaden support was vigorous, imaginative,
and skillful but unsuccessful, for several reasons. First, the center could
get little money from the stations and had to avoid competing with them
for support; second, the presence of the Ford Foundation induced other

national foundations to rule out ETV (except for particular projects or programs); third, support from other sources for particular programs or projects did not provide for basic support; and, fourth, industry and business would not give much money for programs in the two most important areas: public affairs programs and programs for children.

During the first three years under the center's new policy, 1959–61, the center received about $10.3 million from the Ford Foundation and about $3.7 million from all other sources, including fees and payments for services (which usually did not pay for the services rendered). The center's overall annual budget was steadily rising; by 1962 it was nearly $5.25 million. By then outside support was falling, except for specific projects, such as the National Instructional Television Library.[25]

John White began to speak of an endowment of $500 million, which would bring in a steady income. The only possible source for such an endowment would be the Ford Foundation. His discussions of this possibility with the foundation in 1961 came at a time when the foundation was engaged in a self-study, which, completed in 1962, concluded that the development of noncommercial television was among the programs it should support, but that it "should not support a given recipient indefinitely" and could not commit itself "to any fixed outlay of funds over a period of years."[26]

Therefore the foundation began a year-long evaluation of educational television. In the meantime it had granted the center $4.7 million on July 5, 1962 (with an additional $833,000 having been previously earmarked specifically for the Learning Resources Institute, LRI). In the agreement between the NETRC and LRI, signed on June 15, 1962, the center was given the option after June 30, 1963, of using the LRI's corporate structure for instructional television. On July 6, 1962—the day following the foundation's grant—NETRC offered to support the Eastern Radio Network (ERN) for eighteen months on an experimental basis, and ERN accepted. Clearly the center was preparing to adjust its activities according to the outcome of the foundation's evaluation.

As part of the evaluation James Armsey, the liaison with ETV for the Ford Foundation, called a meeting of station managers in Phoenix, Arizona, on December 26, 1962, with no representative of NETRC present. Armsey announced that the foundation was considering another grant to the NETRC that would enable it to eliminate, or at least reduce to a token amount, the stations' affiliation fees, then ranging from $7,200 to $18,700 annually. The station managers, however, were in no mood merely to receive beneficence gratefully. Many strongly recommended that the NETRC limit itself to television programming by eliminating radio and leaving all trade and professional concerns to the NAEB. Some proposed that an affiliated stations senate be created to control all NETRC program policy, with the senate chairman an *ex officio* member of the board. Most of the station managers argued that they should have a voice—some thought the dominant voice—in the center's decisions on programming.

On July 2, 1963, the center announced that it was divorcing itself from educational radio.[27] On October 1, 1963, the NETRC received a letter from the Ford Foundation saying that it was giving the center $6 million for one year, with the unusual comment that it was accepting the center as a possible constant future beneficiary.[28] The foundation grant letter to the center was long and detailed, telling the center how to allocate the grant money.[29] NET was to produce, or otherwise acquire, and distribute to ETV stations five hours per week of high-quality programming, primarily in public and cultural affairs. NET could now produce programs. Its grant income had been substantially increased, but its focus had been sharply narrowed by eliminating radio, instructional television, and ancillary service to the stations and to the field. Each ETV station would be required to pay a nominal annual affiliation fee of $100.

News of NET's new capabilities and restrictions was well known in the field of educational broadcasting at the time of the NAEB annual convention.

The National Association of Educational Broadcasters

When the NAEB opened its annual conference, in Milwaukee on November 17, 1963, it faced a crisis: the danger of breaking into several smaller organizations with specialized purposes; and the opportunity to do much for the entire field of educational broadcasting by holding together as a unifying association.[30] Both the danger and the opportunity were heightened by many developments that had occurred since 1947, most of them advances in educational technology. Concern for educational technology had been sharpened by the shock the Russians gave to the American people by launching the first man-made satellite, Sputnik I, on October 4, 1957. The fear was widespread that the Soviet Union was far ahead of the United States in the exploitation of space and that a major reason for our inferiority was deficiencies in the American educational system.

In late December of that year NAEB President Burton Paulu called a five-day research seminar, the first of its kind, at Ohio State University, financed by the Kellogg Foundation. Twenty-three research specialists made plans and recommendations for research into ways to improve education through broadcasting. They called on educational broadcasters to use research to achieve their objectives and on educational researchers to become more involved in the solutions of the practical problems of educational broadcasters.[31]

Meanwhile, the administration and Congress were rapidly enacting new legislation. The National Defense Education Act of 1958 (NDEA), which became law on September 2, included Title VII—"Research and Experimentation in More Effective Utilization of Television, Radio, Motion Pictures, and Related Media for Educational Purposes." Appropriations for this Title were $3 million for fiscal year 1959, and $5 million for each of the succeeding fiscal years. For more than a decade a shortage of money did not hamper researchers into the utilization of educational broadcasting.

Numerous NAEB and related projects resulted from the NDEA. The first was the conference, reported earlier, with the U.S. Office of Education in September 1959 to explore the feasibility of state and regional networks. A survey headed by Vernon Bronson was financed and became influential in the House's approval of the Educational Television Facilities Act of 1962; the report documented ETV's need for television channels.[32] The evidence of the inadequacy of channels based on the ground revealed the need for another study, this time of the implications that space satellite communication might have for education. The NAEB planned and executed this study, directed by Bronson, in the first half of 1962.[33] The report showed that education had not been considered in policy planning for the use of space satellites. The NAEB recommended that the Department of Health, Education, and Welfare become immediately active in planning for educational uses of space satellites. Thus the association was ready with sharp analyses and hard data at the beginning of the age of communication satellites.

In the light of the report showing the pressing need for television channels for education, the FCC investigated the use of low-power transmission in the 1990–2110 or 2500–2690 mc. band of the electromagnetic spectrum. Adler Electronics in mid-1962 successfully demonstrated in the Northedge School, Bethpage, New York, that telecasts of superior quality could be transmitted at low costs within these bands for distances up to twenty miles. On July 30, 1963, the FCC established the 2500–2690 mc. band for educational uses, giving education thirty-one low-power channels and thereby beginning Instructional Television Fixed Service (ITFS). ITFS is the technical facilities for distributing television lessons

by wireless relay from a production studio to participating school buildings or systems, and also for interconnecting open broadcast and closed-
circuit systems. One licensee may have as many as four channels.

The NAEB undertook two overseas projects in 1961. In April it
signed a contract with the International Cooperation Administration to
send a three-man team, whose chief was Sydney W. Head, to help the Su-
danese government expand and stabilize its radio facilities. Later that
year, under contract with the government of Samoa, the NAEB sent a
survey team to American Samoa to determine the feasibility of using
ETV to upgrade literacy. Vernon Bronson headed the six-week survey,
resulting in recommendations which were later implemented. In May
1963, the contract was extended to help for another year.

The association's primary concern was for broadcasting in the
United States, of course, and by 1963 it had made plans for a semiautonomous division of instruction. On May 13, 1963, the NAEB conducted a
national conference on instructional television at the University of Illinois.[34] In August 1963, as soon as possible after the NETRC had announced it would withdraw from radio, and also in preparation for the
NAEB reorganization, the association and the Educational Radio Network (ERN) affiliates met in Washington to discuss the future of educational radio networking.

The NAEB's 1963 Reorganization

William Harley, program director of the University of Wisconsin's
three stations, guided the association through its reorganization. First, as
elected president for 1960, he led the NAEB to achieve two of its long-
time objectives—headquarters in Washington, D.C., and a full-time paid
president. Then he was elected chairman of the board for 1961. Executive Director Harry Skornia was given the additional title of president. In
June 1960, however, Skornia resigned both positions, explaining that he
had accepted a position within the College of Journalism and Communications at the University of Illinois.[35] In his farewell address, Skornia
gave both a cogent summary of the NAEB's previous decade and a pre-
scient forecast of its next decade:

> In some cases it has identified jobs too big to undertake by itself. In
> each instance, it must be said on its behalf, it has helped to organize the
> mechanism necessary to meet the need—whether this meant fighting for
> frequencies, or helping launch the JCET, or supporting the creation of the
> Educational Television and Radio Center, or helping create an Educational
> Media Council, or supporting the efforts of the U.S. Office of Education,

or a score of others. With its roots in the scholarly community, the NAEB has a responsibility for the advancement of knowledge, not just its distribution.[36]

Harley was asked to assume the permanent full-time paid presidency, and he accepted. The problems of reorganization lay ahead.

The association prepared for the reorganization in a series of steps: a self-evaluation conference and a planning meeting in 1961; simultaneously a drive to increase membership; a 1963 conference on instructional broadcasting; and a board meeting in June 1963, where a new reorganization plan was approved and then distributed to all the members. In the meantime the *NAEB Journal* was carrying several articles discussing the meaning of "professionalism" in educational broadcasting—an idea that seemed to hold, if any single idea did, the binding force of such a heterogeneous association.

At the 1963 convention in Milwaukee, November 17–20, the members unanimously approved the reorganization of the association into four sections—Radio Station Division, Television Station Division, Instructional Division, and Individual Member Division. Each would elect its own board and have its own staff (provided it could some way get the money), and the four boards would make up the full association board. Each division would have its office within the Washington headquarters. The members of each division immediately met and elected their boards.

THE RIFT BETWEEN ETV AND ITV

Educational broadcasters who were interested primarily in television for general audiences (ETV) and those who were interested primarily in television for instruction (ITV) were carried apart by their differing objectives. Several statements indicate the divergence. Vernon Bronson, WTHS FM and TV, Dade County Board of Education, Miami, wrote: "Educational television was born out of the desire of educators to add a new dimension to the instructional process and to extend the benefits of general education to large numbers of people. . . . It is an integral part of the educational system of the country, and it is rapidly becoming a major factor in the revision and improvement of total educational methodology."[37]

In contrast, Hartford Gunn, Jr., WGBH FM and TV (who could not be accused of neglecting instructional broadcasting), in a speech to the NETRC affiliates, questioned the use of "major VHF communications channels in large population centers primarily for narrow instructional purposes. And I particularly question it when the other major communications media are failing to provide the essential information and background without which no intelligent citizen can make informed and useful choices in politics, in business, and in life."[38] A decade later Paul Bosner was to say: "I look upon the relationship between education and educational television, now known as public television, as an illicit love affair carried on for years, using one another, satisfying individual self-serving needs, and all for the wrong reason."[39]

INSTRUCTIONAL TELEVISION

The reservation of channels and the activation of ETV stations coincided with the peak of what many people called "the educational crisis." The crisis in American education began after World War II when enrollments increased in all levels of schools and even larger increases could be forecast. Moreover, the amount of new knowledge to be taught also increased, and the concern heightened to have a larger body of scientific and technological manpower as an element in economic growth and national power. The financial needs of educational institutions surged. Pressures to make American education both more effective and more efficient came in a series of waves. From the mid-forties to the mid-sixties the main pressures were to make teaching more rigorous academically and more productive in the use of resources.

Attempts to improve American education have taken two distinct forms. One was to improve the education and training of teachers, the results of which came slowly. The other was to use new modes of instruction designed to work independently of the average teachers—to use the elite of talented and well educated teachers rapidly and more extensively and to multiply their efforts by means of technology, such as programmed learning and classroom television.

Some educators had quickly recognized the educational potential of television from the time the Bell Laboratory proved in 1927 that a visual image and associated sound could be transmitted over long distances. This demonstration was the beginning of both open and closed-circuit television because Bell used wires between Washington and New York and wireless between Whipanny, New Jersey, and New York. The development by 1938 of a long coaxial cable, which can transmit several signals on a single line, and the development by 1945 of microwave transmission, which can send directional signals through the air, were landmarks in the capability of using television over large areas for many purposes, including instruction. Moreover, many schools adopted closed-circuit television and Instructional Television Fixed Services, both of which are especially suited to instructional television because they can be aimed at precise audiences. Taylor and Gumbert give overviews of instructional television and closed-circuit TV in training and education.[40]

ITV Experiments and Demonstrations, 1954-63

Many and varied experiments in and demonstrations of the use of television for instruction were undertaken during this period. The Fund for the Advancement of Education and the Ford Foundation supported the testing of a variety of approaches to ITV at several educational levels.[41] These activities included the transmission of fifth-grade American history lessons by Montclair State College, New Jersey, to nearby schools; statewide school use in Alabama; a major university program at Pennsylvania State University; the statewide experiment in Texas in training teachers that tied together every teacher-training institution, the state department of education, and nineteen commercial TV stations; the National Program in the Use of Television in the Public Schools; the Midwest Program on Airborne Television Instruction (MPATI); "Continental Classroom,"[42] the countywide closed-circuit TV in-school program of Washington County, Maryland (Hagerstown); and citywide junior college credit and degree courses in Chicago.

These last two projects should be noted especially because they focused on educational goals that television could help attain, rather than merely on the techniques of television.

Wilbur Schramm said: ". . . most visitors come to Hagerstown, Maryland, to view the techniques of closed-circuit television rather than to investigate the accomplished goal of disseminating an articulated 12-year curriculum in science, music, and art throughout a 400-square-mile, rural area."[43] Schramm has documented the substantial improvements in learning achieved in the Washington County Public Schools.[44]

Beginning in 1957 the Chicago public school system offered a complete junior college curriculum by television. Here, too, the significance lies not in television by itself, but in the goal it helped achieve—higher education through integration with other methods. The authors of a final report point out that it was essential to develop, beyond the mailing back and forth of assignments, other response mechanisms, such as telephone and face-to-face conferences.[45] Members of the British Broadcasting Corporation who studied the Chicago junior college experience first-hand, preparatory to the British "Open University," commented that they were not at all interested in the use of television but much interested in the response mechanisms and even more in the relationships between the educators and the broadcasters.

Two promising ventures into ITV began late in the period 1954–63, one on a regional, the other on a statewide basis. Each was independent of the Ford Foundation and The Fund for the Advancement of Education. One was the beginning of the Southern Educational Network; the other, the South Carolina ETV Network.

Through the Southern Regional Education Board, the southern states began in 1958 laying the groundwork for a network to connect more than three hundred colleges and universities in the South—the system to be run cooperatively by the sixteen states to provide programs at various school levels. The Southern States Work Conference, sponsored by six state departments of education and the ten state education associations of the southern region, produced a casebook of programming practices for using television (both open and closed circuit) in the public schools.[46]

The South Carolina General Assembly in 1957 called for a study of the use of television in the public schools. After a pilot project with two courses in one Columbia school during 1958–59 and the extension of three courses to five Columbia-area schools the next year, the assembly in 1960 created the South Carolina Educational Television Commission. Four courses were offered on videotape to thirty-one schools in eleven counties, between cities using microwaves and within cities using closed circuits over commercial lines. During 1961–62 the closed circuit television (CCTV) network was extended to fifty schools in twenty-six counties, and continuing education for physicians and teachers was added. The next year 11 ITV courses were offered to all counties, reaching 155 public high schools, 36 elementary schools, most state colleges, all university extension centers, 5 private colleges, 2 private high schools, and 10 hospitals. During 1963–64 the ETV network signed on two open circuit stations—WNTV in Greenville, and WITV in Charleston—and began broadcasting to the general public. The South Carolina development was a locally initiated response to meet determined needs, carefully building upward and moving outward from a firm base and center. (The next chapter discusses later developments in South Carolina, where the rift between ETV and ITV did not exist.)

Assessment, ITV, 1954–64

Murphy and Gross in 1966 made the following judgment: "After

more than a decade of intensive effort and the expenditure of hundreds
of millions of dollars, has television made a real impact on American
schools and colleges? Has it made a worthwhile contribution to education? The short answer to such a sweeping question would probably have
to be 'No.' . . . In short, TV is still far from fulfilling its obvious promise. Television is *in* education all right, but it is still not *of* education."[47]
This general judgment should not obscure two important facts. One was
that several projects were of major significance for the future; the other
was that the sheer mass of and skillful publicity about the ITV activities
kept hope alive and thereby contributed mightily to the passage of the
Educational Television Facilities Act of 1962 and the Public Broadcasting Act of 1967.

But why did American education remain unchanged in any important way? Paul Bosner thinks that an important reason is that the responsibility has never been placed upon any one set of institutions or agencies:
"To which agency or institution will instructional television be assigned?
It [this question] is basic to understand existing problems and crucial to
future progress. . . . In the U.K. instructional television is the BBC, subject to appropriate cooperation between the Ministry of Education and
the educational system as a whole. In France and Israel, the responsibility for instructional television has been given to the educators and the
program producing organization is part of the Ministry of Education.
What is the solution for the U.S.?"[48] There could be no single "solution
for the U.S.," of course. But insofar as an approach to a solution was apparent by 1964, it was to assign instructional television to educational institutions or agencies that would develop a new breed of broadcast/
educators or educator/broadcasters to fulfill the assignment.

ETV AS AN ALTERNATIVE SERVICE, 1958–63

The first dependable report on ETV audiences was done in 1960 by Wilbur Schramm, Jack Lyle, and Ithiel de Sola Pool.[49] They categorized re-
spondents as: "regular viewers" (who watched at least one ETV-station
program per week and could describe it), "occasional viewers" (who
watched sometimes), and "non-viewers." The following paragraph sum-
marizes results in eight of the nine audiences surveyed (the ninth was a
UHF station in an all-VHF commercial market).

1. There were few ETV viewers. "Regulars" ranged from 24 to 9.4
percent of the persons interviewed. Of the "regulars" interviewed, from
30 to 9 percent had watched one or more of ten specific programs avail-

able to all the stations through the NETRC. Combining the two sets of figures, the conventional commercial "rating" would be a high of about 2 to less than 1 percent of the total TV audiences at any particular hour. 2. ETV viewers were preponderantly highly educated and civic minded. 3. ETV viewers gave as reasons for viewing, in rank: general self-improvement, enjoyment, reaction against commercial TV, and the desire for "something good for children on TV." 4. Nonviewers gave as reasons for not viewing ETV, in rank: wanting only entertainment from TV; no knowledge of ETV; and finding ETV programs dull or unprofessional. 5. Families with grade-school children were more likely to be ETV viewers than families with either younger, older, or no children. 6. ETV "regulars" tended to be highly selective in their viewing—spending less total time watching TV than non-ETV viewers, and tuning in for specific ETV programs. These findings gave ETV stations and the NETRC the first reliable evidence about their actual audiences.

The possibility of ETV becoming a national alternative service was kept alive and nurtured between 1956 and 1963 almost single-handedly by the ETRC-NETRC. The average ETV station received about one-third of its total programming from the center. Considering that about one-third of the total programming of the average ETV station was in-school broadcasting, the center contributed a full half or more of all the programming for the general audiences. This service brought to ETV audiences programs of kinds and standards their local station could not produce or procure by themselves. It also enabled more and more stations to broadcast on weekday evenings, on Saturdays and Sundays, and during summer months—times when they could be most useful to audiences at home.

From October 1958, John White vigorously pursued the goal of making the center the "Fourth Network." Some managers of affiliated stations endorsed and others opposed this goal. But those who opposed it could not agree upon another goal that would have maintained the idea of a national alternative television service for the American people. By the end of 1963, NETRC, stripped down to National Educational Television (NET), was forced to abandon its goal of becoming the "Fourth Network." It did so, however, not because a decision had been made that the goal was the wrong one or because another goal had been set, but because not enough money was available. The Ford Foundation, deciding against endowing NETRC, increased its level of annual support to NET, but specified that higher quality television programming be produced and distributed at the rate of five hours per week. This was a formula for a regular diet of specials, not for a network service.

Nevertheless, this regular diet of specials was to be crucial in the period beginning with 1964. That year the Educational Television Facilities Act began to make grants to activate ETV stations, many of which would be devoted predominantly to ITV. The all-channel receiver act went into effect on May 1, 1964, thereby encouraging the activation of many ETV UHF stations that would broadcast ITV primarily. In 1963 the FCC had authorized Instructional Television Fixed Services, all thirty-one channels of which would be devoted entirely to ITV. ITV had many resources. But the only two national agencies manning the life-support systems of ETV as an alternative service were NET and the Television Stations Division (quickly renamed Educational Television Stations—ETS) of the NAEB.

CONGRESSIONAL ACTS OF 1962

Two federal laws enacted by mid-1962 improved the ETV situation in important ways: the Educational Television Facilities Act provided money to activate and expand ETV stations; and the All-Channel Television Receiver Act eventually increased the number of receiving sets on which viewers could receive UHF signals.

The ETV Facilities Act, May 1, 1962

This amendment to the Communications Act was brought about by the National Association of Educational Broadcasters. Leonard Marks, legal counsel to the NAEB, initiated the idea, first with Democratic Majority Leader Senator Lyndon B. Johnson and then, aided by him, with Senator Warren Magnuson, chairman of the Senate Commerce Committee. Marks helped the committee staff draft bills that passed the Senate in May 1958, in April 1959, and again in March 1961. However, similar bills in the House died in committee until one was approved on March 7, 1962. The decisive area, therefore, was in the House, where until 1962 the problem was not so much opposition as indifference.[50]

Realizing that the struggle would be in the House, the proponents of federal aid for ETV facilities focused on proving the need for and limiting the scope of the legislation. The most persuasive testimony and evidence in the House hearings came from the detailed and authoritative report of plans and financial deficiencies in all fifty states compiled by the NAEB survey directed by Vernon Bronson, "Education's Need for Channels."[51] The major limits to the scope of the legislation were to set a ceiling of $1 million to each state and the District of Columbia over a period of five years, to specify that the aid be for equipment only, and to require that each group receiving aid agree to bear the operating and maintenance costs. Even so, the House insisted upon provision for matching grants. The bill accepted in conference in April, becoming law on May 1, 1962, amended the Communications Act "to establish a program of Federal matching grants for the construction of television broadcasting facilities to be used for educational purposes." Its major provisions were:

1. It authorized the aggregate appropriation of up to $32 million for five fiscal years beginning with 1963 for grants for the construction of ETV facilities. Facilities eligible for grants were defined as transmission apparatus, including what may "incidentally be used for transmitting closed curcuit television programs," and (up to 15 percent) those which may be used to interconnect stations. The grants, made by the secretary of HEW, were to be up to 50 percent of the cost of new facilities and up to an additional 25 percent of the total cost of improving presently owned facilities. No state could receive more than $1 million.

2. Eligible recipients included all four types of ETV stations—university, school, state-agency, and community corporation.

3. The law specified criteria "to achieve (1) prompt and effective use of all educational television channels remaining available, (2) equitable geographical distribution of educational television broadcasting facilities throughout the States, and (3) provision of educational television broadcasting facilities which will serve the greatest number of persons and serve them in as many areas as possible, and which are adaptable to the broadest educational uses."

4. Federal interference of control in any way was prohibited.

When President John Kennedy signed the bill into law, the only persons present other than legislative, executive, and FCC officers and staff members were William Harley, president of the NAEB, and Leonard Marks, the association's counsel. Kennedy, whose practice was to use only one pen and then present it to the bill's chief sponsor, gave the pen to Senator Magnuson, saying, "It's your bill, here's the pen." Magnuson then gave the pen to Marks, saying, "Here, this belongs to you."[52]

The All-Channel Television Receiver Act, July 10, 1962

This amendment to the Communications Act, effective April 30, 1964, gave the Federal Communications authority to require all television sets sold in interstate commerce to be capable of receiving all frequencies.[53] By eventually improving the competitive position of UHF stations, this act was very important to ETV, more than two-thirds of whose reservations are in UHF. FCC Chairman Newton Minow was the mover in this legislation. Convinced that greater diversity and higher quality of programming could come only by the unprecedented utilization of the UHF band, he announced on July 27, 1961, a "package" proposal. It included the separation of UHF and VHF channels in eight TV market areas ("deintermixture"—a change from the mixing of UHF and VHF channels in the same communities), the squeezing in ("shoehorning") of new VHF assignments in eight other TV market areas, and a request for Congress to authorize the FCC to require that all new TV sets be capable of receiving all channels.

In the meantime the FCC was researching UHF reception. In 1961 it requested and received money from Congress to operate an experimental UHF station on Channel 31 for a year, transmitting from the top of the Empire State Building (in company with the transmitters of all seven VHF New York City stations). In July 1962, the Commission reported that almost as many sets with indoor and outdoor antennas could receive a "passable or better picture" from the UHF station as sets with indoor and outdoor antennas could receive from VHF stations. The officials of New York City applied to the FCC to purchase the station; the Commission sold and licensed it to the New York Municipal Broadcasting System, owner and operator of WNYC AM and FM. Thus New York City acquired a second noncommercial station, WNYC TV (Channel 13, WNDT, had gone on the air September 9, 1962). Minow said that Channel 31's success "in the most difficult reception area of the country shows that UHF will work anywhere and paves the way for the growth of commercial and noncommercial TV."[54]

While UHF's reception was being tested in Manhattan, the FCC's "package" proposal was being tested in Washington. The established VHF industry (including, of course, all three networks) disliked the proposal for deintermixture in eight markets and feared that the combined proposals for deintermixture and for requiring all sets to be capable of receiving all channels would pave the way to move all television into the UHF band. The outcome was a compromise. The FCC gave up deintermixture and the addition of more VHF assignments at that time; the VHF industry granted approval of the proposed all-channel sets legislation.

The all-channel act helped the UHF industry and, therefore, it helped ETV also. For example, because of this legislation Community Television of Southern California, a nonprofit corporation, gave up trying to purchase a VHF channel in Los Angeles (which would have cost more than $10 million if one had been available) and applied for UHF Channel 28. The station, KCET, went on the air September 28, 1964.

It would be a mistake to say that the all-channel act removed all handicaps from UHF or that any single additional step (such as higher antennas, more power, or requiring UHF-set click-stop channel tuning) would do so. In a highly technical and carefully guarded analysis, the Corporation for Public Broadcasting in 1974 reported that the problems of UHF are interrelated and can be lessened only by interrelated approaches: "Notwithstanding the fact that significant improvements can, and should be made in the UHF system, it can be said with almost complete certainty, that the day will not arrive when a UHF broadcaster in an intermixed market would not gladly exchange his transmission facilities for similar facilities on a VHF channel."[55]

OPENING OPPORTUNITIES, PERSISTENT PROBLEMS, 1964

By 1964 the capabilities of the electronic media were so varied and flexible that their limits were no longer set by physical means but instead by human beings—their goals, imagination, skills, and ability to cooperate. The challenge to educational broadcasters was to narrow the gap between technical capabilities and effective use. The only possible way for them to attain and maintain common bearings amid proliferating technical capabilities was to pay primary attention to goals held in common.

The only attempt during the period 1956–63 by a national group to grapple with the problem of goals was made by the Educational Media Study Panel, established in 1960 as an official advisory group to the commissioner and Office of Education.[56] The panel was asked "to study the new and rapidly growing developments in the communications and educational media field and to make recommendations to the Commissioner which would be useful in developing sound national policy." The panel quickly narrowed its attention to educational television because that "presented the most immediate and significant national problems." Among the panel's recommendations were: (1) to tie ETV in with the "existing structures of community learning activities"; (2) to conceive of and develop programs "as part of a total systems approach," which will require a "new order of collaboration" between educators and broadcasters; and (3) to provide financial support for educational television "from both public and private funds at the local, state, and national level, to ensure that the necessary new stations will be built, and that the facilities may be operated and programmed to the fullest degree in the public interest."

CUTTING A CHANNEL TO THE BRINK,
LATE 1963–EARLY 1967

O<small>N OCTOBER</small> 1, 1963, the Ford Foundation gave the National Educational Television and Radio Center the first of a series of annual grants for a single purpose: to produce or otherwise acquire five hours per week of high quality television programs and distribute them to ETV stations. The ETRC, divesting itself of radio, instructional television, and ancillary services, became National Educational Television—NET. On January 10, 1967, President Lyndon Johnson said in his State of the Union message: "We should develop educational television into a vital public resource to enrich our homes, to educate our families, and to provide assistance in our classrooms. We should insist that the public interest be fully served by the public's airwaves. I will propose these measures to the 90th Congress." These two events frame the period this chapter covers. The course between the two events was not a straight line but a series of separate advances. The chapter is organized into eight sections: (1) educational radio; (2) ETV stations and networks; (3) communications satellites; (4) instructional television; (5) ETV for general audiences; (6) ETV stations' drive for financial support; (7) the Carnegie Commission on Educational Television; and (8) the Ford Foundation's new moves.

EDUCATIONAL RADIO

In June 1963, the NAEB board proposed that there be a semiautonomous radio division within the association. Although not yet approved by the membership, this proposal took on a new importance when the NETRC announced in July that it was withdrawing support from radio. Officers of the NAEB promptly met with members of the eight stations that made up the Educational Radio Network to discuss the future. At that meeting they conceived what became the Educational Communications System (ECS) project—to study the feasibility of linking U.S. colleges and universities by electronic communications. Plans for both the project and the radio division were advanced at a late January 1964 meeting after the membership of the full association had approved the reorganization plan with four semiautonomous divisions. There the participants voted unanimously to reform and rename the radio division into National Educational Radio (NER), to establish a full-time executive director in the Washington NAEB office, and to pursue with NDEA funds the study of the feasibility of connecting educational institutions throughout the country with a live radio network.

In February Jerrold Sandler, production manager of WUOM FM, University of Michigan, was named NER executive director. In April the U.S. Office of Education gave NAEB a grant ($65,859 for the first two of a four-phase study) to begin the ECS project. In the fall the National Home Library Foundation gave NER $8,000 (the first of a series of annual grants) for creative radio programming. When the NER opened its Washington office, John Witherspoon, formerly program director of KEBS, San Diego State College, became Sandler's associate director of the NER and the CES project. The tape network, renamed the National Educational Radio Network (NERN), was expanded and improved, remaining at Urbana. NER meanwhile sought to resume and extend the live network whose subsidy had been withdrawn by the Ford Foundation and the NETRC.

Significant Programming

Although the ECS project did not result in live interconnection, NER was helped in other ways to achieve a new order of high quality, timely programming, both on its taped NERN and on occasional live interconnection. For example, announcing a series of annual $30,000 grants to NER, Leonard Marks, president of the National Home Library Foundation, said that in this continuing support the foundation "recognizes the leadership role of NAEB through its National Educational Radio Network in providing the American people with programs not readily available through other means." Grants from the Johnson Foundation of Racine, Wisconsin, made possible an extensive NERN series based on

the International Convocation to Study the Requirements of Peace—
Pacem in Terris—and other major series on important international and
national conferences. In September 1965, seventy NER stations had live
interconnection—the first time in the history of educational radio—in a
three-hour broadcast of the returns of the German national election, the
cost borne by the German Information Service. The renamed Eastern
Educational Radio Network (EERN)—eight stations from Boston to
Richmond—managed a few live interconnections, including coverage of
some key sessions of the Fulbright Senate committee 1965 hearings on
the Vietnam war.

A Conference, a Task Force, and a Report

As guests of the Johnson Foundation at its conference center,
Wingspread, Racine, Wis., the NER board of directors decided on a national conference of leaders from many fields to discuss "Educational
Radio as a National Resource" and to plan action. The conference was
held in September 1966 and attended by seventy leaders from industry,
the media, government, universities and colleges, other foundations, and
the arts. The seven recommendations of the conference included steps to
get public support for educational radio at federal, state, and local levels;
the inclusion of educational radio in any proposals for the use of communications satellites for noncommercial broadcasting; the establishment of a national center that would produce high quality educational
radio programs and also train personnel; and the establishment of a NER
public affairs and news bureau in Washington, D.C. The NER directors
immediately retained Herman W. Land, formerly editor of *Television
Magazine,* to help implement the recommendations.

Within a month an informal task force decided that the essential
first step was to gather data on the status, problems, achievements, potential, and needs of educational radio. Guided by Herman W. Land Associates, NER developed a twenty-five-page questionnaire and mailed it
to the 320 educational radio licensees (20 AM and 300 FM) then broadcasting in the United States. By March 1967, returns had been received
from 135 stations, about 50 field interviews had been conducted, and regional meetings had been held. A grant of $38,000 from the Ford Foun-
dation made it possible to organize the data and publish the report *The
Hidden Medium: Educational Radio*[1] in April 1967, just in time for the
hearings of the Senate Commerce Committee on the public broadcasting
bill, which began on April 11, 1967.

The report concluded that the "lines between television and radio, programmed instruction and computers, technology and textbooks, are becoming blurred, and the task, rather than the technique, dictates in what combination the growing number of available resources shall be employed"; and "a network for any single medium can be the substructure upon which multimedia capacity can be constructed for maximal service and flexibility and at minimal cost."

The report made six recommendations, the last of which was the most influential: "Educational radio's ambitions toward national and international coverage should be encouraged and supported. Given commercial radio's unmistakable and perhaps irreversible local trend, there is a decided national stake in building educational radio as a major instrument of national and international communications. The NER Public Affairs Bureau and the NER Network could well serve as the starting point. Radio, moreover, should be included in all plans for satellite communication" (I-17).

Educational Radio Stations: Services, Plans, and Needs

The Land report begins with the statement that educational radio somehow "manages not only to survive and fill its traditional cultural role, but to move forward, innovate, experiment." It is becoming aware that, in addition to serving the needs of those already well endowed, it must respond to the developing needs of the total society. . . . It is beginning to bestir itself on behalf of the special groups . . . such as the disadvantaged, the elderly, the minorities, etc., for whom it appears uniquely equipped to fill the media vacuum that generally prevails." In contrast to the movement in commercial radio toward becoming a *local* medium, educational radio is moving "impatiently toward the day of full live network operations. . . . In the face of a virtual absence of commercial radio from the Washington satellite discussions, educational radio's spokesmen participated in enthusiastic anticipation" (I-1).

The Hidden Medium starkly contrasts how much was being done with what little money it had. Educational radio is not one medium but many media in one. The report specifies with scores of "station profiles," whose concreteness makes summary impossible. Some of the activities have already been noted in the previous chapter of this book: the Albany Medical College's use of two-way radio for physicians was being followed by similar projects in Ohio, North Carolina, Utah, California, and Wisconsin. The Wisconsin State Broadcasting Service had in 1966 installed a Subsidiary Communications Authorization (SCA) system by which two to four signals can be transmitted simultaneously on the same channel—e.g., two stereo, or one stereo and two monaural, or four monaural. There were many plans and even some starts for other state radio networks in Colorado, Florida, Iowa, Kansas, Kentucky, Michigan, Minnesota, Missouri, New York, Ohio, Oregon, Pennsylvania, South Carolina, South Dakota, Tennessee, Texas, and Washington. There were plans for two regional networks—in the Midwest (the "Big Ten") and Appalachia. But almost everywhere the obstacle was lack of money, even where there was a station. "The Southeastern and Southwestern states, along with a number of Plains and Rocky Mountain states are covered inadequately. In short, there is a need to fill in the gaps of existing coverage" (I-2). This summary only indicates some of the gaps. Even when on paper an area might be said to be "generally blanketed with educational radio licensees," it was not necessarily well served by signals. Almost half of the FM stations were 10-watters, and another large percentage had low transmitting towers and low power. Most of the stations with short reach (and some with long reach) were mainly, or solely, providing instructional services or broadcasting campus affairs. Worse, the FCC had crippled educational FM by making no table of reserved FM assignments that would permit the development of local, state, regional, and national services combining 10-watt instructional stations and stations capable of serving larger areas with well-rounded programs.

The report summarized hours of broadcasting. "A large number of stations, mostly in-school, do not broadcast on weekends, and many are silent one day or the other. Educational radio generally broadcasts from noon to midnight. Its service is weakest in the 6 to 9 A.M. early morning hours" (I-3).

What were the circumstances of the responding stations? More than half had budgets under $25,000 per year; about one-third had less than $10,000. More than 75 percent were not adequately staffed; 37 percent had a total salary budget of $10,000 a year or less, and 77 percent had $50,000 or less. "In sum, the starting point for any national building plan must be the stark truth: educational radio, for the most part, is underfinanced, underequipped, underpromoted, and under-researched. That its program service is nevertheless exemplary should not be allowed to obscure its true predicament" (I-16).

Looked at in one way, the Land picture of educational radio in 1966–67 does not differ fundamentally from that given by Tracy Tyler for 1932. But, looked at in another way, there was an important difference. Educational radio had begun to find answers to the basic question of function by defining and performing services that are indispensable and unique.

EDUCATIONAL TELEVISION STATIONS

Local Stations

The number of ETV stations on the air doubled from the end of 1962 to the end of 1967. The figures at the close of each year were: 75 in 1962; 83 in 1963; 99 in 1964; 113 in 1965; 125 in 1966; and 151 in 1967. Late in 1967 for the first time the number of UHF ETV stations exceeded that of VHF ETV stations. By 1967 the FCC had more than doubled the number of reservations made in 1952—from 242 to 632. VHF reserved channels increased from 80 to 116, and UHF from 162 to 516. The allocations plan was designed for educational organizations to develop a greater number of stations by permitting future computer selections and assignments of unallocated channels. However, the percentage of reservations in the UHF band had been increased from 67 in 1962, to 81 in 1966. Thus the future of ETV was even more dependent upon the future of UHF television. Although the 1962 all-channel act gradually improved the UHF situation, experience and research during the following decade would reveal that UHF stations were still at a disadvantage and that measures to relieve the disadvantage would require complex, cooperative, and expensive activities.

ETV Station Activation and Expansion

The ETV Facilities Act of 1962, for which $32 million was authorized in 1963 through the 1967 fiscal year, had by mid-1967 assisted the activation of ninety-two stations and the expansion of sixty-nine stations in forty-seven states, the District of Columbia, and Puerto Rico.[2] By March 1967, the number of ETV stations on the air or under construction was 176, compared with 82 in June 1963, when the program was initiated. Nearly two and one-half times the $32 million was expended in local and state matching funds for facilities. The federal grants ranged from $14,000 to $777,000; the average grant for activation was about $220,000, and for expansion about $170,000. Each of fifteen states received a grant for stations that totalled $1 million (the maximum). The number of grants to each state is significant because each grant was intended to make a critical difference. The states receiving the largest number of grants, each of which resulted in the activation or expansion of an ETV station were: Kentucky, 12; Washington, 9; Florida, 8; and Ohio, 7. California and Pennsylvania each received 6; Alabama, Georgia, Minnesota, Nebraska, New Hampshire, and South Carolina were each granted 5. Nevertheless, many areas had no ETV station or only one or two. As of March 1967, there was no station in Alaska, Montana, or Wyoming; there was one station operating or under construction in each of Arkansas, Colorado, Idaho, Kansas, Louisiana, Maryland, Mississippi, Nevada, New Jersey (counting WNDT), New Mexico, North Dakota, and West Virginia; two stations were operating or under construction in each of Arizona, Iowa (counting WOI TV), Missouri, Oregon, and South Dakota. Many of the communities whose applications for aid could not be granted when funds were depleted in 1967 were small and in sparsely populated areas with few resources for originating programs. One need to establish a nationwide ETV service was to continue the ETV facilities grant program.

Three other needs were the extended use of ETV-ITV libraries; the pooling of resources in the cooperative production of programs; and intrastate, interstate, and regional networks. Federal funds from NDEA were establishing ITV libraries. Federal funds from the ETV Facilities Act were helping to establish interconnection.

State ETV Networks

In April 1968, the FCC reported: "Almost every individual State is in the planning or active stage of an interconnected network, and some 25 States have already linked stations toward eventuation of total intrastate coverage. Complete networks are in operation in such states as Alabama, Connecticut, Georgia, Maine, Nebraska, South Carolina, and Vermont."[3] Although the ETV Facilities Act helped mightily, the initiative had to come from the states. Two states worth special notice are South Carolina and Nebraska.

During 1963–64 the South Carolina Educational Television Commission began broadcasting to general public audiences through two broadcasting stations. The commission had also increased closed-circuit (wired) transmissions to all schools and university centers throughout the state, to most colleges, and to ten hospitals. The next year the legislature appropriated funds for a third ETV broadcasting station, in Columbia. The closed-circuit network expanded, and specialized training for personnel in business and industry was offered by the South Carolina Educational Resources Foundation in response to dramatic economic development in the state. In 1965–66, under the direction of Henry J. Cauthen, the ETV network's in-school and general-audience broadcasting became more diversified. Continuing education programs expanded for members of professions and vocations, including the nation's first statewide program for law-enforcement officers. In 1966–67 WRLK,

UHF Channel 67, Columbia, came on the air, and extensive in-school broadcasting began for the first time over the three open-circuit stations as well as the closed-circuit system. Construction also began on two additional stations for the state's open-circuit network. The next year WJPM, UHF Channel 33, Florence, and WEBA, UHF Channel 14, Allendale, began broadcasting, and a demonstration project of multichannel closed-circuit transmission was begun in forty-six secondary schools in Greenville, Florence, and Darlington counties. This multichannel project resulted in a tenfold increase of in-school ITV enrollment.

With an operating budget of $3.2 million in fiscal 1970–71, South Carolina ETV had a public school ITV course enrollment of 428,000 students; provided a full evening schedule of public and cultural affairs programs; and gave the first master's degree through television courses, other college-level courses, and continuing education series for physicians, teachers, law-enforcement officers, business managers, and many state agency personnel. In 1972 the network reported: "With the National Public Radio Network now in operation, S.C. ETV plans to enter this important field of educational communications. Applications have been made for licenses and funds for initial FM stations in Columbia and Greenville [have been appropriated]. Eventually, FM transmitters will be located at each television transmitter, making public radio available statewide."[4] The state system in South Carolina was probably the best illustration of the complementary development of both ETV and ITV within a concept of life-long learning, and the use of many media and methods for achieving learning objectives.

The Nebraska Educational Television Commission, created by the legislature in 1963, was the result of careful planning and preparation. The activation of ETV station KUON, VHF Channel 12, Lincoln, in 1955, and the organization of the Nebraska Council for Educational Television (a voluntary corporation of public and private schools) in 1961 paved the way for the development of a state network. In 1964 the commission began plans to construct a state network, filing applications for aid under the ETV Facilities Act, which by 1967 had given matching grants for the expansion of the key station in Lincoln and the activation of six other stations.

By 1971 the open-circuit Nebraska ETV Network blanketed the state with nine interconnected stations supplemented by four translator facilities (which boosted power and relayed signals), reaching about 250,000 in-school students from kindergarten through university levels, and offering general broadcasting to the entire population. The Nebraska network is entirely open-circuit, and programming emphasizes public affairs ("Candidates' Forum," coverage of the legislature, and special issues such as constitutional revision), and vocational and professional continuing education (for farmers, ranchers, law-enforcement officers, junior business executives, teachers, pharmacists, dentists, physicians, and nurses). The key leader in this long-term development has been Jack McBride—director of television for the University of Nebraska, general manager of KUON, Lincoln, secretary of the Nebraska ETV Commission, and executive director of the network.

Regional Networks

According to the FCC, "In early 1968, in addition to the Eastern Educational Network, there were five other regional ETV networks in various stages of operation: Central Educational Network, Inc., Chicago and the surrounding area; Midwest Educational Television, Inc., in Minnesota and neighboring states; Rocky Mountain Network; Southern Educational Communications Association; and Western Educational Network. Although some of the stations have . . . interconnection, most stations are serviced by taped program distribution."[5]

The Eastern Educational Television Network (EEN) continued to develop slowly out of common need. By 1964 this mutual network included eleven stations in eight states, was exchanging seventeen series of programs, and was administering the Northeastern Regional Instructional Television Library project (under Title VII of the NDEA). In 1967 the network began full-time live interconnection (in addition to tape exchanges by mail). It had now expanded membership to nineteen stations in eight states, and exchanged eighty-one series of programs, with a self-supporting budget of $163,000. It had completely integrated the instructional library service into its operations, with full self-support. The leaders of the EEN were thinking beyond mere television interconnection: they were planning the origination of programs from many stations and the development of a total communication system, including TV, radio, teletype, teleprint, facsimile, and computer data. They were looking ahead also to the role that regional networks could play as links between individual stations and a national system (and beyond) in the satellite era:

> It is, we believe, an inefficient use of a satellite channel if the program being transmitted is for distribution over a relatively small geographical area such as the EEN. . . . We therefore propose that all member stations in each region be interconnected in a regional network pattern with a ground based system. . . . each regional network headquarters would be equipped with a satellite ground station capable of sending to and receiving

from the satellite. Programs would then be received from the satellite and transmitted through the regional system to all stations. Conversely, programs taken from the regional network could be transmitted to the satellite and made available to all other regions."[6]

By the mid-seventies, of the five regional networks other than the EEN that the FCC named in 1968, three additional ones seemed to be firmly established: Midwest Educational Television, the Southern Educational Communications Association, and the Central Educational Network.

Midwest Educational Television, Inc. (MET), from headquarters in the building of KTCA, St. Paul-Minneapolis, facilitates the sharing of educational resources through operating a privately-owned interconnection system and by acting as agent in producing and broadcasting projects. The leaders of MET, specifically John C. Schwarzwalder and Chris Donaldson, now see its future as a geographical expansion probably to include Montana and possibly the Upper Peninsula of Michigan.

The Southern Educational Communications Association (SECA) began in 1967 when broadcasters from the old NAEB Region II organized to develop and exchange the cultural, educational, and instructional resources of the fifteen states of the South. Primarily an association for the mutual support of the membership (which includes state networks as well as individual stations, ranging from Kentucky and North Carolina to Florida and Texas), SECA is also a production agency for national distribution and produces a weekly regional public affairs series for Southern distribution. Among its services are group purchases of public and instructional programs and the training of personnel. SECA is supported by membership fees, by grants from foundations, and by certain government allocations on a project-to-project basis.

The Central Educational Network (CEN), with headquarters in the building of Chicago's WTTW, differs from the other three regional networks in that it puts less emphasis on the region and more on the common needs of stations and agencies that happen to be in the Midwest. Founded in the spring of 1967, it has four classes of membership: "A"—operation of one or more ETV stations; "B"—production and/or distribution of educational programs to either educational or commercial television stations; "C"—construction of ETV stations; and "D"—those other stations or agencies that help CEN with programs or money. CEN provides a regional program service for acquisition and distribution; a regional interconnected network (using both AT&T wires for live and mails for taped regular programs); help in applying for grants and in administering projects for producing regionally oriented programs; and collective representation with other regional and national organizations involving programs. Its "Class A" members include about thirty ETV stations. Financial support comes from CEN's members—in dues and in freely contributed programs and services. Many of its members are members also of state networks and of Midwest Educational Television. Neither MET nor CEN requires exclusive affiliation.

COMMUNICATIONS SATELLITES

The communications satellite added another dimension to the technology of electronic interconnection. Previously the only alternative to wire or cable connection over long distances was relay repeater stations. These stations must be spaced within line of sight to each other (about thirty miles), they are too expensive for thinly populated areas, and they cannot transmit over large bodies of water. Relay by space satellites overcomes all these difficulties because their line-of-sight signals can be transmitted over one-third of the earth. The early communications satellites had two major disadvantages. One was that because they were small and simple, they were "passive," merely reflecting signals from and to ground stations, and therefore required elaborate and expensive ground stations. The other difficulty was that because they orbited the earth about every ninety minutes, they could be used only during the brief periods when they were within line of sight to the ground stations.

The first difficulty was progressively reduced as larger and more complex "active" satellites were developed, which could amplify, modulate, and focus signals, permitting the ground stations to be simpler and cheaper. The second difficulty was eliminated when the synchronous satellite was developed—one that, circling the earth at exactly the speed of the earth's rotation, was "parked" in an apparently stationary orbit and thus could be used around the clock by all earth stations within its line of sight. Three synchronous (also, when over the equator, called geostationary) satellites parked in apparently stationary places, can give continuous worldwide relay transmission because each is in constant line of sight to earth stations in one-third of the planet and each one of them is in constant line-of-sight relay to one of the others.

Some of these developments came on rapidly before Congress passed legislation to deal with them. In December 1958, the first U.S. communications satellite was launched. In April 1962, a space satellite transmitted the first television picture from California to Massachusetts. In July 1962, "Telstar I," launched and paid for by AT&T, gave the first reliable trans-Atlantic television transmission. When Congress began to consider legislation dealing with space communications, it was facing an accomplished fact—just as it had faced the accomplished fact of an established radio broadcasting system with networks when it passed the Radio Act of 1927.

In 1961 and 1962 a committee of the FCC and committees of both the House and the Senate held long hearings on the support, ownership, operation, and regulation of communications satellites. One group argued that the federal government should own and operate the satellites, and a second group argued that a monopoly should be granted to a communications carrier, such as AT&T. Congress adopted the proposal of a third group of witnesses on August 31, 1962, in the Communications Satellite Act, which established a hybrid public-private commercial corporation, with half of the common stock reserved for authorized common carriers (companies communicating for the public for a fee, such as AT&T and RCA) and half for general public investors.

> The Act sets up a combination government-private corporation responsible for operating an international satellite relay system (Comsat). It represents the United States in the International Telecommunications Satellite Consortium (Intelsat), which it also manages. . . . The FCC shares responsibility for the system with the President and the National Aeronautics and Space Administration (NASA). The latter provides the launch facilities for Comsat's stations. The FCC's role includes ensuring equal access to the system by competing carriers—which in turn requires technical compatibility between the satellites and existing systems—and authorizing the construction of earth stations.[7]

After the Communications Satellite Act was passed, rapid technological progress continued. Within four months television signals were relayed across the Pacific. In less than a year the first successful synchronous satellite was parked. All these satellites were experimental. The next step was to put a commercial, as opposed to an experimental, communications satellite into orbit. This was done in April 1965, when "Early Bird" was placed in synchronous orbit over the Atlantic.

Active, synchronous, commercial communications satellites raised such questions as how they would affect existing wire and cable and ground-based wireless systems (such as AT&T's long-distance lines) and how they could be used to reduce transmission costs by common-carrier customers, such as the commercial broadcasting networks.

The first concrete proposal concerning this second question came from the American Broadcasting Company (ABC). On May 15, 1965, it petitioned the FCC for permission to operate its own satellite system to feed ABC programs to its affiliated stations instead of using the AT&T wire and cable system. The commissioners asked ABC to clarify technical details and to resubmit the application later, and they sent out a notice of inquiry to interested users for submission of comments on a domestic satellite service, with a deadline of August 1, 1966. The most significant comment in terms of educational broadcasting came on August 1, 1966, from the Ford Foundation, whose proposal will be discussed later in this chapter.

INSTRUCTIONAL TELEVISION

ITV Libraries

The institutions considering the activation of ETV channels saw the need for nonlocal programs for general audiences, but to use nonlocal programs for instruction ran against the tradition of institutional autonomy. Nevertheless, the need to do so was forced upon educational institutions by the high cost of producing quality programs. A study financed by NDEA concluded that systematic exchange and distribution were desirable and possible.[8] As a result, one national and two regional instructional television libraries were established on a demonstration basis in 1962 with NDEA funds.

The National Instructional Television Library, first administered by the NETRC-NET in New York City, then by Indiana University, was renamed the National Center for School and College Television (NCSCT) when it moved to Bloomington in 1965. From 1967 until 1970 it received some support from the Indiana University Foundation. By 1970 it had become self-supporting and changed its name to the National Instructional Television Center (NIT). NIT urged educational and broadcasting agencies to pool their ideas, talents, and other resources in consortia to create classroom series beyond the means of any single institution. The success of the first several series of cooperative programs through the American consortia suggested the idea that American-Canadian cooperative enterprises might also be successful. In October 1973, the Agency for Instructional Television (AIT) was established—a nonprofit agency governed by a board of sixteen directors (twelve appointed by the U.S. Council of Chief State School Officers, three appointed by the Canadian Council of Ministers of Education, and the AIT executive director). Edwin Cohen, who had headed the ITV library from its beginning in 1962, was chosen executive director of AIT.

While NIT and AIT were growing, other regional and national instructional television production and distribution agencies were also developing. One of these was the Great Plains Regional Instructional Television Library at the University of Nebraska, which by the close of the 1965–66 academic year had become self-supporting. By that time it had become a national service. In 1966 it substituted "National" for "Regional" in its title —GPNITL (shortened to GPN). It is a permanent educational service agency housed at the University of Nebraska, and its board of directors are national educational and broadcasting leaders.[9]

The Northeastern Instructional Television Library, administered by the Eastern Educational Television Network, undertook to produce ITV programs by stations working cooperatively as its major responsibility from the start in 1962. It succeeded in all its objectives, including self-support, and became an essential part of EEN.

The idea and practice of pooled programs and of cooperative planning, financing, and production for ITV programming spread rapidly. Cooperative enterprises grew by means of a large number of national, regional, and state agreements. These included the videotape library of the ETS division of the NAEB, Midwest Educational Television, the Southern Educational Communications Association, Southwestern Indiana Educational Television Council, and the Central Michigan Educational Broadcasting Council. In addition, the Television Subgroup of the Committee on Institutional Cooperation of the Big Ten Universities and the University of Chicago, the Council on Higher Educational Institutions in New York City, the Texas Educational Microwave Project (TEMP), and the Oregon State Higher Education System were cooperative program exchanges for higher level education instructional broadcasting.

Looking back to the mid-1950s, Jack McBride, chief official of all Nebraska ETV activities, said: "By 1964–65 the local-live/recorded syndrome had come full circle. ETV stations were being activated and initially programmed largely, if not solely, with recorded materials."[10] Looking ahead, he wrote: "The ETV programmer, having analyzed his audiences' needs from every point of view, will want to pick and choose from local, area, state, regional, and national sources, commercial as well as nonprofit, and will need to be supported with sufficient funds to permit such selection."[11]

The Instructional Divison of the NAEB

The role of the Instruction Division was enhanced by the ETV Facilities Act of 1962, the establishment of ITFS in 1963, and the growth of closed-circuit instructional television installations. These three developments all brought about an increase in the number of facilities that were not primarily interested in programming for general audiences, that were not affiliated with the NAEB or NET, but that were keenly interested in improving the quality of instructional television. The Instruction Division's major project was financed by a $600,000 grant from the Ford Foundation, received in December 1964, for a three-year program to improve televised instruction. The grant came a year after the foundation had decided against giving further direct support to ITV operations.

The National Project for the Improvement of Televised Instruction, 1965-68, published its final report, *Toward a Significant Difference,* which concluded that instructional television had not made a significant difference in American education because in any complex situation, "if only one variable is changed, no significant difference results."[12] The report changed the questions facing education and television: not how to improve televised instruction, but how to improve instruction, and how to orient the educational system to the needs of the individual learners rather than to the needs of the administrative instructional system.

The Samoan System

As the previous chapter reported, after a four-man NAEB team headed by Vernon Bronson had proposed a plan for the use of television to improve instruction in Samoa, Samoan Governor H. Rex Lee adopted the Bronson plan and received large increases in appropriations from the U.S. federal government. Three TV channels were in use by October 1964, and three more within a year, and new schools appropriate for the use of television were constructed. At the beginning of 1966 almost two-thirds of the 5,500 elementary and 1,500 secondary school pupils were housed in new schools and being taught by TV. The most striking feature of the system was that television was used to teach the core of the curriculum, not to supplement it. ITV filled almost one-third of all classroom time from first through twelfth grade, and six evenings a week the stations broadcast four hours to adult viewers throughout the islands. "Samoa has in effect created a team-teaching situation in which a small group of highly trained and educated instructors teach the substance of the courses by TV and less well-prepared teachers manage the activities that fill the approximately two-thirds of the class time not devoted to TV. Materials, readings, and exercises are worked out centrally to keep the classroom activities and the TV schedule in phase."[13]

Although the first reports of the Samoan experiment were favorable, the Samoan governor who succeeded H. Rex Lee in 1968 cut back television, saying that it had failed. The administrator of the project explained, however, that the Samoan system will not work because of any inherent value in television but "must be made to work by those who see its validity, understand its demands, and perceive its potential."[14]

Midwest Program of Airborne Television Instruction (MPATI)

In October 1958, officials of the Westinghouse Electric Company proposed to Philip M. Coombs, then educational program director of the Ford Foundation, the idea that videotaped transmissions from airplanes would make possible the broadcasting of instructional courses to schools over wide areas that lacked cables or microwave facilities.[15] Coombs saw the possibilities for the United States and also for underdeveloped countries. The upper Midwest offered the best combination of flat terrain and heavy population for a trial. A conference of educators and engineers, held at Purdue University in May 1959, endorsed the proposal that the Ford Foundation support a three-year experiment. Public schools and university educators formed the Midwest Council on Airborne Television Instruction in October of that year. The Ford Foundation gave a grant of $4.5 million to the council, which contracted with Westinghouse to perform the physical operations. On December 23, 1959, the FCC licensed the council to operate Channels 72 and 76 on an experimental basis for ten years. Additional grants from Ford and other foundations gave the council $8.5 million to operate through May 1962—the end of the three-year experimental period. After preparation (outfitting two DC 6 aircraft, selecting teachers, developing and producing programs, and enlisting schools), regularly scheduled broadcasts of forty hours per week began in September 1961, from a point twenty-three thousand feet above Lafayette, Indiana. The area that could receive the signals included most of Indiana, Ohio, and Illinois; large portions of Kentucky and Michigan; and the southeast corner of Wisconsin.

Affiliated schools paid nothing for the service during the school year 1961–62. However, in January 1962—with the end of the test period near—a not-for-profit corporation replaced the council to continue the program beyond the experimental period, aiming at self-support. Affiliated schools were assessed one dollar per pupil per year. About 1,200 schools had paid membership assessments by the end of the 1962–63 year.

In 1962 the Ford Foundation gave an additional terminal grant of $7.5 million for two years beyond the test period. MPATI was in a critical situation, and on January 15, 1963, it requested the FCC permanently to reserve Channels 72 and 76, and in addition Channels 74, 78, 80, and

82. The FCC delayed decision in order to hold hearings on opposition, particularly by the NAEB.[16]

On June 30, 1965, the FCC denied MPATI's request, recommending instead the use of six channels in the 2500 mc. band. By then MPATI had been forced to raise assessment fees—partly because school systems in Cincinnati, Columbus, Toledo, Cleveland, and Chicago, which were committed to support local ETV stations, did not have the money for both, and partly because many schools "bootlegged" the open-circuit broadcasts without paying. The fees rose to two dollars per pupil for 1963–66, then fifty cents more for 1967–68. Income declined because many schools ended affiliation, and MPATI concluded the broadcasts in May 1968. After three years of operating as a videotape library, it dissolved on June 30, 1971, giving its assets, valued at $250,000, to the Great Plains National Instructional Television Library.

At least three achievements of MPATI should be noted. One is that its daring assaults upon the limits of ITV aided the passage of both the ETV Facilities Act of 1962 and the Public Broadcasting Act of 1967. A second is a precedent for successful cooperation of educational institutions. Finally, it demonstrated that mediocre programs are not good enough.

Instructional Television Fixed Service

When in July 1963, the FCC established a new class of stations—Instructional Television Fixed Service (ITFS)—it stressed that the new service was not a substitute for conventional ETV broadcasting but an important adjunct, making ITV programming available to school systems in communities without ETV stations and easing the spectrum pinch in other communities. In October 1965, the Commission established a National Committee for the Full Development of the Instructional Television Fixed Service, made up of representatives of the FCC and education, to help plan efficient use of the ITFS frequencies.[17] At the end of 1969 ninety-four ITFS systems were in operation, forty-nine others were under construction, and sixteen new applications were pending with the FCC.[18]

EDUCATIONAL TELEVISION FOR GENERAL AUDIENCES—NET

Into the seventies NET remained the chief source of nonlocal programming for the affiliated stations. An average of about one-half of their noninstructional programming came from NET. NET programs were the show case of ETV. The agency aided, or prodded, stations to broadcast more hours, more days, and more weeks, particularly during times suitable for adults and out-of-school young people, and to acquire "color capacity"—a costly necessity to keep pace with commercial stations. Thus it would be difficult to overstate NET's importance in the development of ETV as an alternative national television service.

With the October 1963 Ford Foundation grant, NET for the first time had its own production staff. It began immediately to build that staff, turning frequently to the public affairs departments of the commercial networks. In January 1964, the first of the new progams were going to the stations. "The results throughout the first year were mixed, but by the winter of 1964–65, N.E.T. programming had reached a level of quality it had never attained before, and the consensus seems to be that it has improved steadily ever since."[19] The fact that NET, unlike NETRC, did not have to seek underwriting for public affairs programming from business and industry increased its ability to get underwriting from other sources for cultural and children's programming.[20]

In the 1963–64 reorganization NET replaced the previous programming divisions with three broad program categories—public affairs, cultural affairs, and children's—and built its new program staff accordingly. However, this simplification of content was accompanied by an increasing complexity of delivery. As affiliated stations grew in number, first the block system (in which sets of programs were sent to blocks of stations on a round-robin basis), then the two-unit system (half of the programs going to half of the stations the first week and the other half one or two weeks later), and finally the all-station-release system (with tapes going to all the stations at the same time) were adopted. By the mid-sixties, as the number of stations approached one hundred, the program distribution by mail had become burdensome and costly.[21] The limits of the physical delivery system were driving NET and the Ford Foundation to try to get live interconnection. By 1967 the copying/mailing service cost more than $1 million a year—one-sixth of NET's total annual budget—but the cost of leasing an interconnection network from AT&T for an eight-hour daily schedule would have been $8 million a year.

Interconnection was clearly necessary if educational broadcasting was to develop into an effective nationwide service. But interconnection raises to an unavoidable position the always latent question: Who's in charge? If programs are to be broadcast simultaneously (especially live events), who is to decide which programs go on the network and when? Who is to decide whether they are appropriate and "responsible"? To say that the local station manager has the ultimate authority for what is broadcast is no answer. The program may have already been publicized and scheduled nationally. If the local station manager has not had a chance to preview the program or has no adequate substitute for it, his authority to preempt national programming is meaningless. Therefore, the question, who is in charge of deciding what programs are broadcast nationally, increasingly strained the relationships between the stations and the national programming center from the founding of ETRC in 1952 through 1970. (The situation became critical after the Public Broadcasting Act founded the Corporation for Public Broadcasting, which created the Public Broadcasting Service.) Between 1964 and 1969, before regular live interconnection was achieved, the issue was always resolved by compromises because NET and the stations were mutually dependent. The wonder is not that some managers thought NET's programming too timid while others thought it contentious, and that many thought some of it inappropriate. The wonder, rather, is that in a situation where the stations resented their powerlessness over decisions concerning national programming and during a period when all over the country social unrest was mounting, NET and the stations could stay together.

Much credit should go to John White. He brought to educational television a dynamic practicality and an electrifying sense of high mission that moved it toward becoming (in his words of 1960) "the important force it can be in the world of broadcasting, in the American educational and cultural world." To be important is to be controversial. White introduced some boldness into ETV programming and acted as the "heat shield" for the stations. He converted ETV into a national educational television service, whose potential significance could in 1967 be understood at the highest levels of decision-making.

ETV STATIONS DRIVE FOR SUPPORT

The ETV stations had insisted upon autonomy as a condition for remaining a division of the NAEB when the association was reorganized in 1963. The members of the Television Stations Division adopted the name Educational Television Stations (ETS). Its autonomy included the freedom to withdraw from the NAEB at any time. The station managers asked, what did membership in ETS have to offer ETV stations, and how would ETS be supported? The key individuals involved in finding answers were Richard B. Hull (director, Telecommunications Center, Ohio State University), who was both a member of the ETS board and the chairman of the NAEB overall board; Robert Schenkkan (president and general manager, KRLN, Channel 9, Austin-San Antonio), who was chairman of the ETS board; and William Harley, paid president of the NAEB and also a member of its board.

These three realized that educational television needed to enlist support of social power far beyond the station membership. They sought to employ as head of ETS a person who could command attention in his own right and enlist broad support from the public. Among the individuals they considered were Edward R. Murrow, formerly of CBS and the U.S. Information Agency, and C. Scott Fletcher, formerly president of the Fund for Adult Education and the architect of the base for a national ETV system.

Late in February 1964, Hull, Harley, and Schenkkan appointed Fletcher "executive consultant" to serve as chief executive officer of ETS for one year, "to get the division over a few hurdles." The first hurdle was to win support of the NET Affiliates Committee, which was meeting in New York on March 18. With no money or firm pledges of support, ETS could get substantial financial backing only from the stations affiliated with NET, particularly the big city stations. These stations were as yet undecided whether ETS could offer them services to justify support.

At the March 18 meeting of the Affiliates Committee Schenkkan, as chairman of the ETS board, and Fletcher stated ETS's priorities: (1) effective liaison with government agencies; (2) the improvement of the public image of ETV and the winning of public acceptance through better programming; and (3) effective liaison with national associations and organizations that were interested in ETV. Fletcher said the task of ETS was to build an organization that would win respect and endorsement so as to gain the support of "millions of thinking Americans."[22] Shenkkan asked the members of the Affiliates Committee to support ETS and to persuade the other affiliates to do so, specifically by pledging to pay membership dues, the amounts to be worked out later. The first to pledge was James Robertson, vice-president and general manager, KCET, Community Television of Southern California: "You can count on L.A.: A check will be in the mail."[23]

The ETV stations urgently needed an effective national service organization because NET had withdrawn from all activities except programming. They were able to support one because NET, thanks to the Ford Foundation's increased grant, had reduced each affiliated station's annual fee to $100. The ETV stations gradually became dues-paying members of ETS.

Gerard L. Appy, manager of WGTV, University of Georgia, and

former chairman of the NET Affiliates Committee, in April 1964, began a six-month part-time stint as ETS vice-president with the task of recruiting station-members. This freed Fletcher to concentrate on two other objectives: to establish an ETS program exchange service, which would be necessary to attract members to the organization; and to find long-range financial support for ETV stations.

Hartford Gunn, Jr., manager of the WGBH TV and FM stations, Boston, replaced Appy on the ETS board. A founding member of the NET Affiliates Committee, he had led the stations in attempts to obtain a voice in programming decisions. Therefore, his presence on the ETS board in 1964 gave a big boost to the new division.

Fletcher decided to explore the problem of long-range financing through a conference of key members of the governing boards and the station managers of all ETV stations. ETS, through the NAEB, received a grant of about $65,000 from the U.S. Office of Education to make a survey of the stations' financial situations and to conduct a national conference on long-range financing.

The First National Conference on Financing ETV Stations

This conference in Washington, D.C., December 7 and 8, 1964, was held for the purpose of reaching a consensus on recommended action for long-range station financing. Attendance exceeded 260; more than 200 were from the ETV stations, and almost all the stations were represented by the chairmen of the boards and the chief executive officers.

At a general session Chairman Fletcher read a letter from President Lyndon B. Johnson: "I hope that the sources of support which have been so important to the launching of educational television broadcasting will not only continue to assist this development, but will increase their participation. In addition, I hope that you will find new sources of financial support. In this way, educational television stations will realize their collective potential as the instruments of national purpose in the vast program of social action upon which we are embarked." [24] The conferees did not fail to read in the latter two sentences suggestions of federal aid to programming and also of a possible relationship between ETV and the "Great Society" programs Johnson had initiated. FCC Chairman E. William Henry in a speech at a general session was more explicit: "A Congressional appropriation of federal funds for programming to meet national needs must not be dismissed simply because it raises serious objections and questions fundamental to our society. There should be a debate on this subject, and I urge you to start it." [25]

There was consensus on the need for a national general exchange library, a necessary condition for ETS to remain affiliated with the NAEB. (Within a year Educational Television Stations/Program Service —ETS/PS—was established at Bloomington, Indiana.)[26]

Agenda Item Number 11—"White House Conference or National Citizens Conference (1966 or 1967)" on the long-range financing of ETV stations—received most attention from the conferees. However, Ralph Lowell, Hartford Gunn, Jr., and David Ives, all from Boston, presented an alternative. They proposed a small presidential commission to collect information, listen to testimony, and recommend a national policy. The proposed commission would consist of not more than a dozen outstanding lay citizens; the role of educational broadcasters would be limited to giving testimony. The Lowell statement proposed that the President charge the commission to: (1) determine the role that educational television should play in the nation's mass communication system; (2) assuming that the role should be enlarged, decide how educational television should be strengthened; and (3) recommend methods for financing educational television in its new and enlarged role.[27]

At the final plenary session Lowell proposed: "Immediate attention should be given to the appointment of a Presidential Commission to make recommendations for educational television development, after intensive study of a year or more duration." This proposal was unanimously adopted. When the conference adjourned, Fletcher extended his relationship with ETS as executive consultant to implement the mandates of the conference, particularly the one for a presidential commission.

The Lowell Committee

Soon after the conference, Fletcher and Ralph Lowell formed the "ETS Committee on a Presidential Commission" to persuade President Johnson to initiate a presidential commission or to lend his weight to the creation of a national commission to study ETV. The first would be appointed by the President and financed by the federal government. The second would be privately formed and financed, but Johnson's blessings would be a political necessity.

The committee met in Boston on March 12, 1965, with Fletcher, Hartford Gunn, Jr., and David Ives of WGBH, Boston, to draft a letter to the President. The letter was submitted to the White House in June 1965, through Presidential Assistant Douglass Cater, later a key figure in dealing with the Carnegie Commission and the follow-up legislative proposals. Johnson quickly endorsed the proposal for a national commission privately established and financed.[28]

THE CARNEGIE COMMISSION ON EDUCATIONAL TELEVISION

In his quest for private sponsorship and financing of the commission, Fletcher soon approached the Carnegie Corporation. Its president, John W. Gardner, was then on leave of absence for service with the Johnson Administration. Alan Pifer, executive vice-president of the corporation, approved the project, and the selection of the members was begun.[29] On November 10, 1965, the corporation announced the formation and membership of the Carnegie Commission on Educational Television, with a grant of $500,000. Its mission was to "conduct a broadly conceived study of noncommercial television" focusing its attention "principally, although not exclusively, on community-owned channels and their services to the general public," and to "recommend lines along which noncommercial television stations might most usefully develop during the years ahead." The members included: Chairman James R. Killian, Jr., chairman, Massachusetts Institute of Technology; James B. Conant, former president, Harvard University; David D. Henry, president, University of Illinois; and Leonard Woodcock, vice-president, United Automobile Workers of America.

In November 1965, President Johnson wrote both to Alan Pifer commending the corporation "for sponsoring this valuable study" and to James Killian, saying, "I believe that educational television has an important future in the United States and throughout the world. . . . I look forward with great interest to the judgments which this commission will offer."[30]

THE FORD FOUNDATION'S NEW MOVES

By 1963 the Ford Foundation had invested a total of $80.7 million in ETV —$7.5 million by the Fund for Adult Education, $10 million by The Fund for the Advancement of Education, and $63.2 million by the foundation. It had done so to improve commercial programs (the TV-Radio Workshop), to provide cultural and informational programs for a general ETV audience, and to use television for teaching. The self-study that the foundation made in 1963 led to the decision to discontinue support for classroom TV experimentation and, because there was need for a national noncommercial service, to strengthen National Educational Television and to help broaden the financial resources of community-corporation stations.

In 1965 the foundation initiated a major new program, Matching Grants to Community Stations. Over a four-year period grants ranging from $50,000 to $500,000 were made to help the community stations improve their financial conditions, improve operations, and sustain quality programs. Grants totaling $20.5 million were made to thirty-seven stations and were matched by a total of $42.6 million. But more was needed, the foundation concluded: "Educational television consequently began a serious search for a broader and more secure funding base and for the means to develop a fully interconnected network."[31]

The search for a funding base and a means to finance interconnection began in March 1966, when McGeorge Bundy, President Johnson's Assistant on National Security, became president of the Ford Foundation. The two main efforts the foundation made were to propose a scheme for financing ETV through a domestic communications satellite and to demonstrate the power of interconnection and high quality ETV programming by means of the Public Broadcast Laboratory and thereby win broad approval and financial support from the public.

The Satellite Proposal

On March 2, 1966, the FCC, responding to an application by the American Broadcasting Company,[32] invited interested parties to comment on the broad question of the domestic use of satellite communications facilities by nongovernmental noncarrier entities (e.g., the broadcasting networks). Among the parties that responded were Comsat, AT&T and other communications common carriers, the commercial TV networks, various federal agencies, and the Ford Foundation.

The Ford Foundation proposed the creation of a nonprofit corporation which would own and operate satellite relay facilities for domestic use by commercial and noncommercial television broadcasters. This corporation would pay its initial and operating costs from revenues received from the commercial networks. It would serve noncommercial networks free of charge, and its net surplus from service to the commercial networks (which would be realizing a saving over the alternative use of ground-based interconnection) would be devoted to the support of noncommercial educational television program development and dissemination. Chairman Senator John O. Pastore's Subcommittee on Communications

of the Senate Commerce Committee held hearings on the several proposals on August 10, 17, 18, and 24.[33] Richard B. Hull, the chairman of the
NAEB board, stated: "The real significance of the Ford Foundation proposal is to underline the opportunity this Nation now has to insure the
full development of a dual system of broadcasting, noncommercial and
commercial. . . . The interest of this Committee is to find ways by which
this second service can come into being."[34] William Harley, president of
the NAEB, made an argument for the inclusion of educational radio,
which, he said, "was something of an oversight in the other testimony."[35]

There were other requests by the FCC, other submissions, and
other hearings. The Ford Foundation model was not adopted by the
FCC, but the proposal introduced educational television as a central issue in the intense national debate about the implications of domestic
communications satellites. It set the stage for the development of interconnection for educational television stations and heightened national
interest in the forthcoming report and recommendations of the Carnegie
Commission on Educational Television. It made educational broadcasting (soon to be called public broadcasting) a matter of keen governmental and public interest.

Indeed, not since 1934—when the Senate debated the Wagner-
Hatfield amendment to reserve a percentage of radio channels for nonprofit stations, and the FCC conducted hearings on the proposal—had
educational broadcasting been an issue that engaged the attention of the
entire nation. There was, however, one fundamental difference between
the two occasions, and in 1966 that difference was vastly in favor of educational broadcasting. In 1934 the proposal was *to subtract* from the
physically limited usable electronic spectrum a certain number of channels available to commercial broadcasters. In 1966 the proposal was *to
add to* the entire domestic communications capabilities. The impact of
the Ford proposal was dramatic and sustained. Although some members
of the Carnegie Commission on Educational Television were concerned
that the Ford Foundation proposal might detract from the force of their
recommendations, the consequence was quite the opposite. President
Bundy repeatedly urged that no action on domestic satellites be taken until the publication of the Carnegie Commission report. The Ford Foundation proposal was the best possible psychological preparation for the
Carnegie report. The concern that the impact might be otherwise did,
however, result in a rush for the Commission to put prepublication summaries of the report in the hands of key people in the White House, Congress, the FCC, and the Department of HEW.

The Ford Foundation proposal did something more: it posed the question how to support a national noncommercial educational television system in such a way as to shield it from the political pressures of the executive and legislative branches of the federal government. Testifying before the Senate Subcommittee on Communications, Fred Friendly, who was the originator of the Ford proposal, starkly posed the need to support ETV public affairs and news programming from sources other than congressional appropriations. The Ford proposal, he said, would meet this need by having a portion of the commercial networks' savings support ETV public affairs and news programming and by providing ETV stations with free interconnection:

> I am sure that we must avoid at all costs any situation in which budgets of news and public affairs programming would be appropriated or even approved by any branch of the Federal government. Even the most distinguished and courageous Board of Trustees could not insulate such programs from the budget and appropriation process.
>
> Of one thing we can be certain: public television will rock the boat. There will be—there should be—times when every man in politics will wish that it had never been created. But public television should not have to stand the test of political popularity. Its most precious right will be the right to rock the boat. . . .
>
> To conclude—general appropriations for equipment, trust funds for cultural affairs, but not one cent from these sources for news and public affairs. Last summer Mr. Bundy called the satellite proposal a people's dividend. It can also be a people's safeguard, in perpetuity, with all the checks and balances that our system of separate powers demands.[36]

Announcement of the Public Broadcast Laboratory

On December 12, 1966, the Ford Foundation announced a $10 million appropriation to develop what would become the Public Broadcast Laboratory.[37] "The Foundation . . . established the Public Broadcast Laboratory (PBL) for a two-year demonstration of the power of national interconnection. PBL was also created to show how noncommercial television, when backed by adequate funds for programming, might produce superior cultural and public affairs programs for a nationwide audience. . . . A further $6 million grant for program support was made to NET in 1967 to continue its service for noncommercial channels—five hours of new public affairs and cultural programs weekly. In addition, NET received a special grant to interconnect its affiliated stations for three programs, including an analysis by leading educators and journalists of President Johnson's State of the Union address immediately after delivery."[38]

In that address on January 10, 1967 (with commentary telecast by NET through live interconnection to affiliated stations), President Johnson remarked: "We should develop educational television into a vital public resource . . . We should insist that the public interest be fully served through the public's airwaves. I will propose these measures to the 90th Congress." Educational television had finally cut through to the brink of receiving federal aid for program development.

OVER THE BRINK,
1967

I N JANUARY 1967, with the public release of the Carnegie Commission re-
port educational television was close to receiving federal aid to a national
system of programming for general audiences. In a series of swift moves
President Johnson proposed such measures to Congress in February, by
October both houses of Congress had passed the Public Broadcasting
Act of 1967, which included radio was well as television, and President
Johnson signed it on November 7. This act radically changed the components of and institutional relationships in educational broadcasting in the
United States. It has far-reaching and long-lasting implications for the
entire American system of mass communications and the entire Ameri-
can educational system.

The legislation was enacted with speed because the implications
were evaded or postponed. When suggesting to the Educational Television Stations Conference in 1964 that the appropriation of federal funds
for programming "not be dismissed simply because it raises serious objections and questions fundamental to our society," FCC Chairman E.
William Henry said, "There should be debate on this subject, and I urge
you to start it." No such debate occurred. Most energies were focused on
getting the legislation, few on considering the objections or exploring the
questions.

The American people moved from the FCC's reservation of television channels for educational stations in 1952 to the Public Broadcasting
Act of 1967 step-by-step, none of which anticipated the next, all of which
were primarily concerned with education, not the media of mass commu-

nications, and all of which insisted upon absolute local control. The major steps were two: the National Defense Education Act of 1958, born out of fear of Sputnik I; and the ETV Facilities Act of 1962, whose purpose was "to establish a program of Federal matching grants for the construction of television broadcasting facilities to be used for educational purposes." The act did state that the facilities should be "adaptable to the widest educational use," but the legislative history focused on the benefits that would accrue to *instruction*.

Obviously, between the ETV Facilities Act and the Public Broadcasting Act there was a jump, not only in degree, but also in direction. The jump was motivated by both a stick and a carrot. The stick was evidence that existing means of support for ETV stations were inadequate. The carrot was the vision—vague but luminous—of the potential of the noncommercial television system with federal aid for programming without federal control. The Ford Foundation and Lyndon Baines Johnson said it could and should be done, and the Carnegie Commission proposed a plan to do so.

Although a decisive breakthrough was made into a new and uncharted course, there was no money from the federal government in 1967, nor was there a plan for adequate, insulated, long-range support, not even a sketch of a plan, either in 1967 or (as Johnson promised) in 1968. This chapter follows the sequence of events, with the exception that it puts the Carnegie Commission report first (because it was known to key decision-makers by the first of the year).

THE REPORT OF THE CARNEGIE COMMISSION ON ETV

The Carnegie Commission's report, released on January 26, 1967,[1] was the basis for the Public Broadcasting Act of 1967, although Congress did not adopt the commission's essential financing recommendations. The commission concluded that "a well-financed and well-directed educational television system, substantially larger and far more pervasive and effective than that which now exists in the United States, must be brought into being if the full needs of the American public are to be served." The commission recommended:

> 1. Concerted efforts at the federal, state, and local levels to improve the facilities and to provide for the adequate support of the individual educational television stations and to increase their number.
> 2. Congress act promptly to authorize and to establish a federally chartered, nonprofit, nongovernmental corporation, to be known as the

"Corporation for Public Television." The Corporation should be empowered to receive and disburse governmental and private funds in order to extend and improve Public Television programming.

3. The Corporation support at least two national production centers, and that it be free to contract with independent producers to prepare Public Television programs for educational television stations.

4. The Corporation support, by appropriate grants and contracts, the production of Public Television programs by local stations for more-than-local use.

5. The Corporation on appropriate occasions help support local programming by local stations.

6. The Corporation provide the educational television system as expeditiously as possible with facilities for live interconnection by conventional means, and that it be enabled to benefit from advances in technology as domestic communications satellites are brought into being.

7. The Corporation encourage and support research and development leading to the improvement of programming and program production.

8. The Corporation support technical experimentation designed to improve the present television technology.

9. The Corporation undertake to provide means by which technical, artistic, and specialized personnel may be recruited and trained.

10. Congress provide the federal funds required by the Corporation through a manufacturers' excise tax on television sets (beginning at 2 percent and rising to a ceiling of 5 percent). The revenue should be made available to the Corporation through a trust fund.

11. New legislation to enable the Department of Health, Education, and Welfare to provide adequate facilities for stations now in existence; to assist in increasing the number of stations to achieve nationwide coverage; to help support the basic operations of all stations; and to enlarge the support of instructional television programming.

12. Federal, state, local, and private educational agencies sponsor extensive and innovative studies intended to develop better insights into the use of television in formal and informal education.

The report makes almost no mention of educational radio. The commission's charge, of course, was to make a study of educational television, but it was to be "broadly conceived," and throughout the commission recognized (in the words of President Johnson's letter of endorsement) that our freedom "depends upon the communication of many ideas through many channels." That the commission should not even explain why it ignored educational radio must surely be regarded as one more bit of evidence that the American people during the sixties were obsessed with television.

Despite its contention that "educational television is exactly the subject with which the Commission meant to deal" (p. 15), the commission rejected this term and substituted "Public Television." The coinage was a public relations device. "Justifiably or not it [the name educational television] calls to mind the school room and the lecture hall. It frightens away from educational channels many of those who might enjoy them most" (pp. 14–15). The new tag has gained currency. But just what was "public television" to be exactly? The commission gave no examples, not even any of NET's programs. The report mentions only two specific programming activities—the Ford Foundation's TV-Radio Workshop (more than ten years dead) as an example of the type of experimental programming needed, and Julia Child's "French Chef" as an example of the production of a public television program by a local station for more than local use. What, then, does "public television" mean? Les Brown well called it "a name without a concept."[2]

The commission admitted that it was "ambivalent" concerning instructional television (p. 80). Thus it had a double standard. On the one hand, instructional television was set aside for study because its true potential had "not been realized in practice" (p. 80). On the other hand, public television was advocated as "a great act of faith" (p. 98).

Instruction, of course, is not the same as education. A generation before, John Dewey was perplexed that many modern thinkers did not "take education with sufficient seriousness for it to occur to them that any rational person could actually think it possible that philosophizing should focus about education as the supreme human interest in which, moreover, other problems, cosmological, moral, logical, come to a head." Dewey was in agreement with Plato on this point. Yet the Carnegie Commission, instead of seizing on "education" as an honored word and seeking to elevate it, coined a "name without a concept."

The point drives deeper than the label. The climax of the report is: "If we were to sum up our proposal with all the brevity at our command we would say that what we recommend is freedom. We seek freedom from the constraints, however necessary in their context, of commercial television. We seek for educational television freedom from the pressures of inadequate funds. We seek for the public servant freedom to create, freedom to innovate, freedom to be heard in this most far-reaching medium. We seek for the citizen freedom to view, to see programs that the present system by its incompleteness, denies him" (pp. 98–99). What is missing in this eloquent summary? The producer, the educator, and the "public servant" are all considered. But missing is the explicit inclusion of the citizen's freedom to do more than "to view, to see programs." Missing is his freedom to learn by practicing the government of his affairs, private and public, by his own use of "this most far-reaching medium." The report does not include the concept of television as the people's instrument to present grievances, to be heard and seen, to explain, to express, to use television as a means of communication in action to pursue the most serious personal and social goals.

The commission's recommendation of an excise tax on television sets came at a psychologically inappropriate time. On June 21, 1965, President Johnson had signed, with much fanfare, the Excise Tax Reduction Act, removing excise taxes of 10 percent on more than 1,000 consumers goods (including television and radio sets) and services, which had been imposed as a wartime measure to control inflation and raise revenue. The Excise Reduction Act was the third step in the Kennedy-Johnson Keynesian policy of stimulating the American economy by tax reduction. The first step had been a tax credit for business investments in 1962; the second step had been the reduction of corporate and personal income taxes in 1964. A member of the Carnegie Commission, Joseph H. McConnell, suggested a franchise tax on commercial licensees, which, he said, would probably be passed on to the advertisers, to pay at least part of the cost of public television. But in the report his comment is called a "concurring opinion" and is assigned to a footnote in agate type on page 72. Moreover, the commission may have understated its estimation of the ultimate cost of the proposed public television system for tactical reasons. Burke writes that Hyman Goldin, the commission's staff director, "thought the underestimate was probably made consciously."[3]

MESSAGE ON EDUCATION AND HEALTH

In his Message on Education and Health to Congress on February 28, President Johnson proposed specific measures based on the Carnegie Commission's recommendations, but including educational radio as well. He recommended that Congress provide $9 million in fiscal 1968 as initial funding for the Corporation for Public Broadcasting, saying, "Next year, after careful review, I will make further proposals for the Corporation's long-term financing." However, he warned, "Non-commercial television and radio in America, even though supported by federal funds, must be absolutely free from any federal government interference over programming."

The main reason for Johnson's omitting a plan for long-range, insulated financing, according to Burke based upon an interview with Dean W. Coston, deputy under-secretary of HEW, who was in charge of

drawing up the legislation, was to get the bill through the first session of
the 90th Congress by going to only one committee in each house. "Also
the President himself was against any effort to include long-range financing provisions in the bill initially, feeling that the time was not yet ripe."[4]

The Second National Conference of ETS

The Educational Television Stations division of the NAEB received
a grant in December 1966 from the U.S. Office of Education to hold a
Second National Conference on the Long-Range Financing of Educational Television Stations. The purposes of the meeting were to examine
and respond to the recommendations of the Carnegie Commission and to
make its own recommendations for immediate action. Held on March
5-7, 1967, in Washington, D.C., the conference drew almost 350 participants, most of them chairmen of the boards and managers of the ETS
stations.[5]

The question in everybody's mind was whether the differences between the Carnegie report and the Ford Foundation's satellite proposal
and Comsat's opposition to the Ford proposal would be stumbling
blocks to financial support for ETV. This question was addressed as
quickly as possible by the chief figures. Killian, McCormack, and Bundy
all answered that there was no conflict concerning ends and that differences in means need not be obstructive. James R. Killian, Jr., who had
chaired the Carnegie Commission, said; "In its own way, the Carnegie
Commission sought the same objective as the Ford Foundation; and it
meant what it said in its report that it saw no conflict between the Ford
satellite proposal and the organization and plan presented in the Carnegie report" (p. 41). James McCormack, chairman of the Comsat
board, said: "We can say . . . with propriety and conviction, that both
sets of recommendations are clearly on the right track in commending a
broadly chartered, nonprofit corporation to assist in forwarding the interests of public television" (p. 48). And President McGeorge Bundy
confirmed the Ford Foundation's agreement with the Carnegie Commission's basic proposals, but he predicted: "These things will not end with
this bill. The bill itself is an interim measure, designed to give time for
further study of urgent questions which still have to be resolved. . . . We
in the Ford Foundation expect to be in this business, expect to be concerned with the future of non-commercial television, expect to move towards a greater emphasis upon the needs and upon the understanding of
instructional television" (p. 53).[6]

The proceedings and recommendations of the conference show that it accomplished its two purposes—to give station board members and managers an understanding of the Carnegie report and to achieve a consensus of their approval of and support for the congressional bills that had been introduced because of it. The three points made by individual groups within the conference, however, proposed modification of the Carnegie Commission's recommendations: (1) "It is inappropriate to refer to ETV as 'public' television and leave out of the Corporation title any reference to educational radio; by substituting 'public television' for ETV there is some possible sacrifice of a symbol which has already received wide acceptance and support" (p. 25); (2) "Recruitment and training of more minority group members should be undertaken" (p. 31); and (3) "The distinction between 'Public Television' and 'ITV' is detrimental to public school support of local stations; the totality of educational communications available to a community should be seen as integrated and coordinated" (p. 35).

In supporting the Carnegie Commission report the conferees agreed: "(1) that the recommendations of the Carnegie Commission, in general, should be put into a program of action immediately, and (2) a second commission should be established immediately to study the needs of instructional television and recommend a plan of action for meeting those needs. This commission . . . should be equal to the Carnegie Commission . . . in every way—the stature, . . . the amount of financial underwriting, and Presidential endorsement."[7]

The educational broadcasters found themselves in a delicate position. They wanted what the Carnegie Commission and President Johnson had recommended—a federal act creating a nongovernmental corporation that would receive funds from various sources, public and private, and distribute them for programming without federal control. The bills that were introduced in Congress contained no provision for financing. The educational broadcasters feared that if they made an issue of how the corporation was to be financed they would not get an act creating the corporation. So they evaded the issue. The conference statement said that "actual procedures employed for funding are not important and best left to the wisdom of the Executive Branch and Congress" (p. 5).

THE PUBLIC BROADCASTING ACT OF 1967

Congress quickly passed the Public Broadcasting Act of 1967 because there was little organized opposition to it by the commercial broadcasting interests. Douglass Cater, Johnson's assistant in charge of legislation concerning education, later wrote: "Of all the Johnson legislative initiatives, this one ranked near the bottom in terms of lively interest on Capitol Hill. . . . A potential source of opposition was deliberately avoided: the earmarking of a special tax on TV sets recommended by the Carnegie Commission."[8]

During hearings on the bills, Warren Magnuson, chairman of the Senate Committee on Commerce, and Representative Harley Staggers, chairman of the House Committee on Interstate and Foreign Commerce, favored passage. Key officials in the Department of Health, Education, and Welfare and the Federal Communications Commission testified in behalf of the bills. Educational broadcasters, both television and radio, marshaled an impressive array of proponents. Representatives of all three commercial broadcasting networks supported the bills; President Frank Stanton pledged that CBS would give $1 million to the Corporation for Public Broadcasting when it was established. Leonard Woodcock, vice-president of the United Automobile Workers, who had been a member of the Carnegie Commission, said that his union would give the corporation $25,000.[9]

Because the leaders of the Senate and House committees holding hearings were friendly to the bills and commercial broadcasters did not organize witnesses against them, little of the testimony, questions, and answers touched on the hard issues involved in the proposed legislation, which was the American people's first venture into direct federal support to the content of mass communications.

The testimony and discussions (except for Fred Friendly's) did not come to grips with the valid objections to a proposal that contained no provision for long-range, insulated financing. Nor did they seek to define what the relationship would be between public broadcasting and commercial broadcasting. The only mention of this latter issue was made in *House Report 572*, which said:

> The proponents of this bill, including the presidents of each of the three commercial broadcasting networks, repeatedly emphasized at the hearings that the Corporation will not be in economic competition with commercial broadcasters. It will be filling the gaps that commercial broadcasters do not fill. As Dr. Frank Stanton, president of CBS, observed: "They will do special things that we don't do in quantity at the present time. I would expect that they will appeal at certain times of the day to very small parts of the total audience. Because we are organized as a mass medium, because we have to serve the greatest number of people in order to do our job, they will be able to do special interest kinds of programming that we can't do" (pp. 16–17).

Despite this statement, there would necessarily be competition between public and commercial broadcasting for *audiences*, a competition that the commercial networks might be able to ignore but that would be important to UHF television and FM radio stations. Leonard B. Stevens, the sole witness who opposed the bill before the House committee, on behalf of the All-Channel Television Society stated that "public television programming, federally underwritten and interconnected to give it tremendous appeal and potential, could do irreparable harm to the growing independent UHF stations which, for the time being, are appealing to a smaller share of the audience."[10] At this time almost one-fourth of all UHF TV was reserved for educational stations. The number of commercial UHF stations had dropped to 75 early in the 1960s, then had begun a slow climb to 130 in 1967. That year UHF stations as a group were losing $140 million annually.[11] In this situation the commercial UHF stations were faced with the proposal that ETV stations, which (counting both VHF and UHF stations) already outnumbered them and had 480 reserved channels still to activate, be given substantial federal aid to construct, operate, and interconnect stations, and to produce programs. The Public Broadcasting Act would inevitably be harmful to commercial UHF stations. An argument similar to the one that Stevens made for commercial UHF stations could have been made by commercial FM radio stations. They too were competing for specialized audiences, and as a group they lost money from 1958 through 1967.[12] Surprisingly, no witnesses for commercial FM asked to be heard by either committee.

Ronald Coase, professor of economics, University of Chicago, speculated on why the presidents of the three commercial networks favored the public broadcasting bills. He said that public television would reduce the pressure for pay television and reduce the number of TV channels that would otherwise be commercial, thus raising the value of existing commercial channels. Public television, he said, was

> bound to result in the long run in a much less insistent demand from the intellectual community that the commercial television industry broadcast public service programs and will therefore enable them to concentrate to an even greater extent than they do now on more popular (and more profitable) programs. Indeed, . . . it is very likely that this tendency will be encouraged by those engaged in public television. One of the problems that will be faced by the new federally financed broadcasting system is that its relatively small viewing audience (which it is bound to have if it confines itself to cultural programs, or more generally, those catering to specialized audiences) makes it vulnerable to critics in Congress who will be able to point to how much is being spent for how few and will be able to use this to

threaten the new system's source of funds. There are various ways of blunt-ing such an attack. The one way is to increase the viewing audience by limit-ing the output from the commercial stations of programs competitive with those it transmits (and this is likely to happen, by tacit or even explicit agreement, between those responsible for the two systems, and this not-withstanding any statements which those in charge of the commercial or public television systems may now make.)[13]

Another important issue was whether the existence of a national dual commercial-noncommercial system would improve the overall broadcasting service to the American people. This question was not asked by the witnesses or the members of Congress. It was, however, sensed by the Senate Committee on Commerce. *Senate Report No. 222* contains a reminder: "Your [Senate] committee wishes to make crystal clear that the enactment of this legislation and the growth of noncommercial broad-casting services, will in no way relieve commercial broadcasters of their responsibilities to present public affairs and public service programs, and in general to program their stations in the public interest" (p. 6).

The failure to ask whether the inevitable competition for audiences between public and commercial broadcasting systems would result in bet-ter programming by each was all the more remarkable because a report on the experience of the British people with a dual television system had been available for five years. In 1954 Parliament had established the Inde-pendent Television Authority (ITA) for commercial television to balance the BBC for noncommercial television. In July 1960, the postmaster gen-eral (in charge of all British broadcasting) appointed the Committee on Broadcasting 1960, chaired by Sir Harry Pilkington. The report, com-monly known as the Pilkington report, published on June 5, 1962, de-votes much attention to the reciprocal influences that ITA and BBC had upon one another over a seven-year period. The Pilkington committee reported that many of the British people they had interviewed were con-vinced that the effect of competition was either good and bad mixed or wholly for the worse, and that the range of subject matter presented had not expanded commensurate with the increase in hours of television broadcasting. The committee said that the people interviewed were not criticizing competition as such but competition toward the wrong objec-tives. They believed that where competition had been to improve the techniques and quality of programming, the results had been beneficial but that, where it had been merely to increase the sizes of the audiences, the results had been for the worse.[14]

The U.S. Congress, in deciding to establish a dual commercial-noncommercial broadcasting system, would then pose for the United

States the same question that Great Britain had faced since 1954: how to have the competition between the two components of the system result in higher quality and greater variety in the total programming available.

Purposes and Provisions of the Act

Congress declared: "(1) that it is in the public interest to encourage the growth and development of noncommercial radio and television broadcasting, and (2) that expansion and development of noncommercial radio and television broadcasting and of diversity of its programming depends on freedom, imagination, and initiative on both the local and national levels . . ."

Although both the Senate and the House bills included educational radio in their provisions, the Senate bill included only "public television" in the titles of both the act and the corporation it would create. Both titles, however, were changed to "public broadcasting" during the Senate hearings. The change was occasioned by the good impression that Jerrold Sandler, executive secretary of National Educational Radio, made, presenting the findings of the just completed *The Hidden Medium: A Status Report on Educational Radio in the United States.* The Senate hearings were being broadcast live by educational radio throughout the Northeastern United States and edited copies sent to all NER stations throughout the country, and this fact also called the importance of educational radio to the attention of the Senate committee.

The Public Broadcasting Act had three parts: the construction of stations; the establishment of a nonprofit educational corporation; and a study of educational and instructional broadcasting. The Senate report of the hearings made clear that the central part of the act was the establishment of the corporation to deal with programming because, it said, the station facilities must have something to offer, and the results of the study should become "important secondary benefits" of the legislation.

Title I—Construction of Facilities

The first part of the act was an "extension of duration of construction grants for educational broadcasting." The previous appropriations (for ETV stations only) were used up, there was a large backlog of applications, and the authorization would expire on June 30, 1967. The 1967 act authorized $10.5 million for fiscal year 1968, $12.5 million for 1969, and $15 million for 1970. The increase was only modest, considering that radio was included and that Title II would stimulate communities to activate stations and thus request aid for construction. Other major changes, in addition to the inclusion of radio, were: (1) to provide a more flexible formula for grants to states (no more than 8.5 percent of the total to any one, instead of a flat ceiling of $1 million); (2) to increase matching federal aid to 75 percent (instead of 50 percent); (3) to eliminate a limit of 15 percent of each grant for interconnection; (4) to include the Virgin Islands, Guam, American Samoa, and the Trust Territories of the Pacific as political units eligible for the grants; and (5) to permit the use of federal aid for planning interconnection. The elimination of the 15 percent limit on grants for interconnection and the permission to use federal money for planning interconnection aimed at the development of intrastate and regional interconnection of both ETV and educational radio stations.

Title II—Establishment of Nonprofit Educational Corporation

This part authorized the establishment of the nonprofit Corporation for Public Broadcasting, "which will not be an agency or establishment of the United States Government." Whether the corporation would in fact "not be an agency or establishment" of the federal government would depend primarily upon four key provisions—those concerning the appointment of the board of directors, the financing, programming, and interconnection. In the first three of these respects the act failed to establish an independent corporation, and in the fourth its provision later resulted in sharp conflict between the corporation and the stations.

Concerning the board, the Carnegie Commission had recommended twelve directors, six to be appointed by the President with the concurrence of the Senate and the other six elected by those previously appointed. The original Senate bill proposed a board of fifteen directors, nine appointed by the President, the other six elected by those previously appointed. But the House bill, which prevailed, provided for a board of fifteen, all to be appointed by the President with the concurrence of the Senate, and not more than eight members of the same political party. Thus Congress politicized the board.[15]

The Carnegie Commission had recommended that an excise tax on television sets provide the corporation with public money placed in an insulated trust fund. The act, however, provided for no such sources of public financing independent of and insulated from Congress. Instead, it authorized the corporation "to obtain grants from and to make contracts with individuals and with private, State, and Federal agencies, organizations, and institutions," and it authorized, but did not appropriate, $9 million for the expenses of the corporation for fiscal 1968.

Programming. There are two main issues concerning programming. One is its purposes, the other is restraints upon it.

The act defines educational radio and television programs as those "which are primarily designed for educational and cultural purposes." The House bill contained the additional phrase "and not primarily for amusement or entertainment purposes," but the conference committee eliminated it.

Another provision of the act imposes limits upon the programming that it authorizes the corporation to help develop. There must be "strict adherence to objectivity and balance in all programs or series of programs of a controversial nature." This requirement raises several important questions. One is whether the requirement is the same as or different from the Fairness Doctrine, which the FCC worked out to guide licensees in planning programming on "controversial issues of public importance." If it is the same as the Fairness Doctrine, the requirement would seem to be unnecessary. If it is different from the Fairness Doctrine it gives no guidelines concerning where the responsibility for judging objectivity and balance lies—with the licensee (who must periodically apply to the FCC for license renewal), with the FCC, with the corporation, or with Congress. Moreover, the phrase "in all programs or series of programs" is ambiguous concerning whether it means each *program* or each *series of* programs. A series, of course, can be extended as a result of controversial reaction to a particular program in order to balance the series. The House committee inserted the words "or series of programs" during hearings on the bill to make the requirement more flexible, but issues have arisen that expose both the ambiguity concerning meaning and the ambiguity concerning who is to judge.[16]

A deeper question is raised by Section 399 of the act, which the conference committee inserted. It reads: "No noncommercial broadcasting station may engage in editorializing or may support or oppose any candidate for political office." The phrase "no noncommercial station" applies even to a noncommercial station not receiving federal funds under the act. Most constitutional lawyers agree that the section violates the First Amendment of the Constitution because it imposes prior restraint.[17]

The issue of editorializing goes back to the 1940 Mayflower case. In that ruling the FCC held that "a truly free radio cannot be used to advocate the causes of the licensee." To see that the ruling denies broadcasters the protection of the First Amendment one needs only to change two words, having it read, "A truly free press cannot be used to advocate the causes of the publisher." Some commercial broadcasters protested the ruling at the time, but the industry did not fight it. Not one commercial broadcaster challenged the Mayflower ruling in the courts between 1940 and 1949, when the FCC reversed itself. In the ruling *In the Matter of Editorializing by Broadcast Licensees*, the Commission said that all broadcast stations could editorialize as long as they made available their facilities for the expression of other points of view. Since 1949 the FCC has seemed at times actually to encourage editorializing and the subsequent debate it stimulates. Few commercial stations editorialized at first; however, an increasing number are now doing so, and with more vigor, providing opportunities for responses.

Against this long history there is the short, silent history of Section 399. The proponents of the Public Broadcasting Act of 1967, with a few exceptions, did not object to its inclusion. No noncommercial educational broadcaster has challenged it in the courts. One can concede the propriety and constitutionality of a ban against stations supported in part by public funds endorsing or opposing candidates for political office. One can even make a good case against editorializing.[18] But it is difficult to make a case for a double standard—First Amendment privileges for commercial broadcasters, who are in business to make a profit, and the denial of First Amendment privileges to noncommercial broadcasters, whose purpose is to serve the public interest. Yet noncommercial broadcasters have accepted the double standard. The question is: who is being protected by the prohibition against editorializing? Citing the remarks of seven proponents of the prohibition, documented in the *Congressional Record* for Thursday, September 1, 1967, Toohey concludes: "At least for these gentlemen, the purpose of Section 399 was clear: to prevent Congress from creating a monster that might turn on its creator. Therefore, to achieve its own self-protective ends Congress simply legislated away a significant part of educational broadcasters' right of free speech."[19]

Interconnection. Another important issue concerning programming is who makes the decisions concerning which programs are sent over interconnection. The act denies the corporation the power to "own or operate any television or radio broadcast station, system, or network, community antenna television system, or interconnection or program production facility." Short of this, however, the corporation's powers are very broad. It may "assist in the establishment and development of one or more systems of interconnection to be used for the distribution of educational television or radio programs so that all noncommercial educational television or radio broadcast stations that wish to may broadcast the programs at times chosen by the stations [and] assist in the establishment and development of one or more systems of noncommercial educational television or radio broadcast stations throughout the United States."

The representatives of the Carnegie Commission, the National Association of Educational Broadcasters, and National Educational Television—James R. Killian, Jr., William Harley, and Everett Case, respectively—disagreed on how the implementing paragraph of the section on interconnection should be worded. Nicholas Zapple, counsel for the Senate committee, told them they would have to resolve their differences. The core of the agreement they reached, which was included in the law, was that the responsibility for interconnection should rest with the corporation but that it could exercise that responsibility in several ways, such as appointing an advisory committee, making contractual agreements, or forming a new organization.[20] Thus the act gives the corporation ultimate responsibility for interconnection, but the drafters foresaw the possibilities of conflict between the corporation, the stations, and the producers, and sought to avoid them.

Title III—Study of Educational and Instructional Broadcasting

This part authorized the secretary of HEW to conduct, directly or by contract, "a comprehensive study of instructional television and radio . . . and their relationships to each other and other materials . . . as may be of assistance in determining whether and what Federal aid should be provided for instructional radio and television and the form that aid should take." The study was to be submitted to the President for transmittal to the Congress on or before June 30, 1970. An appropriation of up to $500,000 was authorized.[21]

CLIMAX AND ANTICLIMAX

On November 7, 1967, President Johnson proudly signed the Public Broadcasting Act. However, there were a disappointment and a setback, according to Douglass Cater:

> The President had hoped to use the euphoria of the signing ceremony to announce that the new Corporation for Public Broadcasting would be chaired by Milton Eisenhower, brother of the former President, who would be the nonpartisan centerpiece around which the system could grow in wisdom and strength. But Dr. Eisenhower felt obliged to turn down the chairmanship. This led to a long delay in choosing a head for the Board as well

as other members. It led me to realize the paucity of prominent citizens interested in broadcasting who had enough political savvy to direct this sensitive public enterprise."[22]

On November 17, Defense Secretary Robert S. McNamara disclosed for the first time that the cost of the war in Vietnam that year would be $20 billion instead of the $10 billion that had been estimated in January. President Johnson pointed to the danger that the deficit for 1968 might go as high as $25 billion if tax rates were not raised. Federal Reserve Chairman William McChesney Martin asserted that a sharp spending curb and a steep tax rise were needed to avoid "self-destroying" inflation, pointing out that the U.S. debt was increasing faster than the GNP. He concluded that the country could not continue to wage war in Vietnam and at the same time support all current domestic programs. For this reason President Johnson did not come forth with the plan for long-range, insulated financing for public broadcasting he had promised, and instead he recommended in 1968 an appropriation of only $4 million for the Corporation for Public Broadcasting.

The Public Broadcasting Act of 1967, said Representative Harley O. Staggers, chairman of the Committee on Interstate and Foreign Commerce, could be as important as the Morrill Act of 1862, which granted public lands to help establish a new type of college. The history of the land-grant college movement reveals that it succeeded not because of the land grants (which were wasted) but because it embodied in a new type of social institution "an idea whose time had come." The money that Congress might appropriate would be far more important for public broadcasting than the land grants had been for a new type of college in 1862. But the reality was that in 1967 there was *no* money. A vaguely defined idea had been embodied in half an act—one not providing for long-range, insulated financing but containing serious contradictions and ambiguities. Educational broadcasting, newly named public broadcasting, faced at least a decade of struggle—within the federal government, of course, but also within its own establishment, and, most critical of all, within the American society. It was challenged to demonstrate to the American people that it could perform an indispensable and unique public service.

1968–1978 AND PROSPECTS

Wᴵᴛʜᴵɴ the structure of the Public Broadcasting Act of 1967, which provided federal funds and leadership, both public television and public radio grew enormously during the decade. As was the intent both of the legislators and the local stations, nonfederal financial support increased so that not until the end of the decade did federal finances approach 30 percent of the system's total income, and matching provisions would keep federal funds secondary. Partly because of inadequacies and ambiguities of the 1967 act and partly because of evolution within the public broadcasting system, major points of friction developed that at times seemed to threaten the existence of public broadcasting. However, the dissensions were always allayed, although not removed.

At the end of the decade four new developments were under way that held the opportunity to raise public broadcasting to a new level of importance and effectiveness. These developments were: (1) the introduction of a program delivery system by communications satellites; (2) the appointment of the Carnegie Commission on the Future of Public Broadcasting (commonly called Carnegie Commission II), whose report was scheduled for early 1979; (3) the 1978 Public Telecommunications Act; and (4) revision of the Communications Act of 1934 proposed by the House Subcommittee on Communications. At the end of its first decade, public broadcasting had more of everything than it had ever had before. At the same time it faced more crucial issues than ever before. Probably the most far-reaching issue would be how public broadcasting would adapt to new communications technologies. Historically, public broadcasting was a response to the inadequacies of commercial broadcasting, particularly television. At the close of the 1970s many new technological advances seemed likely to reshape both commercial and noncommercial broadcasting right down to their end-products, which are all the ways the public receives and will be able to receive telecommunications.

THE GROWTH OF THE SYSTEM

The growth of public broadcasting since the passage of the Public Broadcasting Act of 1967 is indicated by some of the latest key statistics available in mid-1978.[1] In 1967 some 125 educational television stations reached slightly more than 6 million homes a week. Viewership unevenly represented the higher income and better educated population. The average ETV station had an annual budget of about $360,000, and total income of the entire system was near $58 million. Contributions from viewers were slightly more than $5 million a year.

In 1967 most of the 296 educational FM radio stations had an annual budget of less than $25,000. Nearly half were low-powered 10-watt stations, and fewer than seventy-five of the 296 stations provided more than limited service for the general public. These stations had no means of regular live interconnection.

By 1978 the number of public television stations had increased to 276, reaching more than 30 million homes a week. Viewership was nearly evenly representative of the American population as a whole. The average public television station's annual budget was $1.9 million, and it was broadcasting eighty-one hours of programs weekly. Total income for the entire ETV system in 1976 was $333 million. Contributions from viewers were $32 million in 1977.

By 1978 there were 200 public radio stations qualified by the Corporation for Public Broadcasting (with qualifications dependent upon minimum criteria with regard to staff, facilities, programming, power, and hours of operation). The typical qualified public radio station had an annual budget of $226,000 and was broadcasting 131 hours of programs weekly. Public radio reached more than 4.3 million people each week, who were nearly representative of the population as a whole.

Concerning the public broadcasting system as a whole, "By 1977, voluntary viewer-listener support exceeded $40 million while income from all sources reached $450 million. . . . Sophisticated national interconnection systems were in operation—both the Public Broadcasting Service (PBS) and National Public Radio (NPR) were distributing nearly

2,000 hours of programs in 1976. Regional and state networks had developed and public broadcasting was about to embark on an even more ambitious and versatile national interconnection by communications satellites."[2]

This growth, however, had absorbed most of the money of the public broadcasting system, leaving the stations and their organizations little margin for making long-range plans or for implementing them. In fact, Stephen White, who was assistant to the chairman of the 1966 Carnegie Commission on Educational Television, wrote in mid-1977: "The system is now more starved for funds than it was in 1967, simply because in a decade it has generated a clearer vision of what it might and must do."[3]

The constant struggle for money and for freedom to use it as the stations wanted to was made more difficult by contentions within the public broadcasting system, which gave Congress incentive to impose detailed restrictions on the use of the funds it appropriates.

THE ORIGINS OF DISSENSIONS

The root cause of contentions within the public broadcasting system is that Congress authorized the establishment of the Corporation for Public Broadcasting, "which will not be an agency or establishment of the United States Government," but has not provided it with the adequate, long-range, insulated financial support that would enable it not to be an agency or establishment of the government. Thus from the beginning there has been a contradiction within Congress' mandate for the corporation "to facilitate the development of educational broadcasting and to afford maximum protection to such broadcasting from extraneous interference and control." The directors of the corporation are appointed by the President and approved by the Senate, with not more than eight of its fifteen members from the same political party, just like any other political governmental agency. Dependent upon the President for appointments and recommended legislation and upon Congress for appropriations, the CPB regards itself and the public broadcasting system as a creature of government. The corporation is prohibited by law from owning or operating "any television or radio broadcast station, system, or network, community antenna television system, or interconnection or program production facility," but it has wide powers to finance program production and to arrange for interconnection facilities.

To arrange interconnection, the Corporation for Public Broadcasting established two entities—the Public Broadcasting Service (PBS, founded in 1969 and operating in 1970) and National Public Radio (NPR, founded in 1970 and operating in 1971). Both were directed by station managers elected by the stations and a few other directors. Now, the management of interconnection can be interpreted narrowly as merely the administration of a distribution system, or it can be interpreted broadly as involving also decision-making concerning which programs are to be distributed and the scheduling of the programs distributed. The differences between these two interpretations sparked the first disagreement between CPB and PBS, with CPB making the narrow interpretation and PBS the broader. (The disagreements between CPB and NPR had never been major, except for the apportionment of money between public television and public radio, because CPB regards radio as less dangerous and it involves much less money than television, and public radio stations are less dependent upon and more flexible in their handling of nationally distributed programs; therefore this discussion will focus on the disputes between CPB and PBS.)

The CPB-PBS dispute began soon after interconnection was operating in 1970. CPB objected to the PBS decision to distribute "off schedule" programs that had been judged unacceptable for the regular program schedule. Negotiations between CPB President John Macy and PBS President Hartford Gunn, Jr., to redefine the respective program decision-making responsibilities of CPB and PBS soon became entoiled in the attack by the Nixon Administration, spearheaded by Clay Whitehead, director of the White House-based Office of Telecommunications Policy, ostensibly against "fourth-network centralization" but actually against interconnected public affairs programming. Soon the localized friction developed into a general battle over basic principles. Some members of CPB took the extreme position that CPB could abolish PBS, which it had founded, and some members of PBS took the extreme position that PBS, as the voice of the nation's public television licensees, was an independent agency properly responsible for all programming decisions, and that CPB was merely a federal funding agency, comparable to a foundation except that it had public instead of private money.

In fact, the legal situation is ambiguous. Congress established the CPB as a "private corporation" but did not permit it to become private. Congress established the CPB to facilitate the development of educational television and radio and "to afford it maximum protection from extraneous interference and control" and did not provide such protection. The Corporation for Public Broadcasting is the only agency mandated by the Act, yet the Act implies the need for other agencies in order to handle interconnection. The other agencies created for this purpose are also the legally constituted representatives of the stations, which are responsible to the Federal Communications Commission and to their communities by authority of the Communications Act of 1934, which stresses the independence of the licensed stations, and which is the governing law of which the Public Broadcasting Act of 1967 is an amendment.

Because the Public Broadcasting Service was able to marshal political influence through the governing boards of the licensed stations and because President Nixon was driven from office, an uneasy detente has been established between the CPB and PBS (mainly because of the need to present an apparently united front before Congress when seeking funds). But the differences are probably irreconcilable. This was illustrated by the only statement of mission, goals, tasks, and responsibilities that the CPB has issued—on November 10, 1976, well after the most heated disputes had been papered over.[4] In that statement the board asserts its broad responsibilities for programming and makes no explicit reference to any agency in public broadcasting except itself. In the first of its brief two-paragraph statement of mission the CPB, referring only to its mission to lead in developing public broadcasting, omits the mission "to afford maximum protection to such broadcasting from extraneous interference and control." In the second paragraph the corporation, referring only to its authority as deriving from Congress, omits reference to the stations' authority deriving from the FCC under the Communications Act of 1934.

Looking at the history of the frictions between the ETV stations and the ETRC-NETRC-NET centers of national programming between 1954 and 1967, considering the fierce sense of autonomy and the diverse natures of the ETV stations, and assuming inevitable evolutions of the components of the public broadcasting system during a decade of enormous growth and many changes, one would expect many points of friction. But there is an important difference between, on the one hand, tensions that are inherent and potentially healthful in a diverse system decentralized in some respects and centralized in others, and, on the other hand, bitter dissensions that threaten dissolution, waste scarce recourses, and invite or even compel other parties to intervene.

Against this summary of the growth of public broadcasting and this diagnosis of the causes of internal dissension during the decade, let us follow the history in some detail. Events can be conveniently divided into four periods; (1) from 1968 through 1972; (2) from 1973 to the passage of the Public Broadcasting Financing Act of 1975; (3) 1976 and 1977; and (4) 1978.

OVERVIEW: 1968–72

Although the events of the decade 1968–78 may for convenience be divided into periods, the factor that influenced most of them was the amount of federal money available to the Corporation for Public Broadcasting. Therefore, it may be useful at the outset to give an overview of the federal funding.

The Carnegie Commission had recommended that federal funds come from a manufacturer's tax on television sets made available to the corporation through a trust fund.

> Shortly after the creation of the Corporation for Public Broadcasting, a meeting was held at the White House office of Douglass Cater, then special assistant to President Johnson. Meeting with Cater were Stanley S. Surrey, assistant secretary of the treasury; Frank Pace, Jr., Chairman of the CPB board; Ward Chamberlain, vice president and general manager of CPB; and Joseph D. Hughes, a member of the CPB board. Mr. Surrey quickly advanced the Treasury Department's traditional position of opposing dedicated taxes, which probably could have been overcome with President Johnson's assistance. However, shortly thereafter, Wilbur Mills, then chairman of the House Ways and Means Committee, announced that such a bill would not clear his committee. The proposal was dropped, and planning turned instead to direct federal funding; and public broadcasting found itself on the annual appropriation treadmill.[5]

The Carnegie Commission had concluded that the Corporation for Public Broadcasting would require from the federal government $40 million its first year, $60 million for each of the next three years, building up to $104 million a year when the system reached an equilibrium after perhaps ten years.[6] Table 8.1 is a summary of congressional authorizations and appropriations for the CPB for the first twelve fiscal years. Figures are in millions of dollars. It will be noted that, except for 1972 and 1977, appropriations have been substantially less than authorizations. Moreover, as will be explained later, the appropriations after 1975 are to be received only after being matched in advance at a ratio of $1 of federal funds to $2.50 raised from nonfederal sources.

Table 8.1

**CONGRESSIONAL AUTHORIZATIONS and APPROPRIATIONS
for the CPB, 1969–1980**

(In Millions of Dollars)

Fiscal Year	Authorization	Appropriation
1969	9	5.0
1970	20	15.0
1971	35	23.0
1972	35	35.0
1973	45	35.0
1974	55	47.5
1975	65	62.0
1976	110	87.5
1977	103	103.0
1978	121	107.2 (plus 12)
1979	140	120.2 (plus 19)
1980	160	152.0 (conditional)

SOURCE: Joseph D. Hughes, "Heat Shield or Crucible? A Blueprint for Carnegie II," *Public Telecommunications Review* (November/December 1977):30. The information in parentheses is from other sources. Congress appropriated another $12 million for 1978 because the system in 1976 raised from nonfederal sources an amount exceeding the minimum necessary for the full appropriation. The CPB has requested another $19 million for 1979 because the system in 1977 exceeded the minimum. The amount appropriated for 1980 is conditional (under the ceiling of authorization) upon the amount the system raises from nonfederal sources in 1978.

Table 8.2 is a summary of Congress' authorizations and appropriations for educational broadcasting facilities. The figures are in millions of dollars. Again, except for the 1963–67 period, appropriations have been substantially less than authorizations, and the facilities grants are made on a matching basis, with a limit of 75 percent for the federal share.

The Educational Broadcasting Facilities Program (EBFP) has been a key instrument in the development of public broadcasting. According to internal NAEB fact sheets, between 1962 and early 1978, 729 grants totalling $132 million have been made in all fifty states, the District of Columbia, Guam, the Virgin Islands, American Samoa, and Puerto Rico. EBFP has funded nearly 80 percent of the full-service public television and radio stations in the nation. Since the beginning of the program in 1962, the number of public television stations has increased from 76 to more than 273. A total of 164 of these stations have been activated with

Table 8.2

CONGRESSIONAL AUTHORIZATIONS and APPROPRIATIONS for EDUCATIONAL BROADCASTING FACILITIES, 1963–1980

(In Millions of Dollars)

Fiscal Year	Authorization	Appropriation
1963	32.0	1.500
1964		6.500
1965		13.000
1966		8.826
1967		3.304
1968	10.5	0.000
1969	12.5	4.375
1970	15.0	5.083
1971	15.0	11.000
1972	15.0	13.000
1973	25.0	13.000
1974	25.0	16.500
1975	30.0	12.000
1976	30.0	12.500
1977	30.0	15.000
1978	30.0	19.000

SOURCE: National Association of Educational Broadcasters, internal fact sheet, "Educational Broadcasting Facilities Program." From 1963 to 1967 the money was for educational television facilities only. Grants for radio facilities were included in the Public Broadcasting Act of 1967. No funds for facilities were requested for fiscal 1968 because of delay in authorizing the appropriation for the 1967 act. The appropriations for fiscal 1977 and 1978 each included $1 million for the Telecommunications Demonstration Grant program, whose goal is to develop new applications of nonbroadcast technology.

aid from EBFP funds, and an additional 330 grants have enabled stations to expand. When radio stations became eligible for facilities grants in 1967, only 67 of the more than 400 noncommercial educational radio stations on the air were capable of providing full service to their communities. As of February 1978, 197 "full-service" public radio stations met the standards set by the CPB. EBFP funds helped activate 72 public radio stations, and 163 additional grants have upgraded nearly 130 stations to full-service capability.

Beyond fostering growth, EBFP has to a large extent shaped public broadcasting. There is no comprehensive nationwide planning for public telecommunications in the United States, and many states and communities have no arrangements for planning. Therefore, the grant-making decisions of EBFP have provided the necessary direction for the television and radio system development.

Moreover, EBFP has vitally influenced public broadcasting in several other ways. For example, every EBFP dollar has stimulated more than $11 in state, local, and private funds, and the technical standards that the EBFP staff set for grant eligibility ultimately affect the entire public broadcasting community, from station managers to the manufacturers of transmission equipment.

From the beginning in 1962 through 1978, the Educational Broadcasting Facilities Program was administered by the Office of Education, Department of Health, Education, and Welfare. However, the 1978 Public Telecommunications Financing Act transferred responsibility (and EBFP staff) to the Department of Commerce (except for the Telecommunications Demonstration Program).

The Formative Years

With this overview, let us look at particular years. In his January 1968 budget message to Congress President Johnson recommended appropriation of only $4 million for the Corporation for Public Broadcasting, less than half the $9 million authorized in the original act. Neither then nor in his February message on education did he offer a plan for long-range financing of the corporation. Thus the founding of the CPB was delayed. Congress, however, appropriated $9 million, with the catch that for fiscal 1969 the corporation would receive not more than $5 million in federal funds.

In February 1968, the President appointed the CPB board of fifteen directors, with Frank Pace, former secretary of the Army, as chairman. The existence of the board qualified the CPB for more than $1 million in private funds that had been pledged to it ($1 million from CBS and $25,000 from the United Automobile Workers). Thus during the spring of 1968 the corporation was able to search for staff and quarters. Not until February 1969 was the president of the corporation named— John W. Macy, Jr., former director of the U.S. Civil Service Commission. Meantime the CPB had formed a skeletal staff, and with the receipt of nearly $5 million in July 1968, it began to plan program grants and interconnection. During this period the greater share of the support for programming and interconnection for the public television system was still being borne by the Ford Foundation, mostly through grants to National Educational Television (NET) and the Public Broadcast Laboratory, which was loosely attached to NET.

In January 1969, the CPB announced that it would oversee a six-month trial interconnection among most of the public television stations in the country, taking advantage of special reduced rates which the CPB and the FCC had worked out with AT&T. NET was to run the operation in cooperation with an Interim Interconnection Group, which was a preliminary mechanism for the permanent interconnection arrangement that CPB was planning. In April 1969, the Ford Foundation and the Corporation for Public Broadcasting made a joint statement in effect signaling that the foundation was yielding leadership to the corporation. The CPB announced that it intended to create the Public Broadcasting Service, which would take over responsibility for interconnection from NET; the foundation announced that it would end support of the Public Broadcast Laboratory in the spring of 1969.

In the meantime, before leaving office in January 1969, President Johnson recommended authorization of $20 million for the CPB for fiscal 1970. In February the new President, Richard Nixon, recommended only $10 million. Not until March 1970 did the White House and Congress agree upon a compromise appropriation of $15 million for fiscal 1970. In September 1970, the White House and Congress agreed upon an authorization of $35 million for the CPB for fiscal years 1971 and 1972. In fact, appropriations for those years were $23 million and $35 million.

The Founding of PBS

The Public Broadcasting Act of 1967 clearly called for the CPB to arrange for some agency other than itself to handle interconnection. The Ford Foundation ended its support to NET in its networking role. The CPB established the Public Broadcasting Service in November 1969, to select and distribute television programming among all public television stations. PBS was not to produce programs but was to help CPB and the Ford Foundation develop among the major production centers suitable programs which PBS would distribute by interconnection. For the PBS board the membership of the Educational Television Stations division of the NAEB was to elect five directors from among the station managers. The presidents of CPB and NET also were to be members, and these seven were to elect two other members from the public.

The title was not Public Broadcasting *Network* but Public Broadcasting *Service,* connoting work done for the stations, which had freedom to accept or reject the programs distributed. (The word *broadcasting* in the title was chosen instead of *television* because at that time no decision had been made on how to arrange distribution for public radio stations.) The title, the composition of the PBS board, and the definition of its functions were the product of a year's negotiations controlled by the CPB with the support of the Ford Foundation. It "resulted in confusion over PBS' origin, role, and position in public television—was it a CPB subsidiary or was it a station organization? . . . The confusion . . . resulted in a situation virtually guaranteeing subsequent changes in the internal structure and external relationships."[7] This documented judgment does not diminish the major accomplishment of the negotiators. They had to make a workable arrangement under pressure of time in an ambiguous legal framework. They had to compromise sharp disagreements inherited from the 1954–67 period, and they were dealing with a new, unstabilized institution.

In February 1970, the PBS board chose as president Hartford Gunn, Jr., who had been general manager of WGBH TV and FM, Boston, and founder and president of the Eastern Educational Television Network. PBS immediately took over the interconnection responsibilities and began preparing a schedule of evening programming for the fall of 1970. Most of the PBS funds would come directly from the CPB, although the Ford Foundation granted $1.2 million at the outset.

The Founding of NPR

The Corporation for Public Broadcasting was required by law to arrange for radio interconnections also. In August 1969, the NAEB proposed that the CPB create an independent national radio production and distribution agency to be known as National Public Radio (NPR). In February 1970, CPB incorporated NPR, which was to distribute programs to its member stations and, unlike PBS, was to produce programs itself as well as acquire them from other sources, particularly member stations. NPR was funded by CPB. The NPR board consists of twenty-five persons, twelve elected by the member stations, twelve selected by these from the general public, and the NPR president. The first president was Donald N. Quayle, former executive director of the Eastern Educational Television Network. NPR began the regular transmission of programs in May 1971, with its continuing news-magazine format series "All Things Considered" and a special full-length coverage of the Senate Foreign Relations Committee hearings on American involvement in Vietnam.

The Continuing Role of the Ford Foundation

Although the Ford Foundation had yielded leadership to CPB, between 1968 and 1972 inclusive, it made more than $90 million of grants and expenditures for public television, compared to Congress' appropriations for the CPB of $78 million in the same period for both television and radio.[8] The foundation's support, in cooperation with CPB and other agencies, was for three objectives: to help establish interconnection; to help develop important television production centers for national programming; and to increase audience support and conduct research into public television viewing so as to build audiences that would contribute money to the television stations. The foundation granted $1.6 million to cover some of the costs of early interconnection. It made program grants primarily to five station-based production centers—in San Francisco, Los Angeles, Boston, New York, and Washington, D.C.—and also to the Children's Television Workshop. Aspects of the grants to these last three production centers deserve special comment.

Before 1970 National Educational Television (NET), in New York City, had no studio, and the New York City-based public television station, WNDT, VHF Channel 13, had no production facilities beyond those it needed for local programming. The Ford Foundation aided the officials of NET and WNDT who wanted to combine the two agencies to do so. In June 1970, the boards of directors of the two agencies were merged; the new organization took WNDT's corporate name, the Educational Broadcasting Corporation (EBC); James Day, former station manager of San Francisco's KQED, replaced both John White, who had been NET president, and J. W. Kiermaier, who had been general manager of WNDT; and EBC established two divisions—the national production center, still to be known as NET, and the station, which changed its call letters to WNET.

WETA, Channel 26, as the public television station in the nation's capital, had a special responsibility to report on national government affairs for the stations in the public television system, but it had no production facilities beyond those for local programming. In 1972 a special National Public Affairs Center for Television (NPACT) was created to handle the coverage of national public affairs, notably with a continuing "Washington Week in Review." In 1973 WETA and NPACT merged their boards of directors. (In 1973 NPACT produced fifty-one days of gavel-to-gavel coverage of the Senate Select Committee on Presidential Campaign Activities—the Watergate hearings.)

The Carnegie Foundation took the lead in developing "Sesame Street." The way to "Sesame Street" began in early 1966 when Lloyd Morrisett, then vice-president of the Carnegie Corporation, which was interested in preschool research, asked Joan Cooney, a producer for WNDT/13, New York, to study the potential of preschool education through television. Cooney presented her report in November of that year, and Morrisett, who later became president of the John and Mary Markle Foundation, sought funds to implement Cooney's recommendations. In 1968 the corporate body that was formed, the Children's Television Workshop (CTW), loosely attached to National Educational Television (NET), with Cooney as president and Morrisett as board chairman, received $250,000 from the Ford Foundation for planning, and in 1969 $1 million for preproduction costs. For the expenses of full production, CTW was given a two-year grant of $8 million jointly from the Carnegie Corporation, the Ford Foundation, the Markle Foundation, Operation Head Start, and the U.S. Office of Education. "Sesame Street" ended its first season over public television on May 29, 1970. The first twenty-six week series was preceded by a year of research into preschoolers' learning and television-viewing habits and also extensive testing of program segments. "Sesame Street" was distributed by PBS, and by 1970 CTW had emerged as an independent national production center for children's programming. In 1970, 1971, and 1972 the Ford Foundation made grants totaling $5 million directly to CTW to continue production of "Sesame Street" and to develop and produce "The Electric Company," a more advanced series to teach reading skills. From the beginning these two program series have accounted for a large fraction of the public television audience. It is significant that they were produced, not as television programs, but as efforts to aid learning by children, and that they came *to,* not *from* public television.[9]

In our chronicle we come now to the momentous year 1972. Before we consider the events that centered around public television, it may be useful to consider the development of public radio, which was involved in the subsequent events only to the extent that was necessary because it was a part of the public broadcasting system.

Public Radio

CPB has treated public radio differently from the way it has treated public television. One reason is that a plan for developing public television was proposed in the Carnegie Commission report, whereas the Land report, *The Hidden Medium: Educational Radio,* while it persuaded Congress to include radio in the titles of the Public Broadcasting Act of 1967, did not propose a scheme for developing noncommercial radio by federal funds. In 1969 the Ford Foundation and the CPB commissioned the Holt study of educational radio.[10] At the time 384 noncommercial FM stations were broadcasting on reserved channels, mostly with low power, over half being 10-watters. The study reported that as a group the stations lacked a consistent concept of their proper role or identity; that more than half operated on an annual budget of less than $10,000; that only about half were members of the National Educational Radio Network of the NAEB and hence could not participate at the national level; and that the proliferation of low-power stations had made it physically impossible in some areas to introduce more powerful stations able to offer wide-area services to the public.

The corporation concluded that, whereas it could build a public television system on the established base of educational television stations, it was necessary to lay the base for a public radio system. Accordingly, in 1970, after establishing National Public Radio, a licensee-controlled production and distribution service, the CPB adopted the "Policy of Public Radio Assistance," which set criteria for grants to individual stations and outlined a five-year development plan, providing specified levels of grants to those stations that could meet the minimum criteria, including standards of power, equipment, staff, hours, and community service. The number of CPB-qualified radio stations increased from 91 in fiscal 1970, to 144 in fiscal 1973.

Noncommercial educational radio stations were much less fearful of being dominated by the White House, Congress, the CPB, or their national interconnection than were noncommercial educational television stations. All the television stations were members of the Public Broadcasting Service and were heavily dependent upon the programs distributed by interconnection or mail. Only a minority of the radio stations were members of National Public Radio, and these were less dependent upon the programs and more flexible in the scheduling of the national distribution system. Moreover, because radio required much less money and was regarded as less powerful than television, the White House, Congress, and the CPB did not subject the radio stations to comparable pressures.

Nixon's Veto and CPB Appointments

The Nixon Administration's specific attack upon public broadcasting began with the speech Clay Whitehead, director of the Office of Telecommunications Policy (OTP), made to the National Association of Educational Broadcasters at their convention in Miami on October 20, 1971. That speech, however, was only a salient in the White House's deliberate assault upon the media of mass communications that had begun well before the establishment of the OTP in the Executive Office of the Presidency in 1970.[11] In that speech Whitehead skillfully exploited the television station managers' inveterate suspicions of national broadcasting agencies by accusing public television of departing from the Carnegie Commission's stress on localism and pursuing a goal of being a national network similar to the commercial networks. To this charge Stephen White, who had been assistant to the chairman of the Carnegie Commission, later replied that the debate of local vs. national "is a strawman and was never anything else. . . . The system absolutely requires both."[12]

On June 22, 1972, Congress sent to the White House a bill authorizing an appropriation for the CPB of $155 million for two years ($65 million for 1973, and $90 million for 1974). On June 30, Nixon vetoed the bill on the grounds that "an organization, originally intended to serve the local stations, is becoming instead the center of power and the focal point of control for the entire public broadcasting system." He asked Congress to enact a one-year extension of the corporation's authorization and to provide it with $45 million. Congress did not override the veto.

Nixon's veto of a bill designed to bring CPB funding to a level approaching that recommended by the Carnegie Commission threw public broadcasting into turmoil. All planning based on the assumption of the higher appropriations for two years had to be abandoned. The components of the system had to scramble desperately to receive supplementary funds during fiscal 1973 at the $35 million level it had received in fiscal 1972.

In addition to this veto, President Nixon exerted his power over public broadcasting by appointments to the CPB board during the summer of 1972. The terms of five directors expired in June, and there was one vacancy to fill. With two reappointments (one of which was Joseph D. Hughes) and three new appointments added to the six he had previously made, Nixon had named eleven of the fifteen directors.

Repercussions within CPB

After the veto, Frank Pace, CPB chairman since the inception, resigned as chairman but stayed on the board. On August 10, John W. Macy, Jr., resigned as CPB president. Nixon filled the vacancy on the CPB board by naming Thomas B. Curtis, former Republican congressman from St. Louis, to the board, expressing his preference that Curtis succeed Pace as chairman. The board dutifully elected Curtis chairman.

He immediately negotiated with Henry Loomis, deputy director of the U.S. Information Agency, to succeed Macy as CPB president. Loomis' appointment was announced on September 11. Curtis and Loomis began efforts to take over from PBS the program planning and scheduling process of the public television interconnection, relegating PBS to a technical distribution role. The first step was for the two agencies to try to negotiate an agreement. By year's end, however, not only had the two agencies drafted sharply different position papers, each side claiming responsibility for national program-making decisions, but these documents had been leaked to the press. The differences expressed themselves also in the two agencies' building up staffs to perform the same role.

Repercussions within PBS

Before 1972 PBS made decisions through an elaborate system of consultation with and evaluation by the station managers and program directors, but President Nixon's veto accelerated two developments within PBS that had begun shortly after its founding in 1970. The first was what PBS President Hartford Gunn, Jr., called a "market plan"— essentially a scheme to involve local stations in the selection and funding of national programs. The plan had been discussed with and favorably received by the stations in June 1972. After Nixon's veto, the PBS board endorsed the refined plan in principle, the Station Program Cooperative (SPC), and Gunn made it public in the *Educational Broadcasting Review*.[13] The plan was to create a mechanism for local stations to select the programs they desired from a pool of available offerings, diminishing central control of national program selection. The Station Program Cooperative would thus increase decision-making by the local stations. It would require that a larger share of the federal allocations to CPB "pass through" directly to the stations in the form of Community Service Grants (CSG). The stations, in turn, would use this money and their local money to "purchase" programs through the PBS, thereby insuring a national programming role for PBS. The Ford Foundation gave $6 million to help support the SPC during its first year.

A second development was also accelerated by the presidential veto. A plan for long-range federal financing would obviously need support from the board chairmen, or "lay representatives," of the local stations. Ralph B. Rogers, a powerful industrialist and chairman of the Dallas community-corporation station, KERA, was invited to chair an informal meeting of several interested board chairmen to determine how they could help secure long-range financing. At the hearings of the

House Subcommittee on Communications in February 1972, he spoke impressively on behalf of the board chairmen of eleven community-owned PTV stations, representing over 30 percent of the available public television audiences, and some committee members urged him to generate greater participation by the system's governing boards. Rogers called a national meeting of lay board chairmen in June 1972. The results were a commitment for greater involvement by local chairmen; an interim sixteen-member coordinating committee representing different types of station licensees in the various regions; and the creation of a small office in Washington, D.C., to handle information. After the presidential veto Rogers called an October meeting of the interim committee in New York City. A new twenty-four-member body, the National Coordinating Committee for Governing Board Chairmen, was created, chaired by Rogers. Rowland concluded:

> In sum, at the very time that the White House was criticizing public television for being overly centralized, this infant system, struggling under severe financial constraints it had never been intended to bear, was in fact developing a unique system that tempered the economically necessary centralization of certain technical distribution processes with a heavy decentralization for program policy-making. . . . Even prior to the initiation of the cooperative in 1973, the amount of station control over the policies and products of the network was at least as great as that of any national broadcasting system in the world and clearly far greater than that of American commercial television.[14]

In contrast, the Corporation for Public Broadcasting, claiming to promote greater decentralization, was trying to establish a national system which, in Rowland's words, "under its tight, direct control, would be much more centralized and politically vulnerable than the then existing structure."

1973 TO THE PUBLIC BROADCASTING FINANCING ACT OF 1975

Temporary Compromise between CPB and PBS

Public statements by the CPB, on the one hand, and by PBS, the Educational Television Stations division of NAEB, and the National Coordinating Committee of Governing Board Chairmen, on the other hand, opened 1973, giving the damaging impression to Congress and the American people that the public broadcasting community was a house divided. A possible way out of the impasse was opened when the CPB board immediately accepted a request from the National Coordinating Committee to meet with the CPB. The meeting was held on February 6, at which time the CPB made clear that accommodation was possible but only if the differences that divided the PBS, the ETS division of the NAEB, and the National Coordinating Committee were resolved. The corporation encouraged, indeed challenged, the Coordinating Committee to take the lead in such a resolution.

Avery and Pepper have described in detail the many and delicate steps that led to a resolution.[15] On March 30, 1973, the public television licensees approved, by a vote of 124 to 1, a new membership organization. Still called the Public Broadcasting Service (PBS), the new organization included what had previously been PBS, ETS, and the Chairmen's Coordinating Committee. Its governing body was revised to include twenty-five lay representatives (board of governors) supported by a second-tier group of twenty-five professional broadcasters (board of managers).[16] The new PBS was both an operating public television agency and a trade association; consequently, CPB supported its interconnection function and dues from members paid for the trade-association function. As a result of the reorganization, the new PBS was not representative of the stations: it *was* the stations.

There were two incidental consequences in other organizations in the field. First, since ETS had lost identity and merged with the new PBS and since public radio stations were already organized in National Public Radio, in 1973 NAEB relinquished its former trade association functions and broadened its professional services to individuals in the field of public telecommunications. Second, since NAEB was no longer a trade association and NPR was strictly an operating agency, public radio stations organized their own trade association, the Association of Public Radio Stations (APRS), also in 1973.[17]

Ralph Rogers, who was named chief executive officer of the new PBS (for at least ninety days, with Hartford Gunn, Jr., titled "chief operating officer"), conducted an offensive from the strength of a united public television field. During the first week of April, Rogers and Curtis had reached agreement on a three-point plan, and each thought he could speak for his organization. In this Rogers was correct but Curtis was not. On April 13, 1973, when the CPB board met to consider the compromise agreement, the directors voted to "defer action" and appointed a new ad hoc negotiating committee. The next day Thomas Curtis resigned as chairman and member of the CPB board, charging that the White House had "tampered with" the board through improper telephone conversations.

On May 9, the CPB board elected James Killian chairman. He accepted the position on two conditions: that the compromise agreement be approved; and that the board reactivate its special committee, the Long Range Financing Task Force, chaired by Joseph D. Hughes. The CPB board approved the compromise agreement, modified slightly, and renewed its efforts to develop a firm funding proposal. On May 17, the PBS accepted the compromise agreement, with revisions to increase Community Service Grants to the stations, which the CPB agreed to do. On May 31, CPB and PBS made public "An Agreement for Partnership."[18]

After Killian had been elected chairman, the Senate passed a two-year $130-million funding bill for public broadcasting. Less than two weeks after the "Partnership Agreement" the House Subcommittee on Communications began hearings on a similar two-year funding bill, which was passed, with final appropriations of $47.2 million for fiscal 1974 and $62 million for 1975.

THE PUBLIC BROADCASTING FINANCING ACT OF 1975

After the 1973 "Partnership Agreement" between CPB and PBS, both CPB, cooperating with PBS and NPR, and the Office of Telecommunications Policy (OTP) submitted five-year financing proposals to Congress. Tables 8.3 and 8.4 permit a comparison for five fiscal years of the long-range financing measures recommended by the OTP and the CPB and the funds Congress appropriated in the Public Broadcasting Financing Act of 1975 (PBFA).

The Public Broadcasting Financing Act of 1975 was a long step

Table 8.3

RECOMMENDED LONG-RANGE FINANCING
and the PUBLIC BROADCASTING ACT of 1975

(In Millions of Dollars)

Fiscal Year	OTP	CPB	PBFA
1976	70	100	87.5
1977	80	125	103.0
1978	90	150	107.2
1979	95	175	120.2
1980	100	200	152.0

SOURCE: Willard D. Rowland, Jr., University of Illinois, personal files.

Table 8.4

RATIOS of FEDERAL FUNDS to MATCHING NONFEDERAL FUNDS

OTP (recommended)—$1.00 to $2.50
CPB (recommended)—$1.00 to $2.00
PBFA (enacted)—$1.00 to $2.50

SOURCE: Willard D. Rowland, Jr., University of Illinois, personal files.

forward in the financing of public broadcasting. For the first time it authorized appropriations for a five-year period and made advanced appropriations for two years. Thus it permitted longer range planning and commitments, and it significantly raised the levels of authorization and appropriation. In the light of the past, these achievements were recognized and appreciated by the public broadcasting community.

Nevertheless, in the light of the original recommendations of the Carnegie Commission and of current and foreseeable needs, the act had serious limitations and drawbacks which Rowland diagnosed. First, supporters did not succeed in preserving the crucial feature of combined five-year authorization *and* appropriation—the cornerstone of the original OTP and CPB versions of the bill. The House Appropriations Committee insisted that the appropriations be provided in separate legislation.

Second, the act stipulated that the CPB board and staff be available at any time to testify before appropriate congressional committees upon request on any matters determined by those committees. This addition to the basic requirement that CPB submit an annual report to the President is an oversight proceeding imposed on all government agencies. In requiring separate appropriation measures and continual oversight, Congress continues to treat the CPB as a government agency, which the 1967 legislation specified it should not be.

Third, the act is at best medium-range, not long-range financing. As soon as one appropriation bill has been passed, public broadcasting must prepare for the next round, and even the principle of renewing the five-year authorization was brought into question well before the end of the 1975–80 period. Fourth, even assuming that the appropriations equal the authorizations, which they rarely do, the amounts provided are well below the documented needs of the public broadcasting system.

Finally, to receive the maximum appropriations the system must in advance raise money from nonfederal sources according to a $1 to $2.50

formula which the system may not be able to meet. In brief, with no dedicated funding sources available, public broadcasting continues to be subject to internal and external pressures not to provide the bold, innovative services that the system was created to offer to the American people.

1976–77

Carnegie Commission II

When he resigned from the CPB board in January 1975, James R. Killian, Jr., relayed the suggestion that another Carnegie-type study of public broadcasting was needed. The idea was advanced by others, including several authors of *The Future of Public Broadcasting,* which was published in 1975. The public broadcasting system finally agreed.

In mid-1976 representatives of the boards of the Corporation for Public Broadcasting and National Public Radio approached the Carnegie Corporation to suggest that it set up a new commission to study public broadcasting and make recommendations for its future. Carnegie soon appointed a small internal task force to analyze the problems of public broadcasting and to discern whether and for what purpose a new commission would be useful. After a six-month study the task force recommended that the corporation appoint and finance a new commission to study issues and make recommendations.[19] On June 14, 1977, the corporation announced the formation of the Carnegie Commission on the Future of Public Broadcasting, funded by $1 million, chaired by William McGill, president of Columbia University. Made up of twenty prestigious members, the commission is scheduled to make its report in January 1979. Congress passed the 1978 Public Telecommunications Financing Act authorizing appropriations for three years instead of five in order to take into account the findings and recommendations of the commission.

Revision of the 1934 Communications Act

In 1977 the House Subcommittee on Communications began a comprehensive review of the nation's telecommunications policy. Its staff prepared, among several such papers, an Option Paper describing alternative legislative solutions to some of the problems of public broadcasting. The subcommittee held three days of hearings on public broadcasting in September 1977. The Option Paper described some of the issues that the subcomittee had to review. These include goals, technology, the structure of the public broadcasting industry, funding, and statutory provisions.[20] The paper does not, of course, indicate what decisions the subcommittee might take. Despite this, three points are notable. First, the subcommittee seems favorable to public broadcasting, although not necessarily in its present form. Second, it sees public broadcasting as only one component in the provision of noncommercial and/or nonprofit telecommunications service to the American people. Third, the subcommittee considers it proper for Congress to concern itself with some of the most detailed aspects of what in an independent public broadcasting system would be internal matters. Whatever the outcome, the revision of the 1934 act will undoubtedly give special attention to public broadcasting because Congress has more leverage on it than on the powerful commercial component.

Carter's Message

On October 6, 1977, President Jimmy Carter submitted to Congress proposals "to strengthen our public broadcasting system and to insulate it from political manipulation."[21] He proposed a renewal of the five-year authorization measure from fiscal 1981 to fiscal 1985; a reduction of the matching level of federal to nonfederal funds from the previous ratio of $1:$2.50 to $1:$2.25; and a five-year authorization for the Corporation for Public Broadcasting—$180 million in fiscal 1981, and $200 million in each of the four succeeding years. He proposed also a separate grant program for facilities—$30 million annually in fiscal 1979 and 1980, and $1 million in fiscal 1979 for telecommunication demonstration projects.

The President noted the duplication of programming functions by CPB, on the one hand, and PBS and NPR on the other, with "unproductive feuds" and the waste of money. In his proposal "CPB's role would be clarified to be that of a system overseer operating much like an endowment or foundation. Based on its planning process, it would make broad allocations among radio, TV, and other distribution systems and among children's, public affairs, minority, and other program types. It would implement these decisions by giving annual or multiyear bloc grants to PBS, NPR, regional and other specialized networks, and production centers."[22]

At the same time Carter proposed legislative prescriptions for certain details of public broadcasting's operations. The point is not that the objectives are wrong but that even a President friendly to public broadcasting sees Congress' power over public broadcasting as appropriately used to intervene in the system's programming decisions.

Communications Satellite Distribution

Just prior to his resignation in 1973, FCC Commissioner H. Rex Lee told the NAEB convention that they were no longer educational broadcasters but in the new profession of public telecommunications. He said that new technologies present many opportunities but, if not taken advantage of, would become "tomorrow's competitors. This may already have happened with satellites. . . . The cost for this inaction will be very heavy."[23] By 1977 the situation was completely reversed: public broadcasting had taken the lead in the use of communications satellites.

The decisions to use domestic communications satellites for public service purposes were made in two separate but parallel developments. Both started with a 1974 study of potentials. One led to action by a group concerned with the use of satellite transmission by consumers—the Public Service Satellite Consortium. The other development led to action by a group concerned with the use of satellite transmission by distributors— the Corporation for Public Broadcasting, Public Broadcasting Service, and National Public Radio.

In December 1974, a preliminary study, initiated by the PBS and financed by the Ford Foundation, indicated that a satellite interconnection system for public broadcasting would be feasible and desirable. That same month a planning group of one hundred people formed an Interim Public Service Satellite Consortium to develop on a permanent basis the kinds of communication services then being demonstrated by Applications Technology Satellite 6 (ATS-6, also called ATS F). Lee, retired from the FCC, was chairman of the planning group and president of the steering group of the consortium. On November 18, 1975, the members of the Public Service Satellite Consortium (PSSC), with a permanent board of directors and John Witherspoon as president, held its first meeting as an operating organization.

The PBS, the CPB, and the Ford Foundation established the Satellite Working Group, which throughout 1975 made detailed analyses indicating that a satellite interconnection system would provide public broadcasting with several advantages.

In 1976 the CPB decided to construct its satellite interconnection. Huge loans were arranged, contracts were signed, and licenses were obtained. For public television, construction of ground stations in the southeastern United States was completed by February 1978, and the use of AT&T long lines in that area was discontinued. The remainder of the public television system is scheduled for completion by November 1, 1978, and all land-line interconnection will be severed. Satellite interconnection for public radio stations is scheduled to be activated early in 1980.

Public broadcasting now has new capacities for delivery. What is now needed are new organizational capacities for handling delivery.

Public television and public radio stations eventually will each be leasing four transponders (devices on a satellite that receive from and send transmissions to ground stations) on Western Union's Westar I, and, if needed, more transponders can be leased from other satellites. Satellite interconnection will give both television and radio transmission high fidelity sound and a capability that can be used for stereophonic music, foreign language translation, or other purposes.

Because satellite transmission has already begun for public television, more information is available about it in mid-1978 than about satellite transmission for radio. Public television will have the nation's first and most extensive system for the regular distribution of programs by way of satellites. By the end of 1978, the system will link together more than 270 local PTV stations, including for the first time those in all fifty states and in Puerto Rico and the Virgin Islands. Picture and sound quality are much better, and new local stations can be brought on the line for the relatively low cost of a new ground terminal.

The most important advantage is that local stations will be able to choose from a wider selection of programs—not only from the PBS main send-and-receive terminal in Virginia but also from six regional send-and-receive terminals around the country. Public television can simultaneously transmit and receive both special coverage events (such as a congressional hearing) and regularly scheduled programs. Access to the satellite transponders not being utilized for the national service will be governed by the newly formed Transponder Allocation Committee (TAC —a special committee of the PBS board). The three transponders being leased in mid-1978 (a fourth will be leased by 1980) will provide about 500 hours a week for program distribution. About 300 hours of these will be needed for existing PBS national program services, including delayed feeds for the various time zones. Priorities for using the remaining 200 hours will be determined by TAC primarily on the basis of the number of potential users of each program.

Any local public television station or group of stations, or other public television entity (such as the Children's Television Workshop) is eligible for access to the excess 200 hours. Also eligible will be all educational broadcast users. The public television satellite system can be expanded virtually without limit by leasing time on other available transponders.

The Public Service Satellite Consortium (PSSC), formed in 1975 to research and facilitate public service satellite utilization, is seeking out high-probability satellite users in order to establish demonstration projects making appropriate use of public broadcasting's underutilized ground facilities. The recently formed Public Interest Satellite Association (PISA), made up of other groups in the noncommercial and/or nonprofit community that might benefit from the satellite system, is conferring with the CPB to see how such groups can use the public ground facilities. Apart from the improved quality and increased flexibility of the PTV service, the satellite system will over time return substantial and continuing savings compared to the ever-increasing costs of leasing longlines from the telephone company.

"It's a foregone conclusion that the medium of television will change rapidly and dramatically over the next twenty-five years. . . . It's exciting that in the midst of all this change, public broadcasting is not being left behind: if anything, the move into satellite networking has put the system at the forefront."[24]

Amid excitement, however, it is sobering to note three facts. First, although the system has the capability for multichannel distribution, that expanded capability ends at the station: a broadcasting schedule of sixteen hours a day will not likely be extended because the range of program choice is wider. Second, although the system has the capability of multiprogram distribution, the cost of producing the extra programs will not be provided or reduced by the mere fact of satellite interconnection. Third, by opening up the capability of providing many more public services by and for many more noncommercial and/or nonprofit groups—through various methods of ground distribution from the satellite terminals, including multichannel cable systems—public broadcasting has opened also a Pandora's box of competition. Because the increased capability for more and wider public services are needed and welcome, public broadcasting will inevitably face increased competition for support from both tax-based and private sources at all levels.

1978

The Environment in Congress

Public broadcasting in 1978 faced a congressional environment very different from the one it was familiar with since the Educational Television

Facilities Act was passed in 1962. Specifically, familiar, friendly leaders, including Senator Warren Magnuson; Senator John Pastore; Nicholas Zapple, chief counsel to the Senate Commerce Committee; Representative Tolbert McDonald; and Representative Harley O. Staggers, had either died or retired or yielded their key positions on key committees. New leaders had moved into the key positions, specifically Senator Ernest F. Hollings, chairman of the Senate Subcommittee on Communications, and his counterpart, Representative Lionel Van Deerlin, chairman of the House Subcommittee on Communications. Van Deerlin has engaged a staff, headed by Harry M. Shooshan III, chief counsel, committed to the philosophy of less government regulation (at least of commercial communications) and of greater reliance upon the forces of competition between old and new technologies. Generally, since the fall of Richard Nixon, Congress has been much more assertive of its powers than it was under presidents Johnson and Nixon. Examples are its treatment of Carter's proposals to conserve energy and reform the tax structure. Thus Carter's message on public broadcasting was not received as a blueprint for legislation; an entirely new bill was introduced.

The Environment in the FCC

The new chairman of the FCC, Charles D. Ferris, in an address to the April 1978 NAEB convention, expressed several principles which he thought should guide the Commission.[25] One was that the FCC "should stimulate excellence through diversity—and diversity through competition. . . . I favor a policy of zero-based regulation. We will rely on competition instead of rules whenever that is promising or possible. . . . A strong noncommercial television and radio service is another means of encouraging diverse services without more regulation. A well-funded system of noncommercial television and radio can relieve the pressure for content regulation of broadcasting in general. It can also provide a useful 'marketplace yardstick' and a competitive prod to . . . commercial broadcasters to strive for excellence and experiment with new ideas and formats. . . . Finally—and perhaps most importantly—I believe that the FCC should encourage new technologies and services, rather than helping any vested interest to hold back."

Ferris seemed to imply that public broadcasting would not have the privileged position with the Commission that it had enjoyed since the reservation of TV channels in 1952, and that public broadcasting would have to compete not only against commercial broadcasting and other technologies but also against other public service applicants for licenses.

This implication was strengthened by the subjects the FCC discussed in a meeting on June 7, 1978, beginning a series of inquiries and rule-making proceedings.[26] One inquiry will examine the standards for eligibility for "noncommercial educational" TV and radio licenses. An alternative is the opening of eligibility to any noncommercial agency found tax-exempt by the IRS. A second inquiry will be into rules that should govern announcements identifying parties contributing services, goods, or money to noncommercial stations and the amount of time that may be devoted to fund-raising programs, including auctions. A third inquiry will be into rules that should govern multiple ownership or noncommercial broadcasting stations. A fourth inquiry will concern the long-awaited Table of Assignments for noncommercial FM radio stations.

The FCC ruled that noncommercial FM stations must have a minimum power of 100 watts and must broadcast at least thirty-six hours per week; stations broadcasting less than twelve hours a day may have their unused time claimed by another group. The Commission created a new FM channel, at 87.9 mc., that can be used in selected parts of the country for low-power noncommercial FM stations.

The Public Telecommunications Financing Act of 1978

The House and Senate Conference Committee on October 12, 1978, reached agreement on the bill. The act was passed by Congress in the final days before adjournment, and President Carter signed it into law.

It authorizes advanced appropriations for the Corporation for Public Broadcasting for only three years—fiscal 1981, 1982, and 1983—not for five years as the Public Broadcasting Financing Act of 1975 did and as President Carter had recommended for the 1978 act. The decision for the shorter period was certainly influenced by the facts that the report and recommendations of the Carnegie Commission on the Future of Public Broadcasting and House and Senate bills to revise the Communications Act of 1934 are both scheduled for 1979, and it was probably influenced also by congressional dissatisfaction with aspects of public broadcasting.

The act has three parts: Title I—Construction and Planning of Facilities; Title II—Telecommunications Demonstrations; and Title III—Corporation for Public Broadcasting.

For the facilities program, the act authorizes appropriations of $40 million for each of the fiscal years 1979, 1980, and 1981. This increase over the $19 million authorization for 1978 will not be as great for public broadcasting as the figures indicate because a wide range of nonbroadcast facilities will also be aided. The act transfers the program from the Department of Health, Education, and Welfare to the Department of Commerce.

Eligibility for grants under the facilities program is broadened to include, in addition to public broadcasting entities, nonprofit educational and cultural organizations primarily engaged in public telecommunications services. Of the funds appropriated for facilities, not less than 75 percent shall be available each fiscal year to extend delivery of public telecommunications services to areas not now receiving them. Because this objective will require concentration in large, sparsely populated areas, the previous ceiling of 8.5 percent to any one state was eliminated. "A substantial amount" is to be available to expand and develop public radio station facilities.

Title II—Telecommunications Demonstrations—continues at the same level a program first authorized for fiscal 1977, with the purpose to promote the development of nonbroadcast facilities and services. One million dollars is authorized for each of 1979, 1980, and 1981. The program remains in HEW.

In Title III Congress authorizes appropriations for the Corporation for Public Broadcasting of amounts not to exceed $180 million for fiscal 1981, $200 million for 1982, and $220 million for 1983. Again, these increases over the $160 million authorization for 1980 will not be as great for public broadcasting as the figures indicate because the monies will be shared by a wide range of nonbroadcast entities and activities. The matching formula, previously $1 of federal funds for each $2.50 from nonfederal sources, is reduced to $1 for $2, with the requirement retained that the matching funds be raised two years in advance. Besides having a matching formula more easily met, the public broadcasting stations may count the value of personal services contributed by volunteers up to 5 percent of nonfederal support, after standards for evaluation have been approved. (The 1978 act retains the prohibition against editorializing and endorsing or opposing candidates for public office and also the requirement that the stations keep for sixty days audio recordings of programs in which issues of public importance are discussed and make them available to anyone.)

Title III broadens the responsibility of the Corporation for Public Broadcasting, in addition to those of public broadcasting, to include public telecommunications technologies, entities, and services so that the title of the corporation might well have been changed to the Corporation for Public *Telecommunications* (just as the title was broadened from *television* to *broadcasting* in the Senate public broadcasting bill of 1967).

The title of the act was, in fact, changed to the Public *Telecommunications* Financing Act, and the significance lies in its broadened scope. The trend in current government thinking, which is expressed also in the proposed House bill to revise the Communications Act of 1934, is away from over-the-air broadcasting as it is known, to what is sometimes called the "wired nation." In the 1978 financing act this trend is seen in definitions of and provisions for facilities to be aided, entities to be supported, and services to be promoted.

"Public telecommunications facilities" are defined to mean "apparatus necessary for production, interconnection, captioning, broadcast, or other distribution of programming, including but not limited to . . ." and there follow ten examples, among them cable, cassettes, and discs. "Public telecommunications entity" means "any enterprise which is (A) a public broadcast station or a noncommercial telecommunications entity; and (B) disseminates public telecommunications services to the public." "Noncommercial telecommunications entity" means any enterprise which "(A) is owned and operated by a State, a political or special purpose subdivision of a State, a public agency, or *a nonprofit private foundation, corporation, or association*; and (B) has been organized primarily for the purpose of disseminating audio or video noncommercial educational and cultural programs to the public *by means other than a primary television or radio broadcast station,* including, but not limited to . . ." and there follows another long list of examples. (Emphasis added.) The inclusion of "nonprofit" entities should be noted, defined as those whose earnings do not benefit any private shareholder or individual. "Public telecommunications services" means, in addition to broadcast programs, "related noncommercial instructional or informational material that may be transmitted by means of electronic communications."

The broadened scope of the act is expressed also in changes in or additions to the statements of purposes. The declaration in Title I adds the phrase "including the use of broadcast *and nonbroadcast technologies.*" Title II adds to the purpose that of promoting telecommunications facilities and services for "*health,* education, and *public or social service information.*" (Emphasis added.) Title III, concerning the Corporation for Public Broadcasting, adds to the declaration the encouragement of "*nonbroadcast* telecommunications technologies." (Emphasis added.)

Moreover, the act contains provisions that seek to promote the achievement of large social goals that go beyond educational broadcasting services. For example, Title I says that in making facilities grants, the secretary of commerce "shall give special consideration to applications which would increase minority and women's ownership of, operation of, and participation in public telecommunications entities." A section in Title III states: "Equal opportunity in employment shall be afforded to all persons by the Public Broadcasting Service and National Public Radio . . . and by all public telecommunications entitites receiving funds . . ."

Much more strongly than previous public broadcasting acts, the 1978 act encourages and requires planning. For example, the facilities program not only requires that the applicant produce evidence of comprehensive planning in its area and a five-year plan for the facilities project, but the act also provides funds for planning. The secretary of commerce "shall develop a long-range plan to accomplish the objectives set forth in the [facilities program]. Such plan shall include a detailed 5-year projection of the facilities required," updated annually. The Corporation for Public Broadcasting "shall create a 5-year plan for the development of public telecommunications services," updated annually.

Probably the most outstanding feature of the 1978 act, and certainly the one that provokes the most criticism, is that it contains many new requirements that put restrictions on the freedom of the public broadcasting system to manage its own affairs. The system accepts most of the objectives, but at the same time the requirements, separately and cumulatively, are inconsistent with the original concept of a "private" corporation that is "not an agency of the Federal government" leading a system of independent stations responsible to the Federal Communications Commission and their local governing boards and communities.

These restrictive requirements include: a limit to Cabinet-level on the salaries that CPB, PBS, and NPR may pay its employees; open meetings (with exceptions) by the governing boards of CPB, PBS, NPR, and the stations; orders to provide "substantial amounts" of money to public radio both for facilities and for programming and other operations; the development by CPB of enforceable uniform accounting principles to be followed by all public telecommunications entities receiving funds; the provision of equal employment opportunities enforceable upon PBS, NPR, the stations, and all public telecommunications entities receiving funds; and provision that public telecommunication entitites other than those of public broadcasting have "reasonable access" to satellite interconnection.

In the conference report by the managers of the House and Senate agreeing upon the final bill, the conferees remark that they "are concerned about the trend toward too much centralization of control in the public television system." They say the danger exists because the Public Broadcasting Service (PBS) both determines what programs will be produced and distributed nationally and acts as a trade association for the stations. "The single, centralized authority of a fourth network perpetuates a 'closed system,' which inhibits access to program production assistance, national distribution, and local broadcast of programs produced. Public broadcasting was created to be a true alternative to commercial broadcasting. . . . Therefore it is imperative that the system remain vigilant to prevent 'creeping networkism.'" These sharp comments have implications not only for PBS, but also for National Public Radio (NPR), which in 1977 merged with the Association of Public Radio Stations (APRS) and thus became, on the model of PBS, both an agency for interconnection and a trade association. Indeed, the implication is even sharper for NPR because it, unlike PBS, also produces programs.

The critics of some restrictive requirements (with the threat of more to come) emphasize that in most cases it is not the objectives but the means that are objectionable—that the public broadcasting system, not the federal government, should solve the problems of the system, and that the greatest danger—from government control—is already present in the Public Telecommunications Act of 1978.

By making advanced authorization of appropriations for CPB for only three years, the 1978 act is clearly an interim measure. Events during this period are likely to determine whether a vigorous, tolerably free public telecommunications system will survive in the United States. The outcome will depend primarily upon four factors: (1) changes in communications technologies and their marketing, and the ability and freedom of public telecommunications to adapt to and use them; (2) the policies of the federal government concerning not only the public component but also the private component of the entire American communications system; (3) how effectively the public telecommunications system is able to influence such federal policies; and (4) how convincingly the public telecommunications system can demonstrate that it is able to deal with its problems in which Congress in the 1978 act has seen fit to intervene.

Review of the 1934 Communications Act

The House Subcommittee on Communications has produced a 217-page bill that has just begun the legislative process during which it will undoubtedly be altered. In July the subcommittee issued a press release of the major provisions.[27] The following are excerpts from that release. The bill:

> 1. Abolishes the Federal Communications Commission, replacing it with a Communications Regulatory Commission, and makes a finding that

regulation should be necessary only "to the extent marketplace forces are deficient."

2. Deregulates radio; licenses would be for indefinite terms, subject to revocation only for violations of technical rules.

3. Extends television license terms from three to five years, but they also would become indefinite ten years after enactment of the bill.

4. Replaces the "Fairness Doctrine" with an "Equity Principle" applicable only to television stations. [The "Equity Principle" is a fairness doctrine without the required affirmative effort to cover controversial issues of public importance, but when TV stations did cover them, they would have to do so in an "equitable manner."]

5. Limits multiple ownership to five radio and five television stations and provides that no individual may own more than three TV stations in the top fifty markets—no divestiture would be required, however; these provisions would take effect at time of transfer or sale.

6. Restricts ownership of broadcasting stations to one per market.

7. Establishes a license fee that would reflect both the cost of processing the license application and the value of spectrum occupied by the user (applies to both broadcasting and nonbroadcasting services).

8. Creates the "Telecommunications Fund" with the license fees collected; the fund would support the Communications Regulatory Commission and new programs for aiding public broadcasting programming, minority ownership of stations, and the development of telecommunication services in rural areas.

9. Prohibits federal regulation of cable television.

10. Frees AT&T from the restraints of a 1956 consent decree under which the telephone company can use its equipment only to provide telephone service and is prohibited from providing unregulated services.

11. Replaces the Corporation for Public Broadcasting with a private nonprofit corporation to be known as the "Public Telecommunications Programming Endowment," the sole purpose of which would be to provide grants for production and acquisition of programming.

12. Removes restrictions on editorializing and endorsement of political candidates by public broadcasters.

Recognizing that this bill will be changed and certain provisions fought fiercely by some powerful, established commercial interests, the proposed bill nevertheless contains at least three possibilities that would profoundly alter the role of public broadcasting in the American society.

First, it would sharply define two components in the U.S. telecommunications system: a commercial component devoted entirely to the pursuit of private gain in the marketplace, and a noncommercial component devoted entirely to serving the public interest. The basic ambiguity of the present law is that commercial stations are supposed to be licensed only to "serve the public interest." If they did so, there would be no need for a public telecommunications system. With the "public interest" requirement removed from the commercial component, the noncommercial telecommunications component would have exclusive mandate to serve the public interest and the justification of the noncommercial component would be an essential part of the legislation.

Second, in the proposed "Telecommunications Fund," part of which would aid "public broadcasting programming," public broadcasting would have a source of funds insulated from Congress (although it would have to share the revenues of the "Telecommunications Fund" with new programs "for aiding minority ownership of stations and the development of telecommunication services in rural areas").

Third, with the creation of the "Public Telecommunications Programming Endowment," whose sole purpose would be to provide grants for the production and acquisition of programming, the present conflict between the CPB and PBS-NPR might be resolved, or, at least, some of the ambiguities in roles might be clarified.

Many of the hopes and fears excited by numerous and far-reaching proposals for changes in FCC regulations and the law regulating communications will not materialize, of course. However, some of the FCC's specific inquiries into rule-making and some specific provisions of the proposed rewrite of the Communications Act contain at least two dangers that are "clear and present." One is that at the very time public broadcasting stations need and can use multiple station outlets in their communities because of satellite transmission, each noncommercial licensee may be prohibited from owning and operating more than one station in its community and state television and radio networks may be curtailed. The other specific danger is that at the very time public broadcasting stations need to broaden and diversify their sources of nonfederal income in order to increase their budgets and to safeguard their independence from Congress, they may be prohibited from receiving money from program underwriters and restricted in their ability to solicit contributions from their audiences.

SOME UNRESOLVED ISSUES

Missions and Goals

It is unrealistic to expect that the public broadcasting system in the United States could and should have a coherent view of *a* mission and *a* set of goals. The system evolved from several different types of licensees in many distinctive communities. To a large extent it has necessarily been reactive to commercial broadcasting, but how it should react is ambiguous: if it tries to attract mass audiences, it is accused of being unnecessary; if it tries to attract special audiences, which usually are small, it is often accused of being inconsequential or "elite." Many local stations have defined their missions and goals well. Their strong sense of peculiar identity and fierce defense of autonomy are among the reasons why *the* mission and goals of the nationwide system cannot be stated.

Yet, since a large fraction of the income of the nationwide system now comes from the federal government, the focus of attention is on its national organizations. Government officials and members of Congress have slight chance to understand the local stations. Even the officials and staffs of the national organizations that in legal fact represent the stations lose touch with them or never acquire the understanding that comes only from experience with local stations.

Public broadcasting has so many missions and goals that it cannot serve them all. One limit is the shortage of money, of course, but one more important is the hours of the broadcast day on a single station.

Commenting on the task of Carnegie Commission II, Stephen White suggested: "Rather than address itself merely to the problems involved in operating an over-the-air system within the limited number of allocations it possesses in the broadcast spectrum, Carnegie II might broach its purview to include the total field of minority programming in terms of the total broadcast capacity, of which over-the-air transmission is but a single and, in the long run, a minor aspect. The question now becomes one of determining how all the needs of all minority audiences, . . . rich and poor, urban and rural, might best be served."[28] That is certainly the question, but an implementing question is how to move toward this vast goal without crippling or starving the present programming for the minorities now being served.

Audiences and Public Participation

The audiences of public broadcasting are growing and becoming more nearly representative of the national population. Still, by commercial ratings they are usually very "small." But what does that mean? For selling soap, an audience of, say, ten million people during a prime hour is "small." Is an audience of, say, fifty million who spend an hour a week watching a public broadcasting program "small"? It depends upon the purpose: whether to sell soap, or to deepen and widen the audience's awareness of themselves and their world. "Public broadcasting ought to be what happens because programs are received."[29] Quoting Sartre as once complaining, "I have readers—but no public," Bermont said: "Replace the word 'readers' with 'viewers' and the quote becomes frighteningly applicable to public television."[30] If over time a public station is able to have as much influence on its audiences as Sarte has upon his readers, the statement should not be frightening. The issue is whether public broadcasting's purpose is merely to engage the attention of its audiences or to try to bring some meaning into their lives. Such influence and meaning cannot be measured directly, but an indirect measurement is the extent to which public broadcasting publics make known that they value the programs offered by the stations. This brings us to the issue of public participation.

Branscomb has put the issue well: "Public broadcasting is asking too much of itself and too little of the public."[31]

In 1969 the Corporation for Public Broadcasting established the Advisory Council of National Organizations (ACNO) to win support from major national organizations representing most of the American public. The ACNO, which started small and constantly grew in size, stated that it was to serve in an "advisory and consultant capacity to the board and president of the CPB." Over the years the role of ACNO changed from being an advisory public forum to trying to be a body of experts, with results unsatisfactory to both sides.[32] In September 1977, its members dissolved ACNO and recommended that CPB "seek new methods and structures to answer the many challenges now facing not only CPB but public broadcasting as well." Accepting ACNO's dissolution, CPB started seeking other ways to achieve public involvement. While it is desirable for CPB to encourage public participation, the system's most important need is to develop a strong, vital rapport with the American people in their local communities, demonstrating that it is responsible through the local stations to their communities, not to political institutions, and generating the public support essential for survival and growth.

Financing

In the formative years of American radio and television, commercial broadcasting found a financial base in the sale of time for advertising. The lack of an adequate financial base drove noncommercial broadcasting eventually to the federal government, which has provided no source of adequate funds insulated from congressional appropriations. Thus the federal government is gradually encroaching on the autonomy of the local stations. Two proposals for insulated federal funding have been made and rejected: the Ford Foundation's satellite scheme and the Carnegie Commission's recommended dedicated fund from a manufacturer's tax on television sets. The need for an insulated source increases with the enlarging concepts of what public broadcasting can and should do. As of mid-1978 the only hint that such a source might become available is in the proposal by the House Subcommittee on Communications that a portion of a franchise charge on the commercial use of the broadcasting and nonbroadcasting spectrum be devoted to public broadcasting programming. When this proposal reaches Congress, the strength of the American publics that support public broadcasting will be pitted against the powerful interests that will oppose it.

Although he was writing only about public television, Gunn's analysis is applicable to all public telecommunications:

> It is time everyone recognized that "insulation"—protection from government and partisan political interferences—cannot be achieved by any single mechanism. . . . Public television should recognize and declare that insulation stems primarily from the local communities, states, and institutions that support public television. The trustees for the public are the local boards of the stations. . . . Therefore, the federal government has three basic options: (a) Stand aside and let public television struggle by itself to serve the public with limited local resources; (b) Offer assistance to achieve a higher quality and more useful public service in a way that supports and encourages local citizens to assume the full responsibility for the public's interest and to strengthen the insulation of this powerful medium from undue political pressures; or (c) Offer alterations to public television that erode local responsibility and trusteeship and pave the way for political intervention. The preferred course is to try to design a federal funding plan which accomplishes everyone's objectives and yet retains and encourages local interest, participation, responsibility, and freedom.[33]

Independence

The relationship between independence and firm, adequate financing from various sources at several levels does not need elaboration. A less obvious aspect of independence is the need for mutual learning in how to accommodate freedom of communications and government financial support. The noncommercial broadcasting system is the American people's first experience with tax-supported media of mass communications. Other countries, such as Great Britain and Canada, over a longer period have learned to live with inherent tensions that are at best endurable and never relaxed. Communicators must learn to accept that complete independence is a myth. Those who hold the purse strings must learn to accept that a large degree of freedom for communicators is essential to a democracy. For example, the restraints upon public broadcasting that Congress included in the 1978 Public Telecommunications Act were viewed by some in Congress, not as restrictions upon the freedom to program, but as the proper exercise of their responsibility to ensure the proper use of public money. On the other hand, some of the officers and staffs of the CPB, PBS, and NPR, who were unfamiliar with the operations of the local stations, did not seem to realize what they were giving away to get money. The outcome might have been different if the spokesmen in the national organizations had candidly conceded to congressional committees that problems exist and persuasively demonstrated that the stations and national organizations were working to solve them.

In the mutually educative process of trying to accommodate freedom of expression and public financing, the courts play a vital role. Examples are decisions on two sections of the Public Broadcasting Act. In one the U.S. Circuit Court of the District of Columbia ruled that the section authorizing the CPB to develop programs "with strict adherence to objectivity and balance in all programs or series of programs" does not create a legally enforceable standard but is simply a goal to which the CPB should aspire. The other case involved the section requiring public broadcasting stations to make a tape of each program "in which any issue of public importance is discussed" and keep it for sixty days for anyone who wants a copy.[34] The U.S. Court of Appeals declared this section unconstitutional because it treats public broadcasting stations differently from commercial stations.

The 1978 Public Telecommunications Financing Act has provisions that treat public broadcasting stations differently from commercial stations, and some of these may be tested in the courts. Moreover, if Congress separates the roles of commercial and noncommercial stations, as the House Subcommittee on Communications proposes, many new issues are bound to come before the courts.

Leadership

Another issue that pervades public broadcasting is the quality of its leadership. With some exceptions, the members of the board of the CPB have not met the standards described in the Public Broadcasting Act of 1967 and that are clearly essential for a vital system. Moreover, recently the managers of many local stations have expressed dissatisfaction with what they consider the uninformed and unresponsive nature of the leadership they receive from PBS and NPR.

During 1978 there were many indications that the stations and agencies of public broadcasting were working to improve the quality and change the instruments of national leadership. These indications were both inside and outside of the Public Broadcasting Service, National Public Radio, and the Corporation for Public Broadcasting.

The board of PBS asked Vice-Chairman Hartford N. Gunn, Jr., to initiate a process of long-range planning for public television. The project was funded and begun in February 1978. In June Gunn completed a report in two volumes—the first titled "Long-Range Planning for Public Television: Overview and Recommendations," the second composed of background and supporting papers that had been commissioned.[35]

In June 1978, the board of the Public Broadcasting Service elected Newton B. Minow chairman to succeed Ralph B. Rogers. In 1973 Rogers achieved the unification of public television agencies in a reorganized PBS, thereby averting a collision between the CPB and PBS that could have been fatal to public broadcasting. Minow gained national recognition during the early 1960s when, as chairman of the Federal Communications Commission, he led many efforts to improve commercial television and to aid noncommercial television. As a private citizen he has been a board member of National Educational Television, an initial member of the National Coordinating Committee of Governing Board Chairmen, and chairman of the Chicago Educational Television Association, of whose board he is still a member.

At the first PBS board meeting under his chairmanship, Minow, feeling that the PBS board was not being adequately informed, created the Managers Resource Group, with the purpose of enabling PBS to deal with two problems: how to handle practical affairs, chiefly in determining the will of the stations concerning issues and effectively advocating them with government, and how to make PBS as much as possible an instrument responsive to the licensees, which it legally represents.

On July 1, 1978, the Rocky Mountain Public Network and the Western Broadcasting Network merged to form the Pacific Mountain Network (PMN), including stations in Alaska, Washington, Oregon, California, Idaho, Montana, Wyoming, Colorado, Nevada, Arizona, New Mexico, Hawaii, American Samoa, Guam, and the Trust Territories. By the fall of 1978 another kind of merger was occurring in the central states. Midwestern Educational Television, St. Paul, was evolving into something else, the nature of which was not yet clear. The television stations in North and South Dakota, which had been members of both MET and the Central Educational Network (CEN), Chicago, remain members of CEN. The big shift was that KTCA TV, St. Paul, which had been MET's key station, also joined CEN.

Moreover, the regional television networks had come together in a consortium. On October 23, 1978, the Eastern Educational Television Network (EEN), the Southern Educational Communications Association (SECA), the Central Educational Network (CEN), and the Pacific Mountain Network (PMN) formed the Interregional Council on Public Television, with a board composed of five managers and five chief operating officers from each region. Its purposes are to use satellite interconnection more fully and flexibly and to help govern the entire public television system more effectively. Thus it is a mechanism for both interconnection and station representation. Concerning interconnection, already the regional networks are renting time on the satellite Westar I beyond the capacity contracted for by CPB and PBS. Concerning representation, many of the stations think that on all matters they can work through the regional associations better than they can through PBS. The Interregional Council intends to move toward building consensus of all PTV stations on the issues they face and to demonstrate that public television stations can handle their own problems.

The formation of the Interregional Council grew out of station dissatisfaction with PBS in much the same way that in 1958 the formation of the Affiliates Committee had grown out of dissatisfaction with the National Educational Television and Radio Center (NETRC), with the important difference that NETRC was not the legal representative of the affiliates, whereas PBS is the legal representative. In September 1978, EEN called a meeting of representatives of the regional networks and proposed that a consortium of the group be created. John Montgomery, executive director of CEN, made a cooperative study of ways to form a consortium, and the result was the Interregional Council. The Council provides new leadership itself and also stimulates changes in the leadership in PBS and the stations. It demonstrates that PBS must become more responsive to the stations, or, if it survives, it may continue as only one of several national programming services. Indeed, it seems likely that there will be more than one national programming services regardless of the changes within PBS. Changes in PBS became apparent immediately. The chairman and vice-chairman of the board recognized the Interregional Council as a legitimate representation of the stations and an agency to deal with in planning and decision-making.

New leadership capacities are being developed in public radio also. The National Federation of Community Broadcasters (NFCB), an organization formed in 1975, is effectively promoting the special interests of many radio stations that have been left out of CPB's qualifications for grants and the general interests of all public radio stations. For example, it is actively trying to secure legislation that will require that all new radio sets, including those in automobiles, be able to receive all channels.[36] (For FM radio "prime time is drive time.")

In October 1978, the board of National Public Radio created the Legislative and Planning Committee, chaired by Ron Bornstein, general manager of the Madison stations WHA TV and FM, with a mandate to create a permanent planning capacity, similar to the mandate that the PBS board had previously given to Hartford Gunn.

In September 1978, the board of the Corporation for Public Broadcasting chose as its new president, effective January 1, 1979, Robben Fleming, president of the University of Michigan. This was the first time the CPB board chose as its chief executive a person outside the federal bureaucracies—the first time, too, that the choice was made without previous knowledge that it was agreeable to the president of the United States. John Macy, Jr., the first president, who resigned in 1972, had been director of the U.S. Civil Service Commission, and Henry Loomis, who in 1978 announced his intention to resign, had been deputy director of the U.S. Information Agency.

However, the greatest need for high leadership is in the boards of the local stations. "Whatever their failings or shortcomings, these local citizens who volunteer their time and resources have the advantage over everyone in government or in public broadcasting in Washington. These local trustees must live in their communities and states. . . . We broadcast our 'failures' just as we broadcast our 'successes' for everyone to see. These local trustees are direct recipients of both the praise and the criticism. They cannot easily walk away; they do not shirk their responsibilities."[37]

Probably the most important factor affecting the quality of leadership of the local boards is the challenge given to exercise their responsibilities with freedom. That is one of the main reasons why the tendency of Congress to erode the independence of the local stations must be reversed. The tendency will not be reversed unless the local stations, individually and through their representative agencies, demonstrate that they can deal effectively with their problems.

SOME PROSPECTS

A Few Present Developments

There are many encouraging features as public broadcasting enters its second decade. For example, the President, Congress, and the FCC are all favorable. The FCC has finally begun to move to give noncommercial

FM radio stations a national table of allocations. Public radio is getting more attention and money.

Public broadcasting audiences are growing in numbers and becoming more nearly representative of the American people as a whole. In general, the American people are becoming more selective in their listening and viewing habits. Most of the local stations are growing in strength and also assertiveness toward their national organizations.

Both television and radio will soon be able to transmit over multichannels in the same spectrum, by which more special audiences can be served in many new ways (including captioned television signals for deaf persons).

The communications satellite interconnection, which is rapidly coming into being for both television and radio, opens up so many capabilities that they cannot yet be even assessed. These include the more rapid expansion of stations in sparsely populated areas; services by and for many groups other than the present public broadcasting communities; and the development of telecommunications centers, some of which are already in early stages of development.

Instructional television is "alive and well,"[38] and the Agency for Instructional Television (AIT), a consortium of thirty-five U.S. state and Canadian provincial agencies, has embarked on a major activity, the Essential Learning Skills Project.[39]

The formation of the Interregional Council on Public Television has already been noted. It could be the root of a new structure within public television that will not only provide more and more varied programming but that will also move to solve problems such as making better use of the talents of independent producers and providing equal employment opportunities—problems which the Public Telecommunications Financing Act of 1978 is trying to solve through restrictive requirements. The public television system is likely to see other configurations of stations organized around special concerns they share independent of geographical location, such as similar types of ownership (e.g., community corporations or universities) and similar types of audiences (e.g., inner city or rural). In brief, the PTV stations are demonstrating their determination to exert control over the directions public television will take and/or supplement PBS with new organizational instruments. These already present and clearly foreseeable developments are toward providing the new organizational capacities to handle the new technical capacities for the delivery of programs that already exist. The combination of these two types of increased capacities may make moot the long-term argument over the dangers of centralized "networking."

Public television and radio stations earned more than $347 million in nonfederal support during fiscal 1977, thereby qualifying not only for the full fiscal 1979 appropriation of $120.2 million but also for an additional $19 million of federal funds for that year. The Public Broadcasting Financing Act of 1975 required that the public broadcasting system raise $2.50 from nonfederal sources for each $1 of federal appropriation and that the nonfederal income be raised and certified two years in advance of the appropriation for the fiscal year. The requirement was first tested for the 1978 appropriation. During FY 1976 the public broadcasting system raised from nonfederal sources nearly $300 million, thereby qualifying not only for the full fiscal 1978 appropriation of $107.2 million but also for an additional $12 million. These performances are encouraging, particularly since the 1978 act has lowered the matching ratio to $2 to $1 and made it possible for the stations to include in nonfederal monies the value of volunteer services up to 5 percent. These performances are encouraging, that is, provided that neither the FCC nor Congress puts restrictions on the amounts and ways the system can raise money from underwriters and solicitations.

Between the passages of the Senate and House versions of the Public Telecommunications Financing Act of 1978 and the final version of the bill that the conference committee agreed upon in October, the spokesmen for public broadcasting and its friends were sufficiently persuasive to bring about modifications in several important provisions that were much less restrictive. The achievement of these modifications seems to indicate both that much of the intent in Congress is to improve the public broadcasting system, not to erode its independence, and that public broadcasting is learning how to deal more candidly with Congress.

By mid-1978 the National Association of Educational Broadcasters had not only survived the traumatic withdrawal of the public television and radio stations in 1973 (to merge with PBS and NPR) but had also developed into an effective professional national association of individuals and a focus for other institutions and agencies in public telecommunications. William Harley, president since 1960, retired in 1975 and was succeeded by James Fellows, who since 1964 had been assistant to Harley in liaison with the association's many projects. In June 1978, the association announced that it had paid off a debt of $160,000 with the help of grants from the CPB and the Ford Foundation matched by $80,000 contributions from members and twenty television stations. The NAEB is the only national organization in public and educational telecommunications, which includes radio and television broadcasting, cable, closed circuit, satellite communications, Instructional Television Fixed Services, and instructional telecommunications. It has more than 1,500 individual members in many professional specialties and an Institutional Associate program. Its fourteen professional councils involve the members in the operations of the association and many other projects throughout the field. To achieve the goals of promoting a high quality of professionalism and to foster new ideas NAEB services are organized into professional training and development, conventions, publications and information, and personnel placement. In 1963, when the NAEB seemed about to break into separate associations, the concern for fostering professionalism was a binding force. After 1973, when the Educational Television Stations and National Educational Radio divisions did withdraw, this same concern provided the basis for rebuilding the NAEB. Amid the fragmenting forces of technology and specialization, the association gives some coherence to the entire field through its pursuit of excellence in the service of shared social goals.

Only persons familiar with the history of educational broadcasting since twenty-five managers of radio stations formed the Association of College and University Broadcasting Stations in 1925 can appreciate how many of public broadcasting's current problems are those of success.

Longer-Range Prospects

The prospects for telecommunications services to the American people for the 1980s are wider than ever before, and the general environment for unhampered development is more open that it has been since the formative period of American radio in 1920–22. For example, the developments of cable services, including the much larger capacity that will be given by fiber optics (light wave technology in which a hair-thin flexible glass fiber is substituted for the copper wire in cable systems to increase the number of channels substantially), will be unrestricted, and AT&T will be able to enter the field. The combination of cable television and computers will enable pay cable systems to charge viewers for the programs they order with the press of a button; a wide range of specialized programs can be expected because they will not require mass audiences. People will be learning to use television differently and to expect different things from it.[40] Additional broadcasting frequencies in the currently available segment of the electromagnetic spectrum will be provided, and new segments are being opened up.

What Sydney Head calls "media symbiosis"—interrelationships among competitive media that in the long run turn out to be mutually advantageous—is working in more complex ways than before. Composite systems of the several media are being developed, as are the cooperative arrangements they require. In important ways commercial and non-commercial activities are reinforcing one another. So are noncommercial and nonprofit activities. Most of the restrictions that the 1978 Public Telecommunications Financing Act imposes on public broadcasting—such as enforcing of services to minorities and the provision of equal economic opportunities—are for socially desirable objectives. At least some of the provisions that may come from the revision of the 1934 Communications Act will serve as stimuli to public broadcasting, which within a decade has become one of the established interests.

If the main provisions of the bill to revise the 1934 Communications Act proposed by the House Subcommittee on Communications—to remove the "public interest" requirement for noncommercial telecommunications—are enacted, for the first time noncommercial telecommunications will have an exclusive mandate from Congress to serve the "public interest." A precise distinction between the roles of commercial organizations, on the one hand, and noncommercial and/or nonprofit organizations, on the other, will be defined. Service to the "public interest" by noncommercial entities will be included as an essential part of the law, instead, as at present, of being regarded as "alternative" or "supplementary" to the commercial services.

On the other hand, the removal of the requirement that the commercial licensees serve the public interest may work to the harm of both the quality and variety of total programs the American people receive and the public broadcasting system. The entire burden of serving the public interest might prove to be a responsibility too great for the public broadcasting system to fulfill. Thus public broadcasting could become the target of the discontents and pressures of all special interest groups in the society. The burden will be made heavier if the FCC or Congress restricts the number of outlets each public station or state system of stations may have in a community or state. Perhaps what is needed is not more outlets for noncommercial educational stations currently broadcasting in a community but more noncommercial/nonprofit stations with licensees different from those of both the commercial and noncommercial educational licensees as we know them.

If these provisions are enacted, another distinction will be defined: that between noncommercial *educational* broadcasting and other types of noncommercial and/or nonprofit broadcasting. Then what is now called "public" broadcasting would have to return to the basic concept of its primary role, which is *education*. "Public" broadcasting would be forced to try to answer three interrelated questions, which have haunted it since its beginning:

1. What essential services can it provide the general society that are more than counterbalances for the limitations and deficiencies of the commercial service?

2. What essential services can it provide education that are more than short-term and/or peripheral counterbalances for the limitations and deficiencies of the traditional educational services?

3. How can it provide these two kinds of essential services in ways that do not waste scarce spectrum space but that, instead, fit into and take advantage of all the other capabilities that exist and are coming on in a technological flood?

A philosophical approach to the answers for these questions was defined more than sixty years ago by Dewey[41] and is today being realized in the concept and practice that education is self-directed life-long learning and that communication is the essence not only of education but also of social life.

> Society not only continues to exist . . . *by* communication, but it may fairly be said to exist . . . *in* communication. There is more than a verbal tie between the words common, community, and communication (p. 5).
>
> Not only is social life identical with communication, but all communication (and hence all genuine social life) is educative. To be a recipient of a communication is to have an enlarged and changed experience. . . . Nor is the one who communicates left unaffected. . . . It may fairly be said, therefore, that any social arrangement that remains vitally social, or vitally shared, is educative to those who participate in it (pp. 6–7).
>
> A democracy is more than a form of government; it is primarily a mode of associated living, of conjoint communicated experience. The extension in space of the number of individuals who participate in an interest so that each has to refer his own action to those of others, and to consider the action of others to give point and direction to his own, is equivalent to the breaking down of those barriers of class, race, and national territory which kept men from perceiving the full import of their activity (p. 101).
>
> There is perhaps no better definition of culture than that it is the capacity for constantly expanding the range and accuracy of one's perception of meanings (p. 145).

Community may be said to exist in communication, but communication is not the same as community. Four of the differences illuminate the justification for a public component of our telecommunications system that is adequately funded and free to serve the public interest solely. The basic one lies in the intent of the transmission, and the other three flow from it. The intent of advertising support of commercial telecommunications is to manipulate the audiences to buy goods and services; in contrast, the intent of public telecommunications is to help the audiences (in Dewey's words) "expand the range and accuracy of meanings." Another difference is between the agent and the source of the communication. Insofar as a commercial telecaster is expressing something only because he or she is paid to do so, that person is an agent for the true source —the sponsor; in contrast, insofar as a public telecaster is expressing something out of personal conviction of its worth, he or she is the source of the communication. Still another difference is in the interpretation of the audience. "If our purpose is art, education, the giving of information or opinion, our interpretation will be in terms of the rational and interested human being. If, on the other hand, the purpose is manipulation, the convenient formula will be that of the masses."[42] A final difference concerns the consequences of the reception. With the purpose to entertain in order to sell, the consequences, if achieved, will be consumers responding to commercials; with the purpose to provide high-quality services of cultural, informational, educational, and instructional programming, the consequences, if achieved, will be human beings fulfilling themselves as individuals and citizens.

NOTES

Chapter 1
SEIZING THE LAST CHANCE

1. Quoted by Harold Hill, *NAEB HISTORY, Volume I—1925-1954* (Urbana, Ill.: National Association of Educational Broadcasters, 1954), p. 60. The phrases "upper band" and "low band" refer to placings in the electromagnetic spectrum. Electromagnetic energy takes such forms as cosmic rays, gamma rays, X-rays, ultra violet rays, visible light rays, infrared rays, and radio waves. All forms travel at the speed of light, and all travel in waves, but the lengths of their waves differ vastly—from many miles to microscopic fractions of centimeters. The wavelengths determine the characteristic properties of the various forms of electromagnetic energy. These waves are measured in two ways: in terms of their lengths (i.e., the distance from crest to crest), and in terms of their frequencies, or cycles, per second. (Frequencies and cycles per second mean the same thing, usually shortened to frequencies or cycles, abbreviated c. Another synonym is Hertz, abbreviated Hz.) The relationship between wavelengths and cycles is inverse, that is, the longer the wavelength, the fewer the cycles per second. When the frequencies of electromagnetic waves are ordered from low to high, they form the electromagnetic spectrum, from low to high (just as refracted visible light rays show a spectrum of light waves from red—less frequent—to violet—more frequent). For broadcast service in the United States, the FCC has allocated the radio spectrum into bands or (subbands) from the lower to the higher frequencies as follows: 535-1,605 kc.—AM radio; 54-72 mc. and 76-88 mc.—VHF TV (channels 2-6); 88-108 mc.—FM radio; 174-216 mc.—VHF TV (channels 7-13); 470-890 mc.—UHF TV (channels 14-83). (In the abbreviations, kc. means thousands of cycles per second, and mc. means millions of cycles per second; one million cycles is called a megacycle. The frenquencies between the allocations listed above are used by nonbroadcast services, such as citizens service, aviation, public safety, and common carrier.)

2. Norman Woelfel and I. Keith Tyler, *Radio and the Schools* (New York: World Book Company, 1945).

3. The powerfully beneficial role that the Rockefeller Foundation and its assistant director, John Marshall, played in the early history of educational broadcasting should be recognized, although it is hard to document because most of it was indirect. For example, the General Education Board of the foundation made grants for research to the Office of Radio Research, Columbia University, and the Bureau of Educational Research, Ohio State University. Robert B. Hudson was specially prepared under a Rockefeller grant before becoming director of the Rocky Mountain Radio Council. Carl Menzer, WSUI, University of Iowa, received a Rockefeller grant. Ralph Steetle entered educational broadcasting because of a Rockefeller fellowship. Harold McCarty was able to study broadcasting in Great Britain in the fall of 1935 under Rockefeller support. Charles Siepmann, director of talks and later director of regional planning for the BBC, was able to visit the United States on a Rockefeller grant, and he later emigrated to this country.

4. Robert B. Hudson, "Allerton House 1949, 1950," *Hollywood Quarterly* 5(3) (1950-51):238-39.

5. Robert B. Hudson, "Allerton House: Twenty Years After," *Educational Broadcasting Review* (February 1970):38.

6. Richard B. Hull, "A Note on the History Behind ETV," *Educational Television: The Next Ten Years* (Stanford: The Institute for Communications Research, 1962), p. 340.

7. This section is based upon *FCC Transcripts,* Official Report of Proceedings before the FCC, Washington, D.C.: Docket 8736—Volumes 24-27. (For guiding me through these numerous pages I am indebted to W. T. Schmid, "A Historical Analysis of the Educators' Request for Non-Commercial Television Channels in the United States" (Ph.D. diss., Ohio State University, 1970). Sources of direct quotations from the hearings are given by volume and page (e.g., 24:16366).

8. S. E. Frost, Jr., *Education's Own Stations: The History of Broadcast Licenses Issued to Educational Institutions* (Chicago: The University of Chicago Press, 1937).

Chapter 2

THE U.S. LAISSEZ FAIRE BROADCASTING SYSTEM

1. The following accounts of foreign systems are based mainly on Walter B. Emery, *National and International Systems of Broadcasting* (East Lansing: Michigan State University Press, 1969).

2. On TV in the USSR, see Ellen Propper Mickiewicz, "Watching the Soviets Watch Television," *New York Times,* Sec. 2, July 9, 1978, p. 1. She says that under Leonid Brezhnev the government has made scientific surveys of TV viewing and its effects. They are remarkably similar to those in the United States, suggesting "that there is something about . . . the magnetism and hypnotic effect of the small screen that changes peoples' lives all over the world."

3. See also Erik Barnouw, *A Tower in Babel* (New York: Oxford University Press, 1966), and *The Golden Web* (New York: Oxford University Press, 1968); Walter B. Emery, *Broadcasting and Government,* 2nd ed. (East Lansing: Michigan State University Press, 1971); and Sydney W. Head, *Broadcasting in America,* 2nd ed. (Boston: Houghton Mifflin, 1972).

4. Barnouw, *A Tower in Babel,* pp. 154-57.

5. Ibid., p. 107.

6. Ibid., p. 187.

7. Ibid., p. 94.
8. Ibid., p. 96.
9. Head, *Broadcasting in America,* pp. 158–59.
10. Louis G. Caldwell, quoted by S. E. Frost, Jr., *Is American Radio Democratic?* (Chicago: University of Chicago Press, 1937), p. 27.

Chapter 3
U.S. EDUCATIONAL BROADCASTING UNTIL *1948*

1. Robert E. Summers and Harrison B. Summers, *Broadcasting and the Public* (Belmont, Calif.: Wadsworth, 1966), p. 53.
2. S. E. Frost, Jr., *Education's Own Stations* (Chicago: University of Chicago Press, 1937), p. 99.
3. See Frank Ernest Hill, *Tune In for Education* (New York: National Committee on Education by Radio, 1942), p. 3.
4. Levering Tyson, *A Study of Radio Broadcasting in Adult Education* (New York: American Association for Adult Education, 1930).
5. U.S. Department of Interior, *Report by the Advisory Committee on Education by Radio* (Columbus, Ohio: Heer, 1930).
6. Levering Tyson, ed., *Radio and Education* (Chicago: University of Chicago Press, 1931–35).
7. The main sources of this section on the National Committee on Education by Radio are Hill, *Tune In for Education* and selected issues of the NCER weekly bulletin, "Education by Radio."
8. Joy Elmer Morgan, "National Committee on Education by Radio," *Education on the Air* (Columbus: Ohio State University Press, Institute for Education by Radio, 1931), p. 6.
9. Tracy F. Tyler, *An Appraisal of Radio Broadcasting in the Land-Grant Colleges and State Universities* (Washington, D.C.: National Committee on Education by Radio, 1933).
10. Tracy F. Tyler, ed., *Radio as a Cultural Agency* (Washington, D.C.: National Committee on Education by Radio, 1934).
11. *Education on the Air,* the institute's proceedings, was published by the Ohio State University Press yearly from 1930 through 1953, with the exceptions of 1935 (when the IER and NACRE met jointly and jointly sponsored the proceedings, *Education on the Air* and *Radio in Education,* published by the University of Chicago Press), and 1945 (when no meeting was held). See also Frank Kelly, "The Institute for Education by Radio-Television" (Ph.D. diss., Ohio State University, 1972). I am indebted to Kelly's manuscript.
12. Other sources of information concerning earlier and then current broadcasting activities by schools are: Carroll Atkinson, *Development of Radio Education Policies in American Public School Systems* (Edinboro, Pa.: Edinboro Educational Press, 1939); Ben H. Darrow, *Radio, The Assistant Teacher* (Columbus, Ohio: Adams, 1932); Margaret Harrison, *Radio in the Classroom* (New York: Prentice-Hall, 1938); and Norman Woelfel and I. Keith Tyler, *Radio and the School* (New York: World, 1945).

The public schools of Oakland, Indianapolis, Cleveland, and Pittsburgh all began broadcasting regular series of programs in 1921. Early test experiments were conducted in 1923 by the Haaren High School, New York City. During the next two years many experimental programs of instruction by radio were tried throughout the country. In the fall of 1926 ambitious programs were begun in both Cleveland and Chicago. Led by Alice Keith, the Cleveland public schools received a music appreciation course over WTAM twice each week; the first listening guide for students was developed for this series. In Chicago Judith Waller, manager of WMAQ, led the preparation and broadcasting of three half-hour instructional programs each week; the Chicago public school officials endorsed and supported these programs in 1929. In 1928 Alice Keith became director of the Education Department of CBS and was instrumental in starting the "American School of the Air" in 1931. That same year Judith Waller helped initiate "The University of Chicago Round Table" over WMAQ; the next year she became the education director of the NBC-Central Division and helped get "The University of Chicago Round Table" over NBC stations in 1933.

In 1945 Woelfel and Tyler summarized school broadcasts still on the air at that time: "First in importance is the American School of the Air, five series of programs broadcast daily from coast to coast over the facilities of the Columbia Broadcasting System. There are regional schools of the air serving the classrooms of Minnesota, Ohio, Oregon, Texas, and Wisconsin. For music classes, the Standard Oil Company of California furnishes a series of weekly half-hour programs to listeners on the Pacific Coast. In some half-dozen cities broadcasts are produced locally to supplement the courses of study in various subjects—notably in Cleveland and Chicago, and, to a less extent, in Rochester, Akron, Indianapolis, Portland, Detroit, Alameda, and New York City" (p. 103).

The "Ohio School of the Air," almost entirely the creation of Ben H. Darrow and initially supported by the Payne Fund, made its first broadcast to schools on January 7, 1929. From then until 1937 it was under the direction of the Ohio State Department of Education, supported by the state legislature, with radio time given free by stations WLW, Cincinnati, and WOSU, Ohio State University. In 1937 the legislature discontinued appropriations because Darrow had refused to have broadcasts to the schools support the candidacy of Governor Martin L. Davey. For two years the program, renamed "The Nation's School of the Air," was subsidized by station WLW. In 1939 Ohio State University took over the program named "Ohio School of the Air" again and broadcast it over the university station, WOSU.

13. W. W. Charters, "Radio in Elementary and Secondary Schools," *Education on the Air,* 1930, pp. 127–35.

14. Levering Tyson, "Contributions of Radio to Higher Education," *Education on the Air,* 1930, pp. 136–38.

15. John Elwood, "Radio and the Three R's," *Education on the Air,* 1930, pp. 22–23.

16. P. O. Davis, "A Centralized Unit in Educational Broadcasting," *Education on the Air,* 1930, p. 70.

17. Round table discussion of Josef F. Wright, "Financing College Stations," *Education on the Air,* 1932, p. 65.

18. Roosevelt's disinterest in radio was evidenced by his ignoring the declaration of principles that emerged from the First National Conference on the Use of Radio as a Cultural Agency. Acting for the NCER, John Henry MacCracken, of the American Council on Education, tried unsuccessfully for a month to get an appointment with the President. See Hill, *Tune In for Education,* p. 65.

19. The summary of this amendment and the Senate debate is made from *Congressional Record,* Vol. 78, pp. 8828 and following, for May 3–20, 1934.

20. A short summary of the hearings and the report are given in Federal Communications Commission, *First Annual Report,* Fiscal Year Ended June 30, 1935, p. 8.

21. Orrin E. Dunlap, "'Court' Opens Tomorrow: Education and Religion Seek Definite Percentage of Radio Waves," *New York Times,* Sec. 9, September 30, 1934, p. 11.

22. Erik Barnouw, *A Tower in Babel* (New York: Oxford University Press, 1966), p. 279.

23. A. G. Crane, "Safeguarding Educational Radio," *Education on the Air* and *Radio and Education,* 1935, pp. 123–24.

24. For a report of the founding meeting see "The Three R's in Radio," *Broadcasting,* June 1, 1935, p. 28. FREC was never dissolved officially but had melted away by World War II. For a summary of its major activities see Leonard Power, "The Activities of the Federal Radio Education Committee, *Education on the Air,* 1940, pp. 237–43; and "FREC Service Bulletin" (Washington, D.C.: The Federal Radio Education Committee, 1938–50).

25. C. S. Marsh, ed., *Educational Broadcasting* (Chicago: University of Chicago Press, 1937–38).

26. Publications by FREC included Paul H. Sheats, *The Groups Tune In* (1939); three by Leonard Power, *Local Cooperative Broadcasting, College Radio Workshops,* and *Public Service Broadcasting* (all 1940); *Radio in the Schools of Ohio* (1942); *Educational Radio Script Exchange Catalog; Directory of Colleges and Universities Offering Courses in R-TV* (1944–45); and the monthly "FREC Service Bulletin" 1 (1939)–12(1950).

27. For details of these activities see the publications cited in note 26, *Educational Radio Script Exchange Catalog; Directory;* Power, *College Radio Workshops*; and Power, *Public Service Broadcasting.*

28. Thomas H. Reed, *Four Years of Network Broadcasting,* A Report by the Committee on Civic Education by Radio of the National Advisory Council on Radio in Education and the American Political Science Association (Chicago: University of Chicago Press, 1937), p. 45.

29. Robert B. Hudson, "Radio Councils," *Education on the Air,* 1941, pp. 177–85.

30. Harold E. Hill, *NAEB History, Volume 1—1935 to 1954* (Urbana, Ill.: National Association of Educational Broadcasters, 1954), pp. 47–50.

31. U.S. Office of Education, "Education's Opportunities in Radio," *Education for Victory* 3 (12) (December 20, 1944):6. *Education for Victory* was the name given to *School Life,* the official weekly publication of the U.S. Office of Education, during World War II. It appeared twice each month from March 3, 1942, to August 8, 1945.

32. U.S. Office of Education, "The Needs of Educational FM Broadcasting for Additional Channels," *Education for Victory* 3(9)(November 3, 1944):5.

33. Testimony in *FCC Transcripts,* Docket No. 6651, 1944–45, pp. 1183–644; see especially pp. 1423–47.

34. Charles Siepmann, *Radio's Second Chance* (Boston: Little, Brown, 1946). Siepmann, as ad hoc consultant, did most of the research in the FCC study that resulted in the "Blue Book."

35. "Educational Radio," FCC INF Bulletin No. 21-B, September 1966, p. 4.

Chapter 4

BUILDING THE BASE OF NATIONAL ETV, 1951-1956

1. FCC Docket 8736, Vol. 27, Part III, Appendix A, March 21, 1951. See also Frank J. Kahn, ed., *Documents of American Broadcasting* (New York: Appleton-Century-Crofts, 1968), pp. 551–53.

2. To distinguish their abbreviating initials the practice was to use "TFAE" for The Fund for the Advancement of Education and "FAE" for the Fund for Adult Education. I will use those distinguishing initials for brevity. "FAE" will appear often in this chapter and "TFAE" in the next.

3. Clarence Francis, chairman of the board of the General Foods Corporation, was FAE chairman 1953–58; Charles Percy, president of Bell & Howell Company, was chairman 1959–61. Other members of the board who were particularly supportive of ETV were Sarah Gibson Blanding, president, Vassar College; Harry A. Bullis, chairman of the board, General Mills; the Rev. John J. Cavanaugh, director, University of Notre Dame Foundation; Milton S. Eisenhower, president, Pennsylvania State University; Clinton S. Golden, executive director Harvard University Trade Union Program; Paul S. Helms, chairman of the executive committee, Helms Bakeries, Los Angeles; Allan B. Kline, president, American Farm Bureau Federation; W. A. Patterson, president, United Air Lines; and Anna Lord Strauss, president, League of Women Voters.

4. FCC Docket 8736, Vol. 24, April 11, 1952. See also Kahn, *Documents of American Broadcasting,* pp. 554–61.

5. The Commission appreciated at least some of the problems of the "intermixture" of VHF and UHF in the same communities when it released the Sixth Report, but it was overly optimistic: "It is reasonable to assume that . . . television receivers will be built to receive VHF and UHF signals." Such receivers were not built in sufficient numbers until legislation required them beginning in 1964, and converters proved to be both expensive and unsatisfactory. The germ of the All-Channels Receiver Amendment Act of 1962 lay within the unresolved "intermixture" of the Sixth Report. However, the inferiority of UHF lies in factors far deeper and more complex than receiving sets. See Hartford N. Gunn, Jr., "The UHF Story," *Public Telecommunications Review* (May/June 1977):4–8.

6. FCC, "Educational Television," INF Bulletin No. 16-B, April 1969, p. 3, says: "The table of channel allocations, including noncommercial educational reservations, has been revised several times since it was first issued in 1952. The most recent revision, issued in June 1965 and corrected in March 1966, provided for 116 VHF and 516 UHF reservations. . . . This table was derived from a computer program, which selected the reservations on an efficiency basis. Deliberately a nonsaturated table, this allocations plan was designed for educational organizations to develop a greater number of stations by permitting future computer selection and assignment of unallocated channels to places where at this time ETV may be completely unanticipated."

7. Paul A. Walker, "The Time to Act Is Now," ed. Carroll V. Newsom, *A Television Policy for Education* (Washington, D.C.: American Council on Education, 1952), p. 31.

8. By October 5, 1955, seventeen ETV stations were on the air, with one other (KTHE 28, Los Angeles) having failed.

9. For an account of the conference see *Educational Television News* (Washington, D.C.: National Citizens Committee for Educational Television), May 11, 1953.

10. *Fund for Adult Education, 1951–1961: A Ten Year Report* (White Plains, N.Y.: 1961), p. 17.

11. See Newsom, *A Television Policy for Education;* especially "A National Commission for Educational Television," pp. 165–66, which organized many of the policy recommendations formulated during the institute; and Raymond Wittcoff, "Proposal for a National Educational Television Network," pp. 232–41.

12. See John Walker Powell, *Channels of Learning: The Story of Educational Tele-*

vision (Washington, D.C.: Public Affairs Press, 1962), pp. 96–103, for details on the Penn State Institute, the conferences by the University of North Carolina, the New York State Board of Regents, the Southern Regional Education Board (SREB), and others, including summaries of actions in seven states taken from the JCET list. John Ivy, Jr., executive officer of the SREB, ran a southern branch of the JCET for about a year, with a special grant from the FAE to promote ETV conferences in the South.

13. Robert R. Mullen, "The Citizen and Educational TV," *AERT Journal* (October 1953):4.

14. For a summary of the committee's three years of activities see "The NCCET—An Enviable Record," *AERT Journal* (February 1956):3. Some people, particularly educators, found the NCCET's "hard sell" methods offensive.

15. Powell, *Channels for Learning,* p. 67.

16. The following bibliography of publications by the NAEB, Urbana, Ill., provides a convenient summary of these activities in professional development: *Lincoln Lodge Seminar on Educational Television,* June 21–27, 1953, edited by Burton Paulu, 1953; *The First NAEB TV Production Workshop for Educational Television,* August 28–September 18, 1953, edited by Edward Stasheff, 1954; *NAEB Educational Television Station Management Seminar,* August 30–September 5, 1953, edited at WOI TV, 1954; *NAEB First TV Engineering Workshop,* October 22–26, 1954, edited by Cecil S. Bidlack, 1955; *The Second NAEB TV Production Workshop for Educational Television,* August 23–September 10, 1954, edited by Edward Stasheff, 1955; *The Third NAEB TV Production Workshop for Educational Television,* August 14–September 3, 1955, edited by Edward Stasheff, 1956; and *NAEB Second TV Engineering Workshop,* September 12–16, 1955, edited by Cecil S. Bidlack, 1956.

17. Robert B. Hudson, "Educational Television Assessment Project Report." One of his generalizations was: "Without exception, the problem of day-by-day programming of an educational television station is the main concern of the informed educators, and the chief deterrent to affirmative action in claiming channel reservations by educational institutions." Another was: "Since the New York Regents' Plan is universally recognized as being an imaginative and bold approach to educational television, its success or failure will strongly influence the development of educational television in the United States in the years immediately ahead." This plan, drawn up by Deputy Commissioner of Education James E. Allen with the aid of Walter Emery, proposed that capital funds be provided by the state legislature and operating costs be shared by the Board of Regents and local participating institutions. It was scuttled by Governor Thomas E. Dewey, who was often at odds with the regents. He set up a study committee, which recommended in February 1953, that the project proceed with private finances, if at all. ("There is no evidence before us that state-owned and operated stations are necessary or desirable.") The network in New York State was not to get under way for a decade. Hudson's report to FAE and ACE, July 1952, was an internal document.

18. See Powell, *Channels for Learning,* pp. 85–95, for details concerning the reasoning behind the conditions.

19. The main source of the information in the vignettes of the stations is material supplementary to "Status Report—1957," by Richard B. Hull (cited in note 38 below).

20. The Lowell Institute, founded in the mid-nineteenth century to give free lectures for the education of workers, had become the center of an interuniversity extension program. In 1947 it took the lead in founding the Broadcasting Council, made up of sixteen universities, colleges, and other institutions, to engage in broadcasting without the burden

of a station. By 1951 the council's broadcasts over commercial stations had received enough of the familiar shifts and cancellations to make it decide to establish its own station. The FCC objected that the council was too loose a federation to be financially responsible. The Lowell Institute and Harvard recruited the Massachusetts Institute of Technology and the Boston Symphony Orchestra as partners in the WGBH Educational Foundation, which became owner and operator of WGBH FM and later WGBH TV.

21. See Powell, *Channels for Learning,* p. 135.

22. The NCCET in a news release dated August 2, 1953, estimated that by then commercial broadcasters had given a total of $1.25 million in buildings, towers, studios, and other equipment to ETV stations. "A Special Report: Educational Television 5 Years and $60,000,000 Later," *Broadcasting,* November 11, 1957, specifically lists the physical or monetary contributions by commercial broadcasters to each ETV station to November 1957, estimating the total value at $6 million and the total value of other contributions (service, counsel, and engineering advice) at an additional $4 million.

23. On April 23, 1952, the group of the NAEB that had taken the lead in forming the JCET submitted to the Fund an elaborate blueprint for a multimillion-dollar enterprise "Educational Television Programs, Inc.," outlining many of the ideas later incorporated in the Educational Television and Radio Center. After the Fund directors had approved Fletcher's plan in principle it was clear that the NAEB was not going to be, directly or indirectly, the agency planning and operating the proposed programming center. The meeting of key persons from the NAEB and the Fund at Gunflint Lodge (University of Minnesota) was to consider the opportunities and dangers of the center that was being founded, and also to retain the cooperation of the NAEB leaders.

24. I. Keith Tyler, "The Educational Television and Radio Center," ed. William Y. Elliott, *Television's Impact on American Culture* (East Lansing: Michigan State University Press, 1956), pp. 225–66, throws light on the early decisions and problems and also some enduring issues and problems.

25. Educational Television and Radio Center, *Presenting National Educational Television* (Ann Arbor: ETRC, 1955). Although not published until 1955, the stated principles, gradually clarified and articulated, guided the center from its conception.

26. The NAEB held the Lincoln Lodge (University of Wisconsin) Seminar with FAE support from June 21–27, 1953. The seminar focused on the role of ETV stations, the nature and needs of their audiences, and the resources from which ETV programs might be developed. See Burton Paulu, ed., *Lincoln Lodge Seminar on Educational Television* (Urbana, Ill.: NAEB, 1953).

27. Fletcher convened the Gunflint Lodge (University of Minnesota) Conference, August 1–8, 1953, to have key persons from the NAEB evaluate the center's plans and early activities. The working paper was Hudson's memorandum on the center submitted in November 1952, just before the incorporation of the ETRC.

28. Two results of the center's grants should be noted: Hideya Kumata, *An Inventory of Instructional Television Research* (Ann Arbor: ETRC, 1956); and Wilbur Schramm, ed., *The Impact of Educational Television* (Urbana, Ill.: University of Illinois Press, 1960).

29. The programs were broadcast Monday through Friday. In the spring of 1957 five thirteen-week series were broadcast ("The American Scene," "Geography for Decisions," "Mathematics," "American Government: Pursuit of Happiness," and "Highlights of Opera History"); and in the fall of 1957 another five thirteen-week series ("The International Geophysical Year," "Camera on Washington," "Arts and the Gods," "Mathematics," and "Survival") were run. In the spring of 1958 three thirteen-week series were broadcast

("Decision for Research," "Briefing Session, and "The Subject Is Jazz"); and in the fall of 1958 two ten-week series ("Ten for Survival," and "Adventuring in the Hand Arts"). The total cost of about $700,000 was shared almost equally by ETRC and NBC.

30. Donald Neal Wood, "The First Decade of the 'Fourth Network': An Historical Descriptive Analysis of the National Educational Television and Radio Center" (Ph.D. diss., University of Michigan, 1963), Appendix F, pp. 501-503, lists all support to the center year by year from December 19, 1952, through July 1962, from the FAE, the Ford Foundation, industry, the U.S. government, and other sources, including earned income. I am indebted to Wood's dissertation in this section on the center and in the next chapter.

31. Erik Barnouw, *The Image Empire* (New York: Oxford University Press, 1970), p. 116.

32. Sydney W. Head, *Broadcasting in America,* 2nd ed. (Boston: Houghton Mifflin, 1972), p. 206.

33. The organizations added to the original seven were the American Association of School Administrators, the Educational Television and Radio Center (which included the group of 106 member units of the Advisory Council), and the National Congress of Parents and Teachers. The Association for Education by Radio-Television, one of the original members of the JCET, merged in 1956 with the NAEB and ceased to exist as a separate organization. For a report of accomplishments and the shift of functions see Joint Council on Educational Television, *Four Years of Progress in Educational Television* (Washington, D.C.: JCET, 1956).

34. By 1957 the NAEB had a total membership of more than 600 (138 radio and 25 television stations), scores of university production centers, and numerous organizations and individuals interested in using and promoting educational broadcasting. The two external factors favoring its growth had been the reservation of channels (FM and ETV) and basic support from the W. K. Kellogg Foundation. Headquarters for the association and the tape network were at Urbana.

With basic-support grants from Kellogg and special-purpose grants from the FAE, the NAEB served educational radio and television stations and personnel by providing legal services; by giving a variety of technical, placement, and management services; by granting fellowships and scholarships; by its monthly *Journal* and other publications; by participating in national affairs (such as the President's Commission on Education Beyond the High School and the Fulbright fellowships program); by involvement in international broadcasting affairs (such as joining the European Broadcasting Union); and, above all, by operating the nationwide magnetic tape radio network. This network was self-supporting by 1955, when it was supplying more than seventy stations with a regular "packaged program" service through a mutual exchange library that contained an increasing number of high quality programs from the United States and Canada and a growing number from other countries. In 1956 the Ford Foundation made its first grant to the NAEB—$64,000 for professional services in engineering and management. For discussion of this period see W. Wayne Alford, *NAEB: History, Volume 2—1954-1968* (Washington, D.C.: National Association of Educational Broadcasters, 1968).

35. Gerard Appy, "NET and Affiliate Relationships," eds. Allen E. Koenig and Ruane B. Hill, *The Farther Vision: Educational Television Today* (Madison: University of Wisconsin Press, 1967), pp.. 98-99.

36. Allan Nevins, *The State Universities and Democracy* (Urbana, Ill.: University of Illinois Press, 1962), pp. 29-34.

37. Joseph F. Wall, *Andrew Carnegie* (New York: Oxford University Press, 1970), p. 816. Carnegie wrote: "I think that an institution has not taken root and is scarcely worth

maintaining unless the community appreciates itself sufficiently to tax itself for mainte-nance."

38. Richard B. Hull, "Educational Television in the United States: A Status Report —1957," p. 26. Fletcher, president of the Fund, initiated and commissioned this ETRC-FAE field survey by Richard Hull and his research assistant, Dorothy E. Hull.

Chapter 5
JERRYBUILDING ON THE BASE, 1956-1963

1. Paul Woodring, *Investment in Innovation: An Historical Appraisal of the Fund for the Advancement of Education* (Boston: Little, Brown, 1970), pp. 74-75, says that after 1956, communication within the foundation was "minimal," and communication between Clarence H. Faust, who was both president of TFAE and vice-president of the foundation, and Alvin Eurich, who was both vice-president of TFAE and executive director of the foundation's Education Division, was also "minimal."

Within the Ford Foundation the persons responsible for working in the field of broadcasting (at first the TV-Radio Workshop and later educational broadcasting) were William McPeak, vice-president, and W. McNeil Lowrey, program director. Within The Fund for the Advancement of Education, in addition to Faust and Eurich, the persons re-sponsible were Philip Coombs, program director; John Scanlon, associate director of edu-cation; and James N. Armsey, director of special projects in education. After Coombs joined the Kennedy Administration in 1961, Armsey became program director of The Fund for the Advancement of Education and also the foundation's liaison person with educa-tional broadcasting until 1966.

2. "The History of Ford Foundation Activities in Non-Commercial Broadcasting" mimeographed (New York: The Ford Foundation, October 1974), pp. 2-4.

3. National Educational Television and Radio Center, *Educational Television Di-rectory* (New York: NETRC, January 1963).

4. See "Statistical Analysis, 1946-63: The Television Industry," table titled "The UHF Story," *TV Factbook* 34(1964):38a. Concerning both converters and all-channel sets, national averages concealed differences between areas. For example, in Buffalo RCA-NBC spent $100,000 to achieve almost 50 percent conversion; in central Illinois, where major network service was provided largely or entirely by UHF stations, the all-channel set rate was 65 to 70 percent. However, the situation was worse for ETV stations in other areas, such as Ohio, where all reservations were UHF and the commercial stations mainly VHF.

5. See Sydney W. Head, *Broadcasting in America,* 2nd ed. (Boston: Houghton Mifflin, 1972), pp. 198-99.

6. Frederick Breitenfeld, Jr., "The Four Faces of Educational Television," in Allen E. Koenig and Ruane B. Hill, eds., *The Farther Vision: Educational Television Today* (Madison: University of Wisconsin Press, 1967), pp. 35-49.

7. ETMA was incorporated for this purpose after the Metropolitan Educational Television Association (META) ceased operations in 1959. META was an ETV production center in New York City, which furnished the ETRC with some of its best series. It tried to gather support for a UHF ETV station in New York City but failed. Carroll Newsom was board chairman; Arthur Hungerford played several key roles. See Arthur Hungerford, "The Demise of META," *NAEB Journal* (March-April 1960):11-14. The organizing com-mittee of the new Educational Television for the Metropolitan Area (ETMA) that raised the

money and got Channel 13 included Howard Shepard (chairman), Devereaux Josephs, John D. Rockefeller III, Arthur A. Houghton, Jr., George Stoddard, and John White. Others, including Frank Stanton of CBS, were also helpful.

8. The details are given by Barbara S. Boekemeier, "The Genesis of WNDT: A Noncommercial Television Station on a Commercial Channel" (M.A. thesis, Columbia University, 1963). The price was $5.75 million for a station whose facilities were estimated as worth $500,000 and which NTA had bought for $4 million in 1957. Money to ETMA for the purchase came from several foundations, including the Ford Foundation, the Rockefeller Brothers Fund, the Alfred P. Sloan Foundation, and the Carnegie Corporation; money came also from all three networks and all six commercial VHF stations in the metropolitan area.

9. My source is Chapter I, pp. 6–26, of an unpublished paper, "Pressures, Programming, Policy: A Mass Communications Case Study, WHYY-TV, Philadelphia," by Willard D. Rowland, Jr., May 1, 1970.

10. See Betty McKenzie, ed., *The Feasibility and Role of State and Regional Networks in Educational Broadcasting* (Urbana: NAEB, 1959).

11. "The Eastern Educational Television Network," (EEN, February 1970); Donald R. Quayle, "The Regional Network," Koenig and Hill, *The Farther Vision,* pp. 107–29, gives a detailed account and analysis of the EEN as a prototype for other regional networks.

12. John P. Witherspoon, "State Public Television—A New Tool for the States," *State Government* (Council of State Governments, Autumn 1971):199. The article gives detailed descriptions of state ETV networks in Kentucky, South Carolina, Nebraska, and Maryland.

13. See John F. White, "ETV and the Next Ten Years," *NAEB Journal* (May-June 1963):61.

14. *In Re Pacifica Foundation* 36 FCC, 147 at 194, January 22, 1964. See also Gene R. Stebbins, "Pacifica's Battle for Free Expression," *Educational Broadcasting Review* (July 1970); and Eleanor McKinney, ed., *The Exacting Ear: The Story of Listener-Sponsored Radio* (New York: Random House, 1966).

15. See E. G. Burrows, Larry Frymire, and Betty McKenzie, eds., *Proceedings of the Seminar for NAEB Radio Network Station* Managers (Urbana: NAEB, 1959).

16. See Betty McKenzie et al., eds. *Live Radio Networking for Radio Stations* (Urbana: NAEB, 1960).

17. During the Newburn administration, Hudson was the only professional broadcaster on the center staff. His earlier activities with the Allerton House seminars, as a member of the Ad Hoc JCET strategy team, as consultant to the Fund for Adult Education, as scout for the most likely places to activate reserved channels, and as the author of the blueprint for the ETRC have been related in previous chapters. He was to remain NETRC (later NET) vice-president for programming until 1965, and then senior vice-president of NET until his retirement in 1969. More than any other person he was the guiding mind of ETV from the day the FCC proposed making no reservations for ETV in 1949 until the Corporation for Public Broadcasting was operating in 1969.

18. NETRC, "Inside Channels," April 1959.

19. For the conference and the speech, see NETRC, "Inside Channels," May 1959.

20. Almost, but not quite all. Three activities were carryovers from the earlier design of the ETRC. One was "extended services"—the promotion of ETRC programs over commercial stations, which continued through 1963. A second activitiy was the NET Film Service for nonbroadcast use. A third activitiy was that of the Department of Utilization,

established as a result of a grant from the Fund for Adult Education in February 1961; the $200,000, matched by the center, was for a four-year project of tying in study and discussion materials with ETV programs.

21. Ralph Steetle, who became director of the Joint Committee on Educational Television in 1951 and remained director after it became the Joint Council on Educational Television in 1955, left in 1960 to become associate dean of university extension of the Oregon State Board of Higher Education, with responsibility for KOAP, VHF, Channel 10, Portland (on the air February 2, 1961).

22. Humble Oil Company underwrote the $250,000 cost for acquisition, duplication, and NETRC promotion, which included a twenty-four-page descriptive booklet in color. The company also put on its own extensive promotion.

23. Summary of talk to Station Managers, October 16, 1960, quoted in Donald Neal Wood, "The First Decade of the 'Fourth Network': An Historical Descriptive Analysis of the National Educational Television and Radio Center" (Ph.D. diss., University of Michigan, 1963), p. 239.

24. John White, "ETV: Forecast for the Future," address on October 17, 1962, to the affiliates meeting, in Wood, "The First Decade of the 'Fourth Network,'" p. 239.

25. Wood, "The First Decade," Appendix F, pp. 501-503, gives detailed figures based on center financial records.

26. *The Ford Foundation in the 1960's* (New York: Ford Foundation, July 1962).

27. Richard F. Shepard, "Educational Radio and TV Split," *New York Times,* July 3, 1963.

28. Richard F. Shepard, "Educational TV Gets New Grant," *New York Times,* October 2, 1963.

29. For official public reports, see Ford Foundation, *1963 Annual Report,* p. 12; NET news release, October 2, 1963; and "N.E.T. News," Fall 1963. From October 2, White and his colleagues referred to their agency as "National Educational Television"—"NET," which had been used as a logo since the mid-1950s. It now became the official acronym when the board changed the name to National Educational Television in early 1964.

30. The main source of the facts in this section is W. Wayne Alford, *NAEB: History, Volume 2—1954-1965* (Urbana: NAEB, 1966).

31. See I. Keith Tyler, ed., *NAEB Research Seminar* (Urbana: NAEB, 1958).

32. Vernon Bronson, "Education's Need for Channels: Report of the NAEB Survey," *Educational Television: The Next Ten Years* (Stanford: The Institute for Communications Research, 1962), pp. 251-65.

33. Vernon Bronson, ed., *The Needs of Education for Utilization of Space Transmission Techniques* (Washington, D.C.: NAEB, 1962).

34. Betty McKenzie, ed., *Instructional Broadcasting* (Washington, D.C.: NAEB, 1963).

35. Skornia had been director of broadcasting at Indiana University, chief of radio for the U.S. armed forces in Austria, and since June 1, 1953, executive director of the NAEB.

36. Harry Skornia, "The NAEB: Past and Future," *NAEB Journal* (January-February 1961):55-62.

37. Vernon Bronson, "ETV: A Proper Home," *Television Quarterly* (Summer 1963):75.

38. Quoted by Robert A. Carlson, "The National Educational Television Network," *Adult Education* (Spring 1967):142-43. For a full statement of Gunn's position,

see his "A Station Manager's View of the Problem of Programming," *Educational Television: The Next Ten Years,* pp. 141–51.

39. Paul Bosner, "Improving Instructional Media Practices," *Public Telecommunications Review* (December 1973):58.

40. Beverly J. Taylor, "The Development of Instructional Television," pp. 133–53; and Gary Gumpert, "Closed-Circuit Television in Training and Education," pp. 155–82, both in Koenig and Hill, *The Farther Vision.* Those interested in comprehensive facts should consult the monumental and sustained *Compendium of Televised Education,* compiled and edited by Lawrence E. McKune, Michigan State University Press, annually from 1954 to 1968.

41. See Judith Murphy and Ronald Gross, *Learning by Television* (New York: Fund for the Advancement of Education, August 1966); and *A Ten Year Report on the Fund for the Advancement of Education* (New York: Ford Foundation, 1961).

42. "Continental Classroom"—nationwide college courses by way of TV—began in 1958, with most of the costs underwritten by TFAE and the Ford Foundation, over more than 150 NBC outlets. The original purpose was to bring high school teachers up to date in their subjects by exposing them to current developments and distinguished scientists and scholars. The special hookup was designed to make the course available to any college in the United States; about 300 of them picked it up the first year. After three heavily subsidized seasons on the air, racking up an impressive record of participating colleges and active viewers, estimated to be about 270,000, the program was discontinued.

No history of educational broadcasting should neglect to mention, if only in a note (it really does not fit into this part of the present history), CBS's "Sunrise Semester." It was started September 23, 1957, in cooperation with New York University, and made a network offering to CBS affiliates beginning September 22, 1963. It is carried by about eighty stations at 6:30 A.M. in New York (where the lectures are repeated in the early evening over WNYU FM). The program reaches an audience estimated at between 1.5 and 2 million. Offered on Mondays, Wednesdays, and Fridays, the course can be taken for college credit through either NYU or one of a national network of other colleges that use it.

43. National Project for the Improvement of Televised Instruction, *Toward a Significant Difference* (Washington, D.C.: NAEB, 1959), p. 39.

44. Wilbur Schramm, *Instructional Television: Promise and Opportunity* (Washington, D.C.: NAEB, January 1967), p. 3.

45. C. C. Erickson and H. M. Chausow, *Chicago's TV College: Final Report of a Three-Year Experiment* (Chicago: Chicago City Junior College, 1960).

46. Southern States Work Conference, *The Public Schools and Television* (Tallahassee: Florida State Department of Education, 1958).

47. Murphy and Gross, *Learning by Television,* p. 9.

48. Paul Bosner, "Improving Instructional Media Practices," *Public Telecommunications Review* (December 1973):59.

49. Wilbur Schramm, Jack Lyle, and Ithiel da Sola Pool, *The People Look at Educational Television* (Stanford University Press, 1963). These findings were modified by later studies of ETV audiences in two important respects: first, the development of "Sesame Street" and "The Electric Company" made children the largest single group of ETV watchers; second, more sophisticated research methods indicated that ETV viewers may watch more, not less, total TV than non-ETV viewers.

50. For details on the history of this act, see John Foster Price, "The Legislative History of Educational Television Facilities Proposals in the U.S. Congress—A Rhetorical Critical Study" (Ph.D. diss., Michigan State University, 1965); and F. H. Roche, C.S.C.,

"Economic Regulation of ETV, 1952 to 1968" (Ph.D. diss., University of Notre Dame, 1968).

51. This study, cited in note 32, was influential partly because it had been endorsed by the National Association of School Boards.

52. John Edward Burke, "An Historical-Analytical Study of the Legislative and Political Origins of the Public Broadcasting Act of 1967" (Ph.D. diss., Ohio State University, 1971), p. 54.

53. For a detailed, yet succinct account of the background, process, and consequences of the FCC's shifts on VHF and UHF, see Erwin G. Krasnow and Lawrence D. Longley, *The Politics of Broadcast Regulation* (New York: St. Martin's Press, 1973), pp. 96–104.

54. Quoted in Walter B. Emery, *Broadcast and Government,* 2nd ed. (East Lansing: Michigan State University Press, 1971), p. 152.

55. Philip A. Rubin, *A Quantitative Comparison of the Relative Performance of VHF and UHF Broadcast Systems* (Washington, D.C.: Corporation for Public Broadcasting, Office of Engineering Research, June 1974), p. 40.

56. See the Educational Media Study Panel, "A National Policy for Educational Television," *Educational Television: The Next Ten Years,* pp. 1–13.

Chapter 6

CUTTING A CHANNEL TO THE BRINK, LATE 1963–EARLY 1967

1. Herman W. Land Associates, *The Hidden Medium: A Status Report on Educational Radio in the United States* (New York: National Educational Radio, National Association of Educational Broadcasters, April 1967).

2. See Senate Committee on Commerce, *Report No. 222,* May 11, 1967 (Public Broadcasting Act), pp. 37–42.

3. FCC, *Educational Television,* INF Bulletin No. 16-B, April 1968, p. 14.

4. *The South Carolina ETV Network* (Columbia, S.C.: South Carolina Educational Television Commission, 1972), p. 10.

5. FCC, *Educational Television,* p. 14.

6. Donald R. Quayle, "The Regional Network," Allen R. Koenig and Ruane B. Hill, eds., *The Farther Vision: Educational Television Today* (Madison: University of Wisconsin Press, 1967), p. 126.

7. Sydney W. Head, *Broadcasting in America,* 2nd ed. (Boston: Houghton Mifflin, 1972), pp. 378–79. For details, see Walter B. Emery, *Broadcasting and Government,* 2nd ed. (East Lansing: Michigan State University Press, 1971), pp. 175–78.

8. See Wesley Meierhenry and Jack McBride, "Exchange of Instructional Television Materials: Report of the Nebraska Survey," *Educational Television: The Next Ten Years* (Stanford: The Institute for Communication Research, 1962), pp. 266–85.

9. See Jack G. McBride, "Trends in Station Programming," Koenig and Hill, *The Farther Vision,* pp. 197–207.

10. Ibid., p. 200.

11. Ibid., p. 205.

12. Lester A. Nelson, *Toward a Significant Difference* (Washington, D.C.: NAEB, 1969, p. 36.

13. Wilbur Schramm et al., *The New Media in Action,* Vol. I (Paris: UNESCO and

International Institute for Educational Planners, 1967), Preface and the first chapter of
"Case Studies for Planners." See also Tom Kaser, "Classroom TV Comes to Samoa," *Saturday Review* (June 19, 1965).

    14. *Toward a Significant Difference,* p. 24.

    15. See Norman Felsenthal, "MPATI: A History (1959–1971), *Educational Broadcasting Review* (December 1971):36–44.

    16. The NAEB argued that granting the six channels would actually subtract a total of eighteen channels because adjacent channels would be unusable, and that ETV ground stations would need these eighteen channels in the future; it proposed that MPATI use six channels in the 2500 mc. band (ITFS) instead. MPATI and supporters (educators, parents, students, and some members of Congress) argued that the upper UHF band would not be used by ground-based UHF stations for years, if ever; that ITFS was unproved; and that conversion costs would be prohibitive.

    17. For details on rules, see the booklet by the FCC Committee for the Full Development of the ITFS, *ITFS: What It Is . . . How to Plan* (Washington, D.C.: National Education Association, 1967).

    18. Emery, *Broadcasting and Government,* p. 197.

    19. Fritz Jauch, "A Brief History of Educational Television in the United States" mimeographed (New York: National Educational Television, February 1968), pp. 11–12.

    20. In the second half of the 1960s NET received about $1 million annually for underwriting programs from businesses, foundations, individuals, or government agencies. One of these grants was for the continuation of "Misterogers Neighborhood." Fred M. Rogers, who in 1954 helped launch WQED, Pittsburgh, created "Misteroger's Neighborhood" with a budget of $30 per program. In 1967 WMVS, Milwaukee, ran out of funds to pay NET's special service fee of $100 for each weekly show and announced that "Misteroger's Neighborhood" would be discontinued. The station immediately received letters with donations, including pennies and nickles, pressed flowers, and a swatch of hair from a favorite toy dog—all to keep "Misterogers" a part of Milwaukee. In all, the station received $6,300, enough for sixty-three more weeks of the program.

    21. *A Progress Report 1967–68* (New York: National Educational Television, 1969), p. 20. "In 1967 alone banks of videotape machines turned out 21,000 individual program copies. In the same year, the film department processed, inspected, and repaired 23,000 film prints in current distribution and provided 2,100 new prints in black and white and 300 in color."

    22. W. Wayne Alford, *NAEB: History, Volume 2—1954 to 1965* (Washington, D.C.: National Association of Educational Broadcasters, 1966), p. 127.

    23. Robertson's initiative was influential because until recently he had been vice-president for network affairs of the NETRC, and he was now head of one of the big city community-corporation stations. His pledge was also daring because KCET was still six months away from going on the air (September 28, 1964); moreover it was a UHF channel in a market with seven VHF commercial stations. Robertson and his directors were gambling that their projected station would succeed because of the All-Channel Receiver Act of 1962, which did not become effective until May 1, 1964.

    24. See Educational Television Stations, *The Long-Range Financing of Educational Television Stations, Second National Conference* (Washington, D.C.: ETS, NAEB, May 1967), p. iii.

    25. Ibid., p. 81.

    26. Hull, Harley, Schenkkan, and Fletcher explained to Leonard Marks, president and board chairman of the National Home Library Foundation, that the establishment of

an ETV program service alternative to NET's was necessary for the survival of ETS. This foundation granted $80,000, 1964–67, for a national television program exchange library. Indiana University offered to provide a home for the center, and Fletcher secured a six-year grant of nearly $350,000 from the W. K. Kellogg Foundation (requested by the NAEB but given to Indiana University) for the establishment of the ETS Program Service. Like the 1951 Kellogg grant to the NAEB to establish a radio tape network at the University of Illinois, the ETS/PS grant was made with the expectation that the service would become self-supporting. The ETS/PS was established in Bloomington in 1965, and was available only to stations that were members of ETS. It was particularly useful to the smaller stations, both for submitting their programs that would not be distributed by NET and for access to a wide range of station-produced programs not available through NET.

    27. *The Long-Range Financing of ETV Stations,* p. 39.

    28. See John E. Burke, "The Public Broadcasting Act of 1967: Part I," *Educational Broadcasting Review* (April 1972):117–18. Burke writes that the President preferred a private commission because the large number of presidential commissions had devalued their prestige (but not their cost) and because Johnson wanted to avoid the possibility that a presidential commission's recommendations concerning ETV could in any way to attributed to the Johnson family's personal interests in commercial broadcasting.

    29. It was obviously important to have a commission in which President Johnson had confidence. Burke, in *Educational Broadcasting Review* (April 1972):118–19, citing as his source an interview with Leonard Marks, writes: "Although the Carnegie Corporation . . . played the primary role in the selection of the members . . . , the White House had some recommendations for membership. Douglass Cater and Leonard Marks were instrumental in naming and/or approving the members of the Carnegie Commission. Certain members were approved or named, with the cooperation of the Carnegie Corporation, for specific reasons. J. C. Kellam, for example, was placed on the Carnegie Commission by Marks not only because he was manager of the radio and television interests of Mrs. Johnson, but also because Marks knew that he would be 'sympathetic and knowledgeable and that the President could turn to him if in doubt and ask him what he thought.' In addition, Mrs. Oveta Culp Hobby, chairman of the board of the Houston Post Company and a former Secretary of HEW, was placed on the Commission because the President knew her, respected her, and could turn to her for advice. John Hayes, manager of WTOP TV in Washington (owned by the *Washington Post*), . . . was placed on the Commission because he was knowledgeable, and it was felt that his direct participation on the Commission would lead to public support through the *Washington Post.*"

    30. *The Long-Range Financing of ETV Stations,* p. iii.

    31. "The History of Ford Foundation Activities in Non-Commercial Broadcasting" mimeographed (New York: Ford Foundation, October 1974), pp. 13–15.

    32. ABC asked for authority to launch its own satellite for affiliated stations, offering free interconnection for educational stations. See Morris Gelman, "The Invisible Shield," *Television Magazine* (February 1966):45–60.

    33. For an account of the Ford Foundation proposal see Fred W. Friendly, *Due to Circumstances Beyond Our Control* (New York: Random House, 1967), pp. 302–22. For an account of the subcommittee hearings see Harold E. Wigren, "TV Via Satellites," *NEA Journal* (October 1966):52. See also Abraham Katz, "Summary Descriptions of Various Proposals for Domestic Satellite Systems," and "Summary Descriptions of Policy Positions of Certain Interested Parties on Issues Relating to ETV and Satellite Communications," in *The Long-Range Financing of ETV Stations,* pp. 76–79, 80–86.

    34. U.S. Congress, Senate, Subcommittee on Communications, Committee on

Commerce, *Hearings, Progress Report on Space Communications,* 89th Cong., 2nd Sess., 1966, p. 230.

35. Ibid., p. 232.

36. U.S. Congress, Senate, Subcommittee on Communications, Committee on Commerce, *Hearings to Accompany S. 1160* (Public Broadcasting Act of 1967), p. 172.

37. Jack Gould, "Ford Acts to Spur Educational TV," *New York Times,* December 12, 1966.

38. *The Ford Foundation Annual Report,* October 1, 1966, to September 30, 1967, pp. 38–40. The original plan—to have PBL placed administratively in the graduate school of journalism, Columbia University—did not work out. In March 1967, PBL was placed as a "semiautonomous" division of National Educational Television (NET).

Chapter 7
OVER THE BRINK, 1967

1. The Carnegie Commission on Educational Television, *Public Television: A Program for Action* (New York: Bantam, January 1967).

2. Les Brown, *Television and the Business Behind the Box* (New York: Harcourt Brace Jovanovich, 1971), p. 319.

3. John E. Burke, "The Public Broadcasting Act of 1967: Part II," *Educational Broadcasting Review* (June 1972):182.

4. Ibid., p. 187.

5. The report of the conference, compiled and edited by Warren L. Wade and Serena E. Wade, "Educational Television Stations," *The Long-Range Financing of Educational Television Stations, Second National Conference* (Washington, D.C.: ETS, NAEB, May 1967) includes the preconference study material, texts of remarks by the major speakers, a roster of special guests and participants organized by groups, findings, and recommendations.

6. The Ford Foundation was as good as Bundy's word. Foundation grants and expenditures for educational broadcasting (primarily television) for the fiscal years 1967 through 1974 were (in round numbers): 1967, $23 million; 1968, $11 million; 1969, $25.3 million; 1970, $17.1 million; 1971, $18.2 million; 1973, $10.7 million; and 1974, $28.85 million. These figures are taken from an appendix to "The History of Ford Foundation Activities in Non-Commercial Broadcasting" mimeographed (New York: Ford Foundation, 1974), which begins: "Since 1951 the Ford Foundation and two organizations funded by the Foundation have made grants to non-commercial broadcasting totaling $273 million. Of this amount, $153 million have been committed since the establishment of the Corporation for Public Broadcasting (CPB) in 1967. The Foundation now [1974] expects to discontinue major grants to non-commercial television within three years since the survival of first-rate non-commercial broadcasting seems assured."

7. *The Long-Range Financing of ETV Stations,* p. 34.

8. Douglass Cater, "The Politics of Public TV," *Columbia Journalism Review* (July/August 1972):9–10.

9. See Burke, "The Public Broadcasting Act of 1967," *Educational Broadcasting Review* (April, June, and August 1972). See also U.S. Congress, Senate Committee on Commerce, Subcommittee on Communications, 90th Congress, 1st Sess., 1967, *Hearings to Accompany S. 1160* (Public Broadcasting Act)—(the House *Hearings* on H. R. 6736 are

largely repetitive); *Senate Report No. 222,* to Accompany S. 1160, May 11, 1967; *House Report No. 572,* to Accompany H. R. 6736, August 21, 1967; and *House Report No. 794,* Conference Report, to Accompany S. 1160, October 18, 1967.

10. House *Hearings* on H. R. 6736, p. 703.

11. Sydney W. Head, *Broadcasting in America,* 2nd ed. (Boston: Houghton Mifflin, 1972), pp. 198–99.

12. Ibid., pp. 320–21.

13. Ronald H. Coase, "Educational Television: Who Should Pay?" *Educational Broadcasting Review* (April 1968):10–11.

14. *Report of the Committee on Broadcasting 1960,* Presented to Parliament by the Postmaster General by Command of Her Majesty (London: Her Majesty's Stationery Office, June 1962), pp. 45–46.

15. "The process of board selection has in fact lent itself to increased politicization to the point that membership on the CPB board is similar to appointment to a federal judgeship—a plum to be pursued through political channels and awarded on the basis of political considerations,"—from Joseph D. Hughes, "Heat Shield or Crucible?" *Public Telecommunications Review* (November/December 1977):17. Hughes is a charter director of the Corporation for Public Broadcasting.

16. See "Black Perspective on the News: Controversy and Comment," *Public Telecommunications Review* (November/December 1977):64–67. Representative Joshua Ellberg objected to a single program and defended Congress' right to oversee it, while Lawrence K. Grossman, the president of PBS, argued that the continuing news series should be judged as a whole and by public broadcasters, not Congress.

17. For discussions of this issue, with citations of cases and rulings, see Walter B. Emery, "Is There a Constitutional Flaw in the Public Broadcasting Act of 1967?" *Educational Broadcasting Review* (February 1968):17–21; Daniel W. Toohey, "Section 399: The Constitution Giveth and Congress Taketh Away," *Educational Broadcasting Review* (February 1972):31–37; and Anne W. Branscomb, "A Crisis of Identity: Public Broadcasting and the Law," *Public Telecommunications Review* (February 1972):16–22.

18. See, for example, Lee Sherman Dreyfus, "The University Station," Allen E. Koenig and Ruane B. Hill, eds., *The Farther Vision: Educational Television Today* (Madison: University of Wisconsin Press, 1967), p. 59.

19. Toohey, "Section 399: The Constitution Giveth and Congress Taketh Away," *Educational Broadcasting Review,* p. 34.

20. This discussion is based on the letters written by Killian, Harley, and Case, reproduced in Appendix B, John E. Burke, "An Historical, Analytical Study of the Legislative and Political Origins of the Public Broadcasting Act of 1967" (Ph.D. diss., Ohio State University, 1971).

21. Congress never appropriated the money. Instead, the secretary of HEW, Wilbur J. Cohen, used department funds to establish the Commission on Instructional Technology, chaired by Sterling M. McMurrin. The secretary's charge to the commission was: "Every aspect of instructional technology and every problem which may arise in the development should be included in your study." The study was directed by Sidney G. Tickton, executive vice-president of the Academy for Educational Development. The result was *To Improve Learning: A Report to the President and the Congress of the United States,* printed for the use of the House Committee on Education and Labor. It was accompanied by a veritable library of valuable papers. For the report and selected papers see Sidney G. Tickton, ed., *To Improve Learning: An Evaluation of Instructional Technology,* 2 vols. (New York: R. R. Bowker Company, 1970).

22. Cater, "The Politics of Public TV," *Columbia Journalism Review,* p. 10.

Chapter 8
1968–1978 AND PROSPECTS

1. These sources are *The Corporation for Public Broadcasting 1977 Annual Report*; "Statement of Public Broadcasting Service (PBS) before the Subcommittee on Communications of the Committee on Commerce, U.S. Senate, May 4, 1978"; and "Testimony of Frank Mankiewicz, President of National Public Radio (NPR), before the Communications Subcommittee of the Senate Committee on Commerce, Science, and Transportation," May 4, 1978." The CPB established PBS in 1969 and NPR in 1970, both representatives of the stations, to handle interconnection.

2. *The Corporation for Public Broadcasting 1977 Annual Report* (Washington, D.C.: CPB, 1977), p. 3.

3. Stephen White, "Carnegie II: A Look Back and Ahead," *Public Telecommunications Review* (July/August 1977):9.

4. See *Public Telecommunications Review* (November/December 1976):73–76.

5. Joseph D. Hughes, "Heat Shield or Crucible? A Blueprint for Carnegie II," *Public Telecommunications Review* (November/December 1977):28.

6. Carnegie Commission on Educational Television, *Public Television: A Program for Action* (New York: Bantam, 1967), pp. 68–69.

7. Robert Pepper, "The Interconnection Connection: The Formation of PBS," *Public Telecommunications Review* (January/February 1976):25.

8. In 1974 the Ford Foundation reported that since 1951 it and its two subsidiary foundations, The Fund for the Advancement of Education and the Fund for Adult Education, had made grants to noncommercial broadcasting totaling $273 million. "Of this amount $153 million has been committed since the establishment of the Corporation for Public Broadcasting. The Foundation now expects to discontinue major grants within three years since the survival of first-rate noncommercial broadcasting seems assured," from "The History of Ford Foundation Activities in Noncommercial Broadcasting" (New York: The Ford Foundation, October 1974), p. 1. Between the date of that report and June 15, 1978, the foundation spent more than an additional $20 million on educational television, primarily for programming.

9. For the early history of CTW, see Richard M. Polsky, *Getting to Sesame Street: Origins of the Children's Television Workshop* (New York: Praeger, 1974).

10. Samuel C. O. Holt, "The Public Radio Study Report" (New York: Corporation for Public Broadcasting, April 1969).

11. See William E. Porter, *Assault on the Media: The Nixon Years* (Ann Arbor: University of Michigan Press, 1976).

12. White, "Carnegie II: A Look Back and Ahead," *Public Telecommunications Review* (July/August 1977):9.

13. Hartford N. Gunn, Jr., "Public Television Financing," *Educational Broadcasting Review* (October 1972):283–308. For an account of how the SPC operated after its initiation, see "Inside the Program Cooperative: An Interview with Hartford Gunn," *Public Telecommunications Review* (August 1974):16–24.

14. Willard D. Rowland, Jr., "Public Involvement: The Anatomy of a Myth," *The Future of Public Broadcasting,* Douglass Cater, ed. (New York: Praeger, 1976), p. 123.

15. Robert K. Avery and Robert Pepper, "Interconnection Reconnection: The Making of the CPB-PBS Partnership," *Public Telecommunications Review* (September/October 1977):5–16. For the complete story of the CPB-PBS controversy, see also the first two articles in this series, "The Interconnection Connection: The Formation of PBS," *Public Telecommunications Review* (January/February 1976), and "Interconnection Dis-

connection: The Evolution of the PBS-CPB Relationship from 1970–73," *Public Telecommunications Review* (September/October 1976).

16. In 1977 the two parts of the board merged.

17. In 1977 APRS merged with NPR, modeling itself on the new PBS, with operating funds provided by CPB and trade association funds coming from member station dues.

18. The "Partnership Agreement" has worked only to the extent of papering over differences between the CPB and PBS well enough to avoid an open split. The basic differences are the result of flaws in the Public Broadcasting Act of 1967, and they can be resolved only by changes in the law. This was recognized by President Carter in his 1977 message on public broadcasting and by the House Subcommittee on Communications in its proposed revision of the Communications Act of 1934, both of which measures will be considered later.

19. See "Carnegie Commission II on the Future of Public Broadcasting," *Public Telecommunications Review* (May/June 1977):9–17.

20. See Harry M. Shooshan III, "Public Broadcasting: A Congressional Review," *Public Telecommunications Review* (May/June 1977):40–51. Shooshan is chief counsel to the House subcommittee.

21. See *Public Telecommunications Review* (September/October 1977):58–62.

22. Ibid., pp. 59–60.

23. H. Rex Lee, "Public Telecommunications: The Task of Managing Miracles," *Public Telecommunications Review* (December 1973):11–12.

24. Richard Gingras, "The PTV Satellite System: Turning Point or High Anxiety?" *Public Telecommunications Review* (May/June 1978):13. This entire article is recommended.

25. Charles D. Ferris, "FCC Regulatory Policies," *Public Telecommunications Review* (May/June 1978):63–67.

26. "FCC Meets on Noncommercial Broadcasting," *NAEB Letter,* June 1978.

27. "Highlights of Communications Act of 1978," *NAEB Letter,* June 1978. For the full text of "Title IV—Broadcast Services" of the bill, its rationale, and the reactions of spokesmen of major groups, see *Broadcasting* (June 12, 1978):29–41.

28. White, "Carnegie II: A Look Back and Ahead," *Public Telecommunications Review* (July/August 1977):10.

29. George E. Bair, "Letters to the Editor," *Educational Broadcasting Review* (February 1970):32.

30. Hill Bermont, "How Blissful Is Ignorance?" *Public Telecommunications Review* (March/April 1978):24.

31. Anne W. Branscomb, "A Crisis of Identity: Reflections on the Future of Public Broadcasting," *The Future of Public Broadcasting,* p. 30.

32. See Steve Millard, "ACNO: CPB and the Public," *Public Telecommunications Review* (March/April 1977):6–13. CPB commissioned Millard's study of ACNO.

33. Hartford N. Gunn, Jr., "Window on the Future: Planning for Public Television in the Telecommunications Era," *Public Telecommunications Review* (July/August 1978):43.

34. Section 399 (b) was added because a PTV station refused to give a U.S. senator the recording of a program with which he was displeased; the station refused on the grounds that he was not an accredited journalist. See "Hearings before the Subcommittee on Communications of the Senate Commerce Committee on S. 1090, The Public Broadcasting Act of 1973," 93d Cong., 1st Sess., Serial No. 93-10, March 28–30, 1974, p. 114.

35. *Public Telecommunications Review* devoted its entire issue of July/August 1978

to Gunn's first volume, which the journal titled "Window on the Future: Planning for Public Television in the Telecommunications Era."

36. See NFCB Newsletter, June 1978. The NFCB address is 1216 Massachusetts Ave., N.W., Washington, D.C. 20005.

37. Gunn, "Window on the Future," *Public Telecommunications Review* July/August 1978):43.

38. See Saul Rockman, "Instructional Television Is Alive and Well," *The Future of Public Broadcasting,* Douglass Cater, ed. (New York: Praeger, 1976), pp. 71–84; see also "Statement of PBS before the Subcommittee of the Committee on Commerce, U.S. Senate, May 4, 1978," pp. 25–28.

39. A periodic bulletin of the project is available from the Agency for Instructional Television, Box A, Bloomington, Indiana, 47401.

40. See Les Brown, "Cable and Pay TV on Eve of Technological Revolution," *New York Times,* July 31, 1978, p. C12.

41. John Dewey, *Democracy and Education: An Introduction to the Philosophy of Education* (New York: Macmillan, 1916).

42. Raymond Williams, *Culture and Society: 1780–1950* (New York: Harper & Row, 1958), p. 304.

INDEX

Carnegie Commission *(cont.)*
252n*29*; conclusions and recommendations, 176–78, 180
Carnegie Commission on the Future of Public Broadcasting, 211
Carnegie Corporation: 56–57, 247n*8*; commission on ETV, 169; took lead in "Sesame Street," 202–203; commission on public broadcasting, 211
Carnegie II. *See* Carnegie Commission on the Future of Public Broadcasting
Carter, Jimmy, 212–13
Case, Everett, 189
Cater, Douglass: 168, 196, 252n*29*; on Congress' disinterest in 1967 public broadcasting bills, 181–82; on Johnson's signing 1967 act, 189–90
Cauthen, Henry J., 153
Cavanaugh, John J., 242n*3*
CBS. *See* Columbia Broadcasting System
CCTV. *See* Closed circuit television
Central Educational Network (CEN), 155–57, 228–29
Chain Broadcasting Regulations (FCC), 74
Chamberlain, Ward, 196
Chamber of Commerce, U.S., 95
Channel 13, Newark–New York: transferred to ETV corporation, 119–20, 247n*8*
Charters, W. W., 61, 62
Chicago, University of, 8
Chicago Educational Television Association, 97, 119
Chicago public schools, 239n*12*
Chicago TV College, 139, 249n*45*
Children's Television Workshop (CTW), 203
Church, Charles, Jr., 24–25
Clark, Delbert, 97
Cleveland public schools, 239n*12*
Closed circuit television (CCTV), 138, 249n*40*
"Closed cities": defined, JCET position on, 15–16; FCC reservations in, 90
Coase, Ronald, 183–84
Cohen, Edwin, 107, 132, 159
Columbia Broadcasting System (CBS): 70, 199; founded, 41–42; filed against ETV channels, 88; pledged $1 million to CPB, 182, 199
Commerce, U.S. Department of: issued licenses to transmit, 35; adopted "broadcasting" as type of station,

Commerce, U.S. Dept. of *(cont.)*
37; policies of, after Washington Radio Conferences, 43
Commercial broadcasting: witnesses for, opposing ETV channels summarized, 15; advertising support, 38; national system of, 45; during Depression, 55; spokesmen for, 67; quality of radio programming, 75–76; industry permitted 1945 reservations of FM, 78–79; support to ETV, 101, 244n*22*
Commission on Instructional Technology, 254n*21*
Committee on Broadcasting (1960) (British), 184
Communications Act (1934), 65–66
Communications satellite: advantages of, 157; before legislation, 157–58; after legislation, 158; questions for users of ground interconnection, 158; study of potential for public broadcasting, 213; use for public broadcasting and other services, 213–15
Communications Satellite Act (1962): history and provisions of, 158
Communications Satellite Corporation (Comsat), 158
Community Service Grants (CSG), 206
Community Television Foundation of South Florida, 101
Community Television of Southern California, 99, 145–46
Comsat, 158
Conant, James B., 169
Conrad, Frank, 39
"Continental Classroom," 139, 249n*42*. *See also* Programs
Coolidge, Calvin, 46
Coombs, Philip, 162, 246n*1*
Cooney, Joan: creator of "Sesame Street," 202–203
Cooper, William J.: conference on educational radio, 57–58
"Cooperative activities": by educators and commercial broadcasters, 70–73
Cooperative Extension Service, 53
Corporation for Public Broadcasting (CPB): 165, 213; on UHF, 146; Congress did not insulate, 186, 193; dispute and détente with PBS, 194, 206–209; 1968–83 authorizations and appropriations for, 197, 217; formation of, delayed, 199; set criteria for grants to public radio stations, 204; repercussions of Nixon's veto, 205–

TO SERVE THE PUBLIC INTEREST

Educational Broadcasting in the United States

.was composed in 10-point Compugraphic Times Roman and leaded two points
with display type in Times Roman by Metricomp Studios, Inc.;
printed offset on 55-lb. Finch Opaque by Dodge-Graphic Press, Inc.;
Smythe-sewn and bound over boards in Columbia Tanoflex,
also adhesive bound with Wyomissing Corvon soft cover
by Maple-Vail Book Manufacturing Group, Inc.;
and published by

SYRACUSE UNIVERSITY PRESS
SYRACUSE, NEW YORK 13210